AT THE SUMMIT

MIKHAIL GORBACHEV

WASHINGTON—MOSCOW—WASHINGTON—MOSCOW

AT THE SUMMIT

WASHINGTON—MOSCOW—WASHINGTON—MOSCOW

Speeches and Interviews
February 1987–July 1988

RICHARDSON, STEIRMAN & BLACK
NEW YORK
1988

Library of Congress Catalog Card Number: 88-061901
ISBN: 0-931933-80-3

Printed in the United States of America
10 9 8 7 6 5 4 3 2 1

Tom Brokaw's "A Conversation with Mikhail
Gorbachev" in the Kremlin on November 30,
1987, is reproduced courtesy of NBC News and
the NBC Television Network.

The May 18, 1988, interview of Mikhail
Gorbachev by editors of the *Washington Post* and
Newsweek is reproduced courtesy of Katharine
Graham and the editors of the *Washington Post*
and *Newsweek* magazine.

CONTENTS

III. PRE–MOSCOW SUMMIT STATEMENTS

IV. THE MOSCOW SUMMIT

V. POST–MOSCOW SUMMIT SPEECHES

AT THE SUMMIT

I

PRE-WASHINGTON SUMMIT STATEMENTS

February 16–October 1, 1987

1

"For the Sake of Preserving Human Civilization"

Speech Before the International Forum for a Nuclear-Free World

Moscow, February 16, 1987

Ladies and gentlemen,
Comrades,
The destiny of the world and the future of humanity have concerned the best minds of various lands ever since man first began to think about the morrow.

Until rather recently reflections on these and related topics have been viewed as an imaginative exercise, as the otherworldly pursuits of philosophers, scholars and theologians. In the past decades, however, these problems have moved onto a highly practical plane. I think that the reasons for this are obvious to everyone present here.

As a result of the development and subsequent stockpiling beyond all reasonable bounds of nuclear weapons and their delivery vehicles, man has become technically capable of terminating his own existence. The simultaneous accumulation of acute social problems in the world, and attempts to continue tackling forcefully, using methods from the Stone Age, the problems of a fundamentally changed world make catastrophe highly likely in political terms as well. The militarization of the mind and of the way of life weakens and even removes altogether any moral inhibitions with regard to nuclear suicide.

We have no right to forget that the first step, which is always the most risky, has already been made. Nuclear weapons have been used against human beings and they have been used twice. There are dozens—I repeat dozens—of recorded and acknowledged incidents when the possibility of using such weapons against other countries was seriously considered. I am not saying this by way of criticism or condemnation, although this is more than appropriate here. I am saying this to stress once again how close mankind has come to the point-of-no-return.

The First World War shocked those who lived at that time for its unprecedented scale of destruction and suffering, for the brutality and impersonal, technical process of annihilation. But as appalling as the wounds inflicted by WW I might have been, the Second World War surpassed its "records" many times over, if the word "record" may be used here at all.

One strategic submarine today has a destructive power equivalent to several Second World Wars. There are scores of such submarines and they are by far not the only weapons with nuclear systems. It is impossible to imagine the hell that will be created and to what extent the very idea of humanity will be negated if any part, however small, of the present nuclear potential is used.

The Second World War (like WW I) was followed by attempts to arrange the world in such a way as to preclude a repetition of the wholesale slaughter of peoples. Although these attempts have not quite lived up to expectations, they have nevertheless left their mark. There is the United Nations Organization. There are regional and other structures for relations among states, nongovernmental organizations and individuals, structures that did not exist before. In brief, the political search continues for ways of delivering the international community from the vicious "logic" that led to the two world wars.

After a nuclear war there will be no problems and there will not be anyone left to sit down at the negotiation table, or even at the negotiating tree-stump or stone. A second Noah's ark will not emerge from a nuclear deluge. Everyone seems to understand this. So it is time to realize that we can no longer expect things to take care of themselves. There are still many people in the world, however, who do expect things to take care of themselves. International relations and the policies of governments and states must, without delay, be brought into line with the realities of the nuclear age.

The question stands like this: if political mentality is not geared to the requirements of the times, civilization and life itself on earth will come to an end.

In all human affairs, and especially in international politics, we should not for a moment forget the currently dominant contradiction—that between war and peace, between the existence and nonexistence of humanity. And we must work to resolve this contradiction in favor of peace as soon as possible.

This requires us to seek out, foster and share with each other all the best that history has produced, to look for new, creative approaches to chronic problems.

The very survival, and not just progress, of the human race depends on whether or not we find the strength and courage to overcome the threats lurking in the modern world. We believe that there are grounds to hope for this.

A notable feature of recent decades is that mankind as a whole, and not only individuals, has begun for the first time in history to feel that it is one entity, to see global relationships between man, society and nature, and to assess the consequences of material activities.

And as these feelings began to emerge, the struggle began to remove the nuclear threat. And it cannot be denied that this struggle has already become a great moral and political school in which great numbers of people and whole nations are learning the difficult but necessary art of living together in peace; of striking a balance between general and particular interests; of looking at the present and future boldly, square on, of comprehending the present and future, and in doing so, of drawing timely conclusions for action. Your forum is evidence of this.

Ladies and gentlemen,

Comrades,

Before describing the substance of all these problems in detail, I wish, on behalf of the people and the government of the Soviet Union, to extend cordial greetings to all of you, to all the participants in the Moscow forum—politicians, journalists, businessmen, scholars, doctors, people engaged in culture and the arts, writers and representatives of various churches.

We value and appreciate the fact that such a forum is being held and that such a great number of famous and influential people from all over the world have gathered for it. We understand that every one of you has duties and commitments. Nevertheless you put them aside and travelled thousands of kilometers to come here and voice your concerns, to share your thoughts with people worried about the same problems.

This alone is significant, for the forum includes representatives of various sectors of the population, people from all continents and from dozens of states.

The forum is a true embodiment of world public opinion.

The ideas of the forum, the cares and sentiments that have brought you here, are near and dear to the Soviet people. It is in this spirit that I once again address words of greeting and gratitude to you for the work which you have done these past days and which has been described here by representatives of all Round Tables. And I think that the voice of this forum, of each of us, will be heard some time or other.

We are encouraged by the fact that for all the diversity of opinions, views, positions and evaluations, the salient feature of this forum has been a common desire to pool all efforts in the struggle against the nuclear threat, and in the attempts to resolve other global issues before mankind.

It is very important that the ideas and spirit of the forum reach the public at large and political circles and, even more important, be reflected in the work of those who are in positions of state leadership. It must be this way, because these ideas pertain to the most vital and essential issue—how to save the future of mankind.

I have a few things to say on the matters discussed at the forum and I would like to present our government's point of view. But before doing this, I'd like to draw your attention to the following.

You have come to the Soviet Union at a time when basically revolutionary changes are taking place here. These changes are of immense significance for our society, for socialism as a whole, and for the entire world. It is only by understanding the content, meaning and aims of these changes that one can form a correct opinion about our foreign policy. Before my people, before those present and before the whole world, I state with full responsibility that our foreign policy is today to a greater extent than ever before determined by domestic policy, by our interest in concentrating our efforts on constructive activities aimed at improving our country. And that is why we need a lasting peace, predictability and constructiveness in international relations.

We have heard about the alleged threat stemming from the USSR and we continue to hear about it—the "Soviet threat" to peace and freedom.

I must note that the restructuring, which we have launched on such a large scale and which is irreversible, shows to everyone: this is where we want to direct our resources, this is what our thoughts are concentrated on, these are our actual programs and intentions and this is what we intend to spend the intellectual energy of our society on.

Our main idea is to bring out the full potential of socialism by activating all the people's energy. To do this it is necessary that all our public and state agencies, all our production collectives and creative unions, function fully and freely. We need to create new forms of civic activity and to restore those which have been unfairly forgotten. In brief, we seek the broad democratization of our entire society. This is the main guarantee that the ongoing processes will be irreversible. We seek more socialism and therefore more democracy.

This is how we are carrying on the cause of our great

Revolution. And our people have welcomed this enthusiastically.

To preclude any idle talk and speculation (we get a lot of this from the West), I wish to emphasize that we are going about our reforms in accordance with our own socialist choice, on the basis of our ideas about social values, and are guided by the criteria of the Soviet way of life. We measure our successes and our mistakes solely by socialist yardsticks.

But we want to be understood and we hope that the world community will at last acknowledge the fact that our ambition to improve our country will bring no harm to anyone; the world will only gain from this.

The restructuring is an invitation to all social systems to compete with socialism peacefully. And we will be able to prove with our actions that such competition benefits universal progress and world peace. But for such competition to take place in civilized forms, forms worthy of mankind in the 21st century, we must have a new outlook and overcome the mentality, stereotypes and dogmas inherited from a past that will never return.

Our society and the Soviet leadership did not develop an interest in a new mode of thinking overnight. We thought about this a great deal. We criticized ourselves and others and asked ourselves difficult and challenging questions. And finally we saw things as they are and became convinced that new approaches and methods are required for resolving international problems in today's complex and contradictory world, a world that stands at a crossroad.

We came to conclusions that made us review something that had once seemed axiomatic, for after Hiroshima and Nagasaki, was (at any rate world war) ceased to be a continuation of politics by other means. And a nuclear war will incinerate the architects of such policy as well.

We forced ourselves to face the fact that with the stockpiling and sophistication of nuclear armaments, the human race is no longer immortal. Its immortality can be regained only if nuclear weapons are destroyed.

We rejected the right of the leadership of any country, be it the USSR, the U.S.A. or any other country, to pass a death sentence on mankind. We are not judges and billions of people are not criminals to be punished. So the nuclear guillotine must be taken apart. The nuclear powers must overstep their nuclear shadow and enter into a nuclear-free world, thus ending politics' isolation from the general ethical standards of humanity.

A nuclear tornado will sweep away both socialists and capitalists, both the righteous and sinners. Is this situation moral? We Communists do not think so.

It could be said that we took the hard way to acquire a new outlook which is being called upon to bridge the gap between political practice and universal moral and ethical standards.

Last year at the Party congress, the highest forum of Soviet society, we set forth our vision of the world, our philosophical concept of its present and future. We did not just proclaim our theoretical doctrine, but on the basis of this doctrine, formulated a definite political platform for an all-embracing system of international security. This is a system based on the principle that one's own security cannot be ensured at the expense of others'; it is a system that organically connects all the main areas of security—the military, political, economic and humanitarian.

In the military and political domain, we put forward a program to abolish nuclear weapons by the year 2000. This program was announced on behalf of the Soviet people thirteen months ago, on January 15, 1986. And we are convinced that this date will go down in the history of the struggle to save civilization from destruction. Prior to this we came forward with the initiative that all nuclear explosions be halted and repeatedly extended the unilateral moratorium we had announced. It was our idea to have the Reykjavik summit meeting and we brought to that meeting initiatives which, had the other side responded, would have meant an end to the arms race and a radical turn towards disarmament and elimination of the nuclear threat. Along with our allies, we took bold and large-scale steps on the issues of confidence-building measures and the reduction of conventional arms and armed forces in

Europe. We expressed our readiness to have chemical weapons totally abolished.

In Vladivostok we invited Asian and Pacific countries to join us in the search for security for each and every state in that huge region of the world coming into its own and in the search for mutually advantageous and equal cooperation. We signed the Delhi Declaration, in which our philosophical and political approach to the establishment of a nonviolent world free of nuclear weapons merges with the approach of great India and the billions of people represented by the nonaligned movement.

As firm advocates of a new world economic order, we formulated and submitted for universal consideration a concept of international economic security.

Last, our new approach to the humanitarian problems from the "third Helsinki basket" is there for all to see. And I must disappoint those who think that this has been the result of pressure on us from the West, that we want to suit someone's fancy in pursuit of some ulterior motives. No, we have no ulterior motives. Our new approach is also a result of our new way of thinking.

Thus, we seek to translate in every way possible our philosophical vision of the world into practical politics.

Naturally, a new edifice of international security can be erected only upon a foundation of trust. We understand: reaching this trust is not simple, and it's not only we who need to have trust, although we, if you recall our history, have greater cause for mistrust.

I will not delve into this now. Let me just state that along with a lack of new attitudes everyone feels a lack of confidence as well. I am not going to look into the reasons for this situation on a wider plane, although a lot might be said. We must now look forward and must not be captives of the past.

Trust must be built up through experience in cooperation, through knowing each other better, through solving common problems. It is wrong in principle to say that first comes trust and then everything else follows: disarmament, cooperation and joint projects. Trust, its establishment, its consolidation and development, comes from common endeavor. This is the rational way.

And I repeat: everyone must begin with himself. It is not the pose of a self-appointed supreme judge of the whole world that international relations need so badly now, but rather respect for others and an unbiased and self-critical view of one's own society.

One of the chief results of the reconstruction efforts in the Soviet Union has been a general and universal boost in confidence in our society. And this strengthens our conviction that it is possible to establish trust in the realm of international relations as well.

The new mode of thinking is still laboring to break through in world politics. Trust is making ground very slowly. And I think this is why more and more people are realizing that the fate of the most important cause of our time should not be left to politicians alone. This cause concerns not only politicians. And we are witnessing the emergence and rise of a huge movement worldwide which includes scientists, intellectuals of varying professions, clergymen, women, young people, children (more and more!), and even ex-members of the military and former generals, who know full well what modern weapons are. And this is all because people are becoming increasingly more aware of how very dangerous a point the world has come to and how very real the threat hanging over it is.

I believe that your forum is a major contribution to the worldwide movement for a nuclear-free world and for mankind's survival, and I welcome this contribution.

I would like to say a few words here about the Reykjavik meeting. It was not a failure. It was a breakthrough. Reykjavik was not just another round of negotiations, but rather a moment of truth: an opportunity arose to embark upon the path leading to a world without nuclear weapons.

The Reykjavik meeting made such a great impression throughout the world because we approached the issue of reducing nuclear arsenals in an entirely new conceptual way; we approached it as a political and psychological problem rather than just a military and technical one. And we almost found a solution. But what are we to do with that "almost" which stopped us from reaching the finish line in Reykjavik?

I will not discuss here the reasons for this to happen. I hope you are already familiar with our view. What I want to say is that when both sides agreed at Reykjavik to make sweeping cuts in their nuclear arsenals and then eliminate them entirely, they recognized for all practical purposes that nuclear weapons can no longer guarantee security effectively.

What happened in Reykjavik irreversibly changed the nature and essence of the debate about the future world. However, some people were scared by the new opportunities and are now trying to make a fast retreat. But as attractive as the past may be, there is no returning to it. I am sure mankind can and will quite soon free itself of the chains of nuclear weapons. But this will require a fight and a hard fight.

The new political outlook is bound to raise civilization to a qualitatively new level. This alone serves to show that this is not a one-time adjustment of position but a methodology for conducting international affairs.

There is probably no one in this hall or elsewhere who considers nuclear weapons harmless. However, quite a few people sincerely believe that they are an evil necessary to prevent a greater evil, war. This is the viewpoint underlying the doctrine of nuclear deterrence.

Let me say the following.

First, even if we stick to this doctrine, we will have to admit that the "nuclear safeguard" is not 100 percent effective and not without a time limit. This doctrine can at any moment become a death sentence for mankind. The bigger the nuclear arsenals, the less the chances are that they will remain "obedient." Proliferation, increasingly sophisticated nuclear weapon systems, the greater scale of transportation and the constant risk of technical error, human failure or malice are all chance factors on which the survival of mankind depends.

Second, if we look at deterrence from a different angle, we see that it is, in fact, a policy based on intimidation. Each model of behavior has its inner logic. When threats become a political means, naturally there is the hope that each threat such as this will be taken seriously. But to achieve this, threats must always be backed up by definite actions. Here this means military force. The only conclusion that can be drawn is that the policy of deterrence, considered in a historical context, does not reduce the risk of military conflict. In fact, it increases that risk. Nevertheless, even after Reykjavik, some leaders continue to cling to such a doctrine.

And the most adamant supporters of that doctrine are those who are inclined to teach us morality. But how do they themselves look from this point of view—from the point of view of today's generally accepted morality? They are convinced that threats, force and the use of force are the only language that can be used in dealing with others and make no secret of the fact that this is the only language they know. How would you react if you met such a person in the street? How can educated leaders consider behavior generally considered unacceptable in relations between people normal for relations between states?

Third, when disarmament is discussed a common thesis is that man is violent by nature and that war is a manifestation of human instinct.

Is war the perpetual concomitant of human existence then? If we accept this view, we shall have to reconcile ourselves to the fact that ever more sophisticated weapons of mass destruction will continue to be developed.

Such thinking is unacceptable. It is reminiscent of times when ever more sophisticated weapons were invented and used to conquer other peoples and to enslave and pillage them. That past is neither reason nor model for the future. Man living at the threshold of the 21st century knows a great deal and can do a great deal. That is why he must realize the need for the demilitarization of the world. We believe that it is possible to build such a world and we shall do everything to ensure the accomplishment of what is perhaps the most ambitious social goal ever.

There is another aspect to the question of nuclear deterrence. In politics one must not ignore the problem of the rational and the irrational. This is particularly relevant in our complex world where the very content of such notions is subject to the great influence of the specific historical experience of the peoples, very different political cultures, traditions and many other factors. It is no easy matter to find a common denominator which would seem rational to all. And this confirms the fact that the more nuclear weapons there are, the greater the risk of a fatal error.

Nevertheless, the development of more powerful and sophisticated, of what is cynically called exotic weapons, continues.

The uniqueness, I might even say the dramatic character, of the situation is emphasized by the threat of the arms race spreading to outer space. If this should happen, the very idea of arms control would be compromised. Distrust, mutual suspicion and the temptation to be ahead in deploying still new weapon systems would increase tremendously. Destabilization would become a reality and might well bring on a crisis. The risk of an accidental outbreak of war would increase several times over.

We regret that continued American testing has put an end to our moratorium. Yet our initiative has not been wasted.

By our moratorium we have shown the world that it is quite possible not to carry out nuclear weapon tests, provided there is the necessary political will.

I wish to assure this authoritative audience that the Soviet Union will not abandon its efforts to have nuclear testing banned and bring about major reductions and eventually elimination of existing nuclear stockpiles.

Now I would like to say a few words about the passions that flared up in recent days over the deployment of a first layer of SDI. The advocates of the deployment insist on a "broader interpretation" of the ABM Treaty. Incidentally, while debates on this subject are going on in Washington and between the NATO allies, the U.S. Administration has already officially suggested in Geneva that such an interpretation be formally endorsed. Whatever the pretexts used to justify this, the aim is clearly to wreck the ABM Treaty. From the very start the political and, if you like, philosophic significance of the Treaty has consisted in ensuring stability based on the absence of antimissile defense and in this way ending the eternal competition between the sword and the shield, which is particularly dangerous in a nuclear epoch. If the Treaty should be annulled, the nuclear missile race would acquire new dimensions and would be accompanied by an arms race in outer space, the inevitable consequences of which I have just mentioned.

In November 1985, President Reagan and I made the following pledge in Geneva: ". . . to prevent an arms race in space and to terminate it on earth, to limit and reduce nuclear arms and to enhance strategic stability." This is recorded in the joint statement adopted in Geneva. By undermining the ABM Treaty, the U.S. Administration shows scorn for that pledge and for the signature the United States put to that Treaty of unlimited duration 15 years ago.

What the situation requires is stricter observance of international law rather than attempts to undermine it or throw out of it some of its major elements.

Another matter we are considering now is why some countries arrogate to themselves the right to invent and develop new weapon systems which, even if not deployed or used, threaten other countries and peoples. Most likely, you are bound to ask the same question. This problem transcends the boundaries of national sovereignty. It is an international problem.

Or consider another question. At present the national sovereignty of a state extends to the airspace above it. And every state has the right to defend it from intrusion. A far greater threat will come from outer space if weapons are placed there as intended. The aim of such plans is to create a new instrument of blackmail against independent states. Isn't it high time to consider making a ban on the deployment of weapons in space, over the heads of the people in other countries, a part of international law?

Now permit me to deal with another important reality of our time. It also requires a new way of thinking. I refer to the unprecedented diversity and at the same time growing interconnection and unity of the world. Our world is united not only by the internationalization of economic life and powerful information and communications media, but also by the common threat of nuclear death, ecological catastrophe and global explosion of the contradictions between poverty and wealth in its different regions.

The world today is a community of states, each with its own unique history, traditions, customs and way of life. Each people and country has what it considers to be truth, its own national interests and its own aspirations. This is a most important reality of the modern world; there was nothing of the kind thirty or forty years ago. It has been brought about by the people themselves who have chosen independent development and free national advancement.

However, the development of this process has outstripped some politicians who fail to grasp the meaning of irreversible changes. In the sphere of nuclear weapons, as in some other spheres, they live by old notions.

The way out also lies in overcoming the gap between the fast pace of events and the realization of the state of things, of what is actually happening and what consequences it may have. And this must be done before it is too late.

We know that some people still regard the world as their private domain and declare zones of their "vital interests" wherever they like. This in turn stimulates the arms race because such views stem from a policy of strength, without which it is impossible to attain political and economic domination. This is stereotyped thinking belonging to a time when it was considered "right" to exploit other peoples, to manage their resources and arbitrarily to decide their destinies.

Such views lead to new regional conflicts and incite hatred. The conflicts assume dangerous proportions, involving more and more countries as their interests are affected directly or indirectly. Regional conflicts have a very negative impact on international relations as a whole. People are being killed in wars declared and undeclared, at the front and in the rear. Countries suffering from dire poverty and mass hunger are being drawn into the abyss of a wasteful arms race.

The settlement of regional conflicts is an imperative of our time. And our initiatives on the Middle East may serve as an example of our approach to the problem. The Middle East is a

major nerve center of our planet. The interests of many nations, and not only the Arabs and Israel, intertwine there. It is
a crossroad of histories, religions and cultures. Therefore, a
very responsible, cautious and even delicate approach is
needed. Power politics, piratical raids and constant threats to
use force are unacceptable.

This is what we propose: let us search and act together. This
applies to the Iran-Iraq war, the crisis in Central America, the
Afghan problem and the situation in the south of Africa and in
Indochina. The main thing is to respect the rights of the peoples to decide their own destiny and not to interfere in the
internal affairs of other states.

We are against attempts artificially to disrupt historical ties.
Yet, justice requires a regulation of international economic activities so that the rich will not rob the poor. Can one live
unperturbed in a world where three-quarters of the countries
are deep in debt, while a handful of states are playing the role
of omnipotent usurers? The preservation of such a situation is
fraught with a social explosion also capable of destroying modern civilization.

A just political settlement of regional conflicts is dictated by
the same logic about an interrelated and integral world. This
logic also demands the solution of other global problems, such
as food, ecology, energy, and worldwide literacy, education
and medical care.

Another plight of the modern world is terrorism. It is a
great evil. Yet, as I have said recently, attempts to put an end
to it by state-sponsored terrorism are a still greater crime
against humanity. This "method" leads to more deaths and
undermines international law and the sovereignty of states, not
to mention moral principles and the principles of justice. It
creates a vicious circle of violence and bloodshed, and the
overall situation deteriorates.

We have already declared at the United Nations and other
international forums—and I would like to repeat it today—
that we are prepared to cooperate with other countries in the
fight against all forms of terrorism.

All the problems I have spoken of here today are important

and when they are solved new vistas will open up before human civilization. Yet, their dependence on one another is not identical: without halting the arms race we will not be able fully to solve any other problems.

The Soviet Union and the Soviet people consider themselves part of the international community. The worries of mankind are our worries, its pain is our pain and its hopes are our hopes.

With all the differences between us, we must all learn to preserve our one big family of humanity.

At our meeting in Geneva, the U.S. President said that if the earth were threatened by an invasion by extraterrestrials, the United States and the Soviet Union would join forces to repel such an invasion. I will not dispute the hypothesis, though I think it is too early to worry about such an invasion. It is more important to ponder over the problems which are already facing us. It is more important to realize the need to eliminate the nuclear threat and accept the fact that there would be no roof, either on earth or in space, to save us if a nuclear storm broke out.

Our idea of creating a comprehensive system of international security and our other initiatives clearly show that the Soviet Union is willing and ready to renounce its nuclear power status and reduce all other armaments to a level of reasonable sufficiency.

The USSR does not want anything it would deny others and does not seek an ounce more security than, say, the United States has. However, the Soviet Union will never agree to an inferior status or discrimination against it.

Take all our proposals. There are no weapons of ours that are not subject to negotiations. Our principle is simple: all armaments should be limited and reduced, and mass-destruction weapons should be eventually scrapped. Such is our firm position. If there is any imbalance, we must restore the balance, not by letting the one short of some elements build them up, but by having the one with more of them scale them down. The historic goal before us—a demilitarized world—will have to be achieved stage by stage, of course. At each stage, there must definitely be respect for mutual interests and a balance of reasonable sufficiency whose level should be constantly lowered. Everybody must realize and agree on this: parity in the capability to destroy one another several times over is madness and an absurdity.

It is important, in our view, while lowering the level of military confrontation, to carry through such measures as would make it possible to lessen, or better still, altogether exclude the possibility of a surprise attack. The most dangerous offensive arms must be removed from the zone of contact. Quite naturally, military doctrines must be of a strictly defensive nature.

I have already had occasion to point out that since we are now coming to consider major measures for actual disarmament affecting a most sensitive area—that of national security —the Soviet Union will be working for the strictest system of supervision and verification, including international verification. There must be complete certainty that the commitments are honored by all. Could not we take the Soviet-American experiment at Semipalatinsk as a prototype of such supervision?

There is yet another aspect to the question of verification. It is common knowledge that the United States has numerous military bases on the territory of other countries. We would like to have access to them in order at least to carry out the necessary inspection and make sure that no activity is taking place there that is prohibited under any possible agreement. This would apparently require cooperation on the part of the states on whose territory those bases are situated.

Of course, it will be better still to consider again the old idea of dismantling foreign bases and bringing the troops back home. We apply this to ourselves, too. We have already taken the first practical steps. As you know, some of our forces are being withdrawn from the Mongolian People's Republic in accordance with an agreement reached with our Mongolian friends. We have withdrawn six regiments from Afghanistan, and we shall withdraw the whole of our military contingent within as short a time as possible. But there has to be reciprocity on the part of the United States and Afghanistan's neighbors, as well as international efforts aimed at resolving this problem.

We do not claim to know the ultimate truth. We readily respond to proposals made by other countries, political parties, public movements and individuals. The Soviet Union has supported the idea of a nuclear-free corridor in Central Europe, and nuclear-free zones in Northern Europe, the Balkans, the South Pacific and other regions. We are ready to hold consultations on all proposals in order to find the best variant, one that would suit everybody.

Dear guests,

Comrades,

A promising and noble idea has been expressed at your forum—that of setting up a "Human Survival Fund." Such an institution could be used for open discussion of the nuclear war threat. The Fund could encourage research into the burning international issues and contribute towards drafting projects on the global problems facing humanity, including the combatting of new lethal diseases.

We would be glad to see the Soviet public take an active part, both on a material and intellectual plane, in the work of such a Fund.

I do not doubt that the good seeds your forum has sown will yield a good crop. The forces of militarism—and they are often synonymous with the forces of ignorance and intellectual blindness—are not omnipotent.

The movement of scientists for the elimination of the nuclear threat, the fervent and most competent speeches by physicians, environmentalists, cultural figures and workers in the arts, and the appearance of various antinuclear groups and associations are all clear evidence of the determination of sober-minded people everywhere to save the precious gift of life on Earth, perhaps the only one of its kind in the universe.

I see politicians and political scientists in this audience. And I wonder whether we can, with the knowledge and the experience we have today, move step by step towards more balanced and harmonious international relations, and towards an all-embracing system of international security, one that is dependable and equal for all. I think we can and must do that.

I believe it is the hope and desire to find a positive answer to this question that has brought you to this forum.

Our great scientist, Vladimir Vernadsky, warned back in 1922 (just think, 65 years ago!): "It will not be long before man gets hold of atomic energy, such a source of power as will enable him to build new life as he wishes. . . . Will man be able to use that power for his own good, not for self-destruction? Is he wise enough to be able to use that power which science will certainly give him? Scientists must not close their eyes to the possible implications of their research effort and of scientific progress. They must feel responsible for the consequences of their discoveries. They must link their work to better organization of all mankind."

Let us ponder over these words. Earlier man had tried, without too much thought, to subdue the forces of nature. Now, invading nature without considering all the possible consequences might turn nature into a deadly enemy of humanity. The Chernobyl accident reminded us of this, and Chernobyl was a tragedy of relatively local proportions. While the nuclear arms race is inexorably pushing us towards a universal tragedy.

For centuries men have sought immortality. It is difficult to accept the fact that we are all mortal. But it would simply be impossible to reconcile ourselves to the doom of all humanity, of human reason itself.

Unfortunately, many of our generation have grown accustomed to nuclear weapons. Many have come to regard them as a kind of idol demanding more and more sacrifices. Some even went so far as to declare that the nuclear arms race is a guarantee of peace.

Alas, nuclear weapons have in many ways molded the image of the times we live in. Naturally, destroying them does not mean going back to what was before. Renunciation of nuclear deterrence must not give free rein to trigger-happy individuals. This is by no means an idle question. Some would say that the answer lies in upgrading other components of military power, conventional arms. But that would be a wrong way.

Humanity must become stronger and overcome the nuclear sickness and then enter the post-nuclear age. It will acquire an immunity to violence and to attempts to dictate to others. Today, international relations are made soulless by the worship of force and the militarization of consciousness. Hence the goal of humanizing international relations.

Is that possible? Some believe it is, others think not. There is no use arguing about it at this moment. I think life itself will give the answer. On the whole, the people are coming to realize that. They already realize that a nuclear war must never be fought. So let us take the first big step: reduce the nuclear arsenals and keep outer space weapon-free. Let us start from the vantage ground of Reykjavik, move on from there and see how that will affect the international atmosphere. My own feeling is that each such step will create greater confidence and open fresh vistas for cooperation. And more democratic thinking at the international level, equality, and independent and active participation of all nations, large, medium and small, in the affairs of the world community should help the process.

To "humanize" international relations, there have to be appropriate actions in the humanitarian field, too, specifically as regards information, human contacts, professional exchanges, etc. That will help create moral guarantees for peace and thus contribute towards working out the material guarantees. The information aggression practiced by some countries not only leads to spiritual degradation, but obstructs normal contacts between people of different countries and hinders mutual cultural enrichment. It gives rise to ill feelings and alienation between peoples. On the other hand, you will agree that a people that knows and values the culture and art of other peoples can have no ill feelings towards them.

Ladies and gentlemen,

Comrades,

In view of the growing danger of a new spiral in the arms race and of the drastic aggravation of regional and so-called global problems, we must waste no more time trying to outplay each other and to gain unilateral advantages. The stake in such a game is too high—the survival of humanity. Therefore, it is now important to take the crucial factor of time into account.

So may the ideas of this forum reach every corner on Earth, hasten enlightenment and broaden mutual understanding. May your efforts help bring about a nuclear-weapon-free and nonviolent world, for the sake of preserving human civilization!

2

"Realities and Guarantees for a Secure World"

Pravda, September 17, 1987

The 42nd session of the United Nations General Assembly opened a few days ago. That fact led to this article.

Objective processes are making our complex and diverse world more and more interrelated and interdependent. And it increasingly needs a mechanism capable of discussing common problems in a responsible fashion and at a representative level. This mechanism needs to be a place of mutual search for a balance of differing, contradictory, yet real, interests of the contemporary community of states and nations. The United Nations Organization is called upon to be such a mechanism by its underlying idea and its origin. We are confident that it is capable of fulfilling that role. This is why in the first days of autumn, when vacation time is over and international political life is rapidly gathering momentum, when an opportunity for important decisions in the disarmament field can be discerned, we in the Soviet leadership deemed it useful to share our ideas on the basic issues of world politics at the end of the 20th century. This seems all the more appropriate since the current session of the United Nations General Assembly is devoted to major aspects of such politics.

Naturally, what we would like to do first of all in this connection is to try to see for ourselves what the idea of a comprehensive system of international security—the idea advanced at the 27th CPSU Congress—looks like 18 months after the Congress. This idea has won backing from many states. Our friends—the socialist countries and members of the nonaligned movement—are active co-authors.

This article deals primarily with our approach to the formation of such a system. At the same time it is an invitation for the United Nations member-countries and the world public to exchange views.

I

The last quarter of the 20th century has brought changes in the material aspect of being—changes revolutionary in their content and significance. For the first time in its history, mankind became capable of resolving many problems that had hindered its progress for centuries. From the standpoint of the existing and newly created resources and technologies, there are no impediments to feeding a population of many billions, to educating it, providing it with housing and keeping it healthy. Despite the obvious differences and potentialities of the various peoples and countries, a prospect has arisen of befitting standards of living for the inhabitants of the Earth.

At the same time dangers have emerged which put into question the very immortality of the human race. This is why new rules of coexistence on our unique planet are badly needed, rules which conform to the new requirements and the changed conditions.

Alas, many influential forces continue adhering to outdated notions concerning ways for ensuring national security. As a result the world is in an absurd situation whereby persistent efforts are being made to convince it that the road to the abyss is the most correct one. It would be difficult to appraise in any other way the point of view that nuclear weapons make it possible to avert a world war. It is not simple to refute it, precisely because it is totally unfounded. One has to dispute something which is being passed off as an axiom—because no world war has broken out since the emergence of nuclear weapons, those weapons have averted it. It would seem more correct to say that a world war has been averted despite the existence of nuclear weapons.

Some time back the sides had several scores of atomic bombs apiece, then each came to possess a hundred nuclear missiles, and finally, the arsenals grew to several thousand nuclear warheads. Not long ago Soviet and American scientists made a special study of the relationship between strategic stability and the size of nuclear arsenals. They arrived at the unanimous conclusion that 95 percent of all U.S. and Soviet nuclear arms can be eliminated without stability being disrupted. This is a killing argument against the "nuclear deterrence" strategy that gives birth to mad logic. We believe that the 5 percent should not be retained either. And then the stability will be qualitatively different.

Not laying claims to instructing anyone and having come to realize that mere statements about the dangerous situation in the world are unproductive, we began seeking an answer to the question of the possibility today of a model for ensuring national security which would not be fraught with the threat of a worldwide catastrophe.

Such an approach was in the mainstream of the concepts formed during the evolution of a new mode of political thinking which is permeated with a realistic view of what is surrounding us and happening around us and of ourselves; this view is characterized by an unbiased attitude towards others and an awareness of our own responsibility and security.

The new thinking is bridging the gap between word and deed. And we have embarked on practical action. Sure that nuclear weapons are the greatest evil and pose the most horrible threat, we announced a unilateral moratorium on nuclear tests, which we observed, let me put it straight, longer than we might have done . . . Then came the January 15, 1986 Statement putting forth a concrete program for the stage-by-stage elimination of nuclear weapons. At the meeting with President Reagan in Reykjavik we came close to understanding the desirability and possibility of complete nuclear disarmament.

And then we took steps making it easier to approach an agreement on the elimination of two classes of nuclear arms—medium- and shorter-range missiles.

We believe this to be possible and realistic. In this connection I would like to note that the Government of Federal Germany has assumed a stand conducive to this to a certain extent. The Soviet Union is proceeding from the premise that a relevant treaty could be worked out before the end of the current year. Much has been said about its potential advantages. I will not repeat them. I would only like to note that it would deal a tangible blow to concepts of the limited use of nuclear weapons and the so-called "controllable escalation" of a nuclear conflict. There are no illusory intermediate options. The situation is becoming more stable.

This treaty on medium- and shorter-range missiles would be a fine prelude to a breakthrough at the talks on large-scale—50 percent—reductions in strategic offensive arms under strict observance of the ABM Treaty. I believe that, given the mutual striving, an accord on that matter could become a reality as early as the first half of next year.

While thinking of advancing towards a nuclear-weapon-free world it is essential to see to it even now that security be ensured in the process of disarmament, at each of its stages, and to think not only about that, but also to agree on mechanisms for maintaining peace at drastically reduced levels of non-nuclear armaments.

All these questions were included in proposals set forth jointly by the USSR and other socialist countries at the United Nations—proposals for the establishment of a system of international peace and security.

How do we see this system?

The security plan we proposed provides, above all, for continuity and concord with the existing institutions of the maintenance of peace. The system could function on the basis of the UN Charter and within the framework of the United Nations. As we see it, its ability to function will be ensured by the strict observance of the Charter's demands, additional unilateral obligations of states, as well as confidence measures and international cooperation in all spheres—politico-military, economic, ecological, humanitarian and others.

I do not venture to foretell how the system of all-embracing security will appear in its final form. It is only clear that it can become a reality only if all means of mass annihilation are destroyed. We propose that all this be pondered by an independent commission of experts and specialists, which would submit its conclusions to the United Nations Organization.

Personally, I have no doubt about the capability of sovereign states to assume obligations even now in the field of international security. Many states are already doing this. The Soviet Union and the People's Republic of China have stated that they will not be the first to use nuclear arms. The Soviet-American agreements on nuclear armaments are another example. They contain a conscious choice of restraint and self-limitation in the most sensitive sphere of relations between the USSR and the United States. Or take the Treaty on the Non-Proliferation of Nuclear Weapons. What is it? It is a unique example of the high sense of responsibility of states.

In reality "bricks" which can be used to start building the future system of security already exist today.

The sphere of the reasonable, responsible and rational organization of international affairs is expanding before our very eyes, though timidly. Previously unknown standards of openness, of scope and depth for mutual monitoring and verification of compliance with adopted obligations, are being established. An American inspection team visits an area where exercises of Soviet troops were held; a group of United States Congressmen inspects the Krasnoyarsk radar station; American scientists install and adjust their instruments in the area of the Soviet nuclear testing range. Soviet and American observers are present at each other's military exercises. Annual plans of military activities are published under the accords within the framework of the Helsinki process.

I do not know a weightier and more impressive argument in support of the fact that the situation is changing than the stated readiness of a nuclear power to renounce nuclear weapons voluntarily. References to an aspiration to replace them with conventional armaments in which there supposedly exists an imbalance between NATO and the Warsaw Treaty in the latter's favor are unjustified. If an imbalance and disproportions exist, let us remove them. We do not tire of saying this all the time and we have proposed concrete ways of solving this problem.

In all these issues the Soviet Union is a pioneer and shows that its words are matched by deeds.

The question of comparing defense spending? Here we will have to put in more work. I think that, given proper effort, within the next two or three years we will be able to compare the figures that are of interest to us and our partners and which would symmetrically reflect the expenditures of the sides.

The Soviet-American talks on nuclear and space arms, and the convention on the prohibition of chemical weapons, which is close to being concluded, will intensify, I am sure, the advance to détente and disarmament.

An accord on "defense strategy" and "military sufficiency" could impart a powerful impulse in this direction. These notions presuppose a structure for a state's armed forces in which these forces would be sufficient for repulsing any possible aggression but inadequate for conducting offensive actions. The first step towards this could be a controlled withdrawal of nuclear and other offensive weapons from borders, with the subsequent creation along borders of strips of sparse armaments and demilitarized zones between potential, let us put it this way, adversaries. And in principle we should work for the dissolution of military blocs, the elimination of bases on foreign territory and the return home of all troops stationed abroad.

The question of a possible mechanism to prevent the outbreak of a nuclear conflict is more complex. Here I approach the most sensitive point of the idea of all-embracing security: much will have to be thought over further and improved. In any case the international community should work out agreed-upon measures for the event of a violation of the all-embracing agreement on the non-use and elimination of nuclear arms or of an attempt to violate this agreement. As for potential nuclear piracy, it appears possible and necessary to consider in advance and prepare collective measures to prevent it.

If the system is sufficiently effective, then it will provide even more effective guarantees of averting and curbing non-nuclear aggression.

The system proposed by us presupposes precisely definite measures which would enable the United Nations Organization, the main universal security body, to ensure its maintenance at a level of reliability.

II

The division of the world's countries into those possessing nuclear weapons and those not possessing them has split also the very concept of security. But for human life security is indivisible. In this sense it is not only a political, military and juridical category, but also a moral one. And contentions that there has been no war for already half a century do not withstand any test on the touchstone of ethics. Who said there is no war? There are dozens of regional wars raging in the world!

It is immoral to treat this as something of secondary importance. But the heart of the matter lies in more than just impermissible nuclear haughtiness. The elimination of nuclear weapons would also be a major step towards a genuine democratization of relations between states, towards establishing their equality and their equal responsibility.

Unconditional observance of the United Nations Charter and the right of peoples to choose for themselves the roads and forms of their development, revolutionary or evolutionary, is an imperative condition for universal security. This applies also to the right to a social status quo, which is exclusively an internal matter. Any attempts, direct or indirect, to influence the development of other than one's own country, to interfere in such development, should be ruled out. Just as inadmissible are attempts to destabilize existing governments from outside.

At the same time the world community cannot remain an outsider to interstate conflicts. Here it could be possible to begin by fulfilling the proposal made by the United Nations Secretary General to set up under the United Nations Organization a multilateral center for lessening the danger of war. Evidently, it would be feasible to consider the expediency of setting up a direct communication line between the United Nations headquarters and the capitals of the countries that are permanent members of the Security Council, and the location of the Chairman of the nonaligned movement.

It appears to us that, in the interests of greater trust and mutual understanding, a mechanism could be set up under the aegis of the United Nations Organization for extensive international verification of compliance with agreements on lessening international tension and limiting armaments, and of the military situation in conflict areas. The mechanism would use various forms and methods of monitoring to collect information and promptly submit it to the United Nations. This would provide an objective picture of the events taking place and timely detection of preparations for hostilities; it would impede sneak attacks, make possible measures to avert any armed conflict, and prevent such conflicts from expanding and becoming worse.

We are arriving at the conclusion that wider use should be made of United Nations' military observers and United Nations' peace-keeping forces for disengaging the troops of warring sides and for ensuring that ceasefire and armistice agreements are observed.

And, of course, at all stages of a conflict, extensive use should be made of all means of peaceful settlement of disputes and differences between states, and good offices and mediation should be offered with the aim of achieving an armistice. The ideas and initiatives concerning the setting up of nongovernmental commissions and groups which would analyze the causes, circumstances and methods of resolving various concrete conflict situations appear to be fruitful.

The Security Council permanent members could become guarantors of regional security. They could, on their part, assume an obligation not to use force or the threat of force and to renounce demonstrative military presence, because such a practice is one of the factors fanning regional conflicts.

A drastic intensification and expansion of cooperation between states in uprooting international terrorism is extremely important. It would be expedient to concentrate this cooperation within the framework of the United Nations. In our opinion, it would be useful to create under its aegis a tribunal to investigate acts of international terrorism.

More coordination in the struggle against apartheid as a destabilizing factor of international magnitude would also be justified.

As we see it, all the above-stated measures could become an organic part of an all-embracing system for peace and security.

III

The events and tendencies of the past decades have expanded this concept, imparting new and specific features to it. One of them is the problem of economic security. A world in which a whole continent can find itself on the brink of death from starvation and in which huge masses of people are suffering from almost permanent malnutrition is not a safe world. Neither is a world safe in which a multitude of countries and peoples are being strangled in a noose of debt.

The economic interests of individual countries or groups of them are indeed so different and contradictory that consensus with regard to the concept of the New International Economic Order seems hard to achieve. We do hope, however, that the instinct of self-preservation will start working here as well. It is certain to manifest itself if we manage to determine the priorities and realize that there are circumstances that are menacing in their inevitability, and that it is high time to abandon the inert political mentality and views of the outside world inherited from the past. This world has ceased to be a sphere which the big and strong divide into domains and zones of "vital interests."

The imperatives of the times compel us to elevate to the rank of politics many common sense notions. It is not philanthropy which prompted our proposal for reduction in interest payments on bank credits and the elaboration of extra benefits for the least developed nations. This holds benefit for all, namely—for a secure future. If the debt burden of the developing world is alleviated, the chances for such a future will grow. It is also possible to limit debt payments by each developing country to the share of its annual export earnings without detriment to development; to accept export commodities in payment for the debt; to remove protectionist barriers on the borders of creditor nations; and to stop adding extra interest when payments on debts are deferred.

There may be different attitudes to these proposals. There is no doubt, however, that the majority of international community members realize the need for immediate actions to ease the developing world's debt burden. If this is so, through concerted effort it would be possible to start working out a program.

The words "through concerted effort" are very important for today's world. The interconnection between disarmament and development, confirmed at the recent international conference in New York, can be used in practice if none of the strong and the rich keep themselves aloof. I have already expressed the view that the Security Council member states, represented by their top officials, could jointly discuss this problem and work out a coordinated approach. I confirm this proposal.

Ecological security. It is dangerous in the direct meaning of the word when currents of poison flow along river channels, when poisonous rains pour down from the sky, when an atmosphere polluted with industrial and transport waste chokes cities and whole regions, when the development of atomic engineering involves unacceptable risks.

Many have suddenly begun to perceive all that not as something abstract, but as quite a real part of their own experience. The confidence that "this won't affect us," characteristic of the past outlook, has disappeared. They say that one thorn of experience is worth more than a whole forest of instructions. For us, Chernobyl became such a thorn . . .

The relationship between man and the environment has become menacing. Problems of ecological security affect all—the rich and the poor alike. What is required is a global strategy for nature conservation and the rational use of resources. We suggest starting its elaboration within the framework of the UN special program.

Countries are already exchanging relevant information and notifying international organizations of the state of affairs. We believe that this practice should be turned into a law by introducing the principle of annual reports by governments about their nature conservation activity and about ecological incidents, both those that have already occurred and those that were prevented on the territory of their countries.

To realize the need for opening a common front of economic and ecological security and to start its formation mean defusing a delayed-action bomb planted deep inside mankind's existence by history, by people themselves.

IV

Human rights. One can name all the top statesmen of our times who have threatened to use nuclear weapons. Some may object: it is one thing to threaten and another to use. Indeed, they haven't used them. But campaigning for human rights is in no way compatible with threatening to use weapons of mass destruction. We hold it unacceptable to talk about human rights and freedoms while intending to hang up "chandeliers" of exotic weapons in outer space. The only ordinary element in that "exoticism" is the potential possibility of mankind's annihilation. The rest is in dazzling wrapping.

I agree: the world cannot be considered secure if human rights are being violated. I will only add: it cannot be considered secure if a large part of this world lacks elementary conditions for a life worthy of man, if millions of people have a full "right" to go hungry, to have no roof over their heads and to be jobless and sick indefinitely, since treatment is something they cannot afford, and if, finally, the most basic human right, the right to life, is disregarded.

First of all, it is necessary that national legislation and administrative rules in the humanitarian sphere be brought into accordance with international obligations and standards everywhere.

Simultaneously, it would be possible to start coordinating a broad range of practical steps; for instance, to start working out a world information program under UN auspices to familiarize peoples with the life of others, life as it is and not as someone would like to present it. That is precisely why such a project should envisage ridding the flow of information of "enemy image" stereotypes, of bias, prejudices and absurd concoctions, of deliberate distortion and unscrupulous violation of the truth.

There is much promise in the task of coordinating unified international legal criteria for handling in a humanitarian spirit issues of the reunion of families, marriages, contacts between people and organizations, visa regulations and so on. What has been achieved on this account within the framework of the all-European process should be accepted as a starting point.

We favor the establishment of a special fund of humanitarian cooperation of the United Nations formed from voluntary state contributions through reductions in military spending and private donations.

It is advisable that all states join the UNESCO conventions in the sphere of culture, including the conventions on the protection of the world cultural heritage and on the prohibition and prevention of the illicit import, export and transfer of ownership of cultural property.

Alarming signals of recent times have pushed to the top of the agenda the idea of creating a worldwide network of medical cooperation in treating the most dangerous diseases, including AIDS, and combatting drug addiction and alcoholism. The existing structures of the World Health Organization make it possible to establish such a network relatively quickly. The leaders of the world movement of physicians have valuable ideas on this account.

Dialogue on humanitarian problems could be conducted on a bilateral basis, within the forms of negotiations that have

already been established. Furthermore, we propose holding
such dialogue within the framework of an international conference in Moscow. We made that proposal at the Vienna meeting
in November last year.

Pooling efforts in the sphere of culture, medicine and humanitarian rights is yet another integral part of the system of
comprehensive security.

V

The proposed system of comprehensive security will be effective to the extent to which the United Nations, its Security
Council and other international institutes and mechanisms effectively function. It will be necessary resolutely to enhance
the authority and role of the UN and the International Atomic
Energy Agency. There is a strong need for a world space organization. In the future it could work in close contact with the
UN as an autonomous part of its system. UN specialized agencies should also become regulators of international processes.
The Geneva Conference on Disarmament should become a
forum that would internationalize the efforts for a transition to
a nuclear-free, nonviolent world.

One should not forget the possibilities of the International
Court of Justice either. The General Assembly and the Security Council could approach it more often for consultative conclusions on controversial international legal issues. Its manda-
tory jurisdiction should be recognized by all on mutually
agreed upon conditions. The permanent members of the Security Council, taking into account their special responsibility,
should make the first step in that direction.

We are convinced that a comprehensive system of security is
at the same time a system of universal law and order which
ensures the primacy of international law in politics.

The UN Charter gives extensive powers to the Security
Council. Joint efforts are required to ensure that it could use
them effectively. For this purpose, it would be expedient to
hold meetings of the Security Council at Foreign Ministers'
level when opening a regular session of the General Assembly

to review the international situation and jointly search for effective ways towards its improvement.

It would be useful to hold meetings of the Security Council not only at the headquarters of the UN in New York, but also in regions of friction and tension as well as to alternate among the capitals of the Security Council permanent member states.

Special missions of the Council to regions of actual and potential conflicts would also help consolidate its authority and enhance the effectiveness of the decisions adopted.

We are convinced that cooperation between the UN and regional organizations could be considerably expanded. The aim is to search for a political settlement to crisis situations.

In our view, it is important to hold special sessions of the General Assembly on the more urgent political problems and individual disarmament issues more often so as to improve the efficiency of the latter's work.

We emphatically stress the need for making the status of important political documents passed at the United Nations by consensus more binding morally and politically. Let me recall that they include, among others, the final document of the 1st Special Session of the UN General Assembly on Disarmament, and the Charter of Economic Rights and Duties of States.

In our opinion, we should have long ago set up a world consultative council under the UN auspices to bring together the world's intellectual elite. Prominent scientists, political and public figures, representatives of international public organizations, cultural workers, people in literature and the arts, including winners of the Nobel Prize and other international prizes of worldwide significance, and eminent representatives of the churches could greatly enrich the spiritual and ethical potential of contemporary world politics.

To ensure that the United Nations and its specialized agencies operate at full capacity it should be realized that using financial levers to pressure it is inadmissible. The Soviet Union will continue to cooperate actively in overcoming budget difficulties arising at the United Nations.

And, finally, about the United Nations' Secretary General. The international community elects an authoritative figure en-

joying everybody's trust to that high post. Since the Secretary
General is functioning as a representative of every member
country of the organization, all states should give him the
maximum of support and help him in fulfilling his responsible
mission. The international community should encourage the
United Nations' Secretary General in his missions of good offices, mediation and reconciliation.

*　*　*

Why are we so persistent in raising the question of a comprehensive system of international peace and security?

Simply because it is impossible to put up with the situation
in which the world has found itself as the third millennium
draws nearer—facing the threat of annihilation, existing in a
state of constant tension, in an atmosphere of suspicion and
strife, spending huge funds and the labor and talent of millions
of people to increase mutual distrust and fears.

We could speak indefinitely about the need for terminating
the arms race and uprooting militarism, and about cooperation. Nothing will change unless we start acting.

The political and moral core of the problem is the trust of
states and peoples in one another, respect for international
agreements and institutions. And we are prepared to switch
from confidence measures in individual spheres to a large-scale
policy of trust which would gradually shape a system of comprehensive security. But such a policy should be based on one-
ness of political statements and real stands.

The idea of a comprehensive system of security is the first
project of a possible new organization of life in our common
planetary home. In other words, it is a pass into a future where
the security of all is a token of the security of each. We hope
that the current session of the UN General Assembly will
jointly develop and elaborate on this idea.

3

Speech in Murmansk

October 1, 1987

Dear Comrades,

I have come to you to familiarize myself with the life of the Soviet Polar Region, to get first-hand information about your work and concerns and, most important, to fulfill the honorary mission entrusted to me by the CPSU Central Committee and the Presidium of the USSR Supreme Soviet and present the Hero City of Murmansk the high award of the Homeland.

Murmansk's glorious history is a bright mirror reflection of the destiny of our country. Soviet power was proclaimed here on the second day after the armed uprising in Petrograd. Today, recalling those days, we admire the heroism and selflessness displayed by working people in the Far North during those legendary days and years.

Throughout the hardships of the Civil War, when the very existence of the Soviet Republic was at stake, Murmansk's workers, together with revolutionary soldiers and seamen, bravely fought against the interventionists and White Guards. They prevented the transformation of the Kola Peninsula into a staging area for an offensive on red Petrograd.

Large-scale construction in keeping with the plans for industrialization was begun in the first five-year-plan periods.

The Great Patriotic War was a stern test for city dwellers as

it was for all Soviet people. The defense of the Soviet Polar
Region lasted 40 months. The plans of the German fascist
command to seize Murmansk failed. The city not only held
out, it paralyzed the enemy's strike forces and steadfastly defended the state border.

Communists and Komsomol members were the first to take
up arms. The troops of the Karelian front (which included the
"Polar division," set up in Murmansk) played a decisive role
in defeating the alpine regiments of the fascists on the Bol-
shaya Zapadnaya Litsa River. The marines and guerrilla units
carried out devastating raids behind the enemy lines. Men,
fighting at the front, were replaced at machine tools by women
and teenagers. Murmansk fishermen caught fish under enemy
fire.

Murmansk during the war was a major center of cooperation of the countries of the anti-Hitler coalition. And Murmansk again saw men in American and British uniforms, but
in a quite different capacity, not what they had been twenty
years before—this time they were allies. We have not forgotten, nor shall we ever forget, how Allied convoys with weapons and equipment for the Soviet Army broke their way
through the Hitlerite blockade to reach Murmansk. The courage of Soviet, British and American sailors who made this
operation possible remains a vivid symbol of cooperation between our peoples in the period of the Second World War.

The memory of those events sears us with the burning truth
of selfless heroism. The great courage of Soviet troops and
workers on the home front was especially manifest here on the
Kola Peninsula, in the rigorous conditions of the Far North.
Their profound feeling of civic responsibility for the future of
the socialist land gave the Murmansk people the strength to
surpass the limits of human endurance. These patriots will
never be forgotten. What was the Valley of Death will remain
in popular memory forever as a Valley of Glory.

The heroic defenders of Murmansk had absorbed the forti-
tude and gallantry as well as the wisdom of many generations
of northerners, starting from the ancient Russian Pomors. Let
us recall, for example, that it was here at Murmansk, in the

arduous fishing trade, that a great son of Russia, a scientist of genius and an ardent patriot, Mikhail Vasilyevich Lomonosov, spent his youth. It is to these parts, to the Kola Peninsula, that Pugachyov's men were sent to eternal exile. This was the place that the families of many political exiles, revolutionaries, chose to take refuge during the years of the czarist autocracy.

The October Revolution opened a new chapter in the history of this region and created favorable conditions for the tapping of its natural wealth. Inspired by the ideas of social progress, the people enthusiastically embarked on sweeping changes in order to advance along the path of socialism.

Murmansk today is among the biggest ports in the USSR. It has become a base for Arctic development, pioneering a northern sea route, exploring the Kola Peninsula and surrounding seas, and exploiting their riches. New cities have sprung up in the region. A number of major scientific centers and industrial enterprises such as the Severonikel combine and the Apatit amalgamation have been built. It is here that the Red-Bannered Northern Fleet carries out its duties. It is here that our nuclear-powered ice breakers have their main base. Murmansk fishermen are making a considerable contribution to the country's food resources.

The military and industrial contributions of the people of the region and the city have won them high awards. Murmansk is a city with a heroic past and a radiant future, a city of fine revolutionary traditions and labor accomplishments which are continued today. It was, is, and we are sure, will remain, the nation's dependable outpost in the Arctic.

Permit me, dear Comrades, to fulfill the mission entrusted to me and to present to Murmansk the Order of Lenin and the Gold Star Medal.

Comrades,

On behalf of the CPSU Central Committee, the Presidium of the USSR Supreme Soviet and the Council of Ministers of the USSR I heartfully congratulate you, participants in this solemn meeting, all inhabitants of the city and region, the soldiers of the local garrison, the sailors of the Northern Fleet with the high well-deserved award and the conferring of the honorable title "Hero City" on the city of Murmansk.

We convey our cordial gratitude and appreciation to the participants in the Great Patriotic War—to those who fought at the front, to the partisans and workers of the rear. I wish you good health and creative forces, glorious veterans of war and labor.

It is a great honor to be a citizen of and to live in a Hero City. It means, I think, first of all, to be keenly aware of one's responsibility for the state of affairs, not only in this city, but also in the country as a whole, to be a citizen in the loftiest sense of the word and set an example of steadfast patriotism and real service to the interests of the people and fidelity to the cause of socialism.

To live and work in a Hero City means not only to develop production. It means to build not only high-rises, but also social relations of a new kind. It means fighting shortcomings, breaking inertia and initiating everything new and progressive that is associated today with restructuring, renewal, democratization and openness.

To be an inhabitant of a Hero City, in short, means to enhance its honor and glory everywhere and in all respects, the honor and glory of every factory and organization, of every work collective.

And you have people on whom you can rely. In the national economy of the Murmansk Region there are quite a few collectives noted for their ability to work. There are hundreds of real past masters in their jobs who show the highest responsibility in their work and put their hearts into it, who actively draw on all that is new in the life of the country.

Among those whose labor is especially productive and who are noted for their social activity are:

—head of a building team, USSR State Prize winner Semyon Konstantinovich Shitov;

—depot engine driver, Honorable Railwayman Boris Vasilyevich Kozlov;

—worker of the Murmansk fish-packing plant and deputy of

the RSFSR Supreme Soviet Melguzova Antonina Alekseyevna;

—Hero of Socialist Labor, Merited Doctor of the RSFSR Pyotr Andreyevich Bayandin;

—Merited School Teacher of the RSFSR Zinaida Ivanovna Dmitriyeva;

—delegates to the 27th Party Congress, Murmansk shipyard pipelayer Yuri Grigoryevich Baskakov, fishing fleet captain Nikolai Ivanovich Gutskalov and many, many others.

I heartfully congratulate you, Comrades, with your successes. I congratulate all front-rank workers, innovators and restless, daring and exploring people.

I have had a lot of meetings and conversations with working people recently. They were businesslike and open. The talk was about restructuring, its successes and difficulties, about problems and ways to resolve these problems, and about work which is directed towards the future.

It was very important for me, for the Political Bureau of the Central Committee, to be reminded again and again that Soviet people realize the necessity and urgency of the changes that have been started. The spirit of renewal is manifested ever more clearly in the life of your city and this is the main thing now.

Our meeting is held not long before a great national day, the anniversary of the October Socialist Revolution.

The path we have traversed over these seven decades has been far from smooth. It was a truly heroic path. The Soviet people have proved equal to resolving the huge tasks of restructuring society on new socialist principles.

The creation of a mighty power, our common home, in which scores of nations and peoples live and work shoulder to shoulder, is the crowning result of the work and struggle of all generations of Soviet people.

We take pride in the achievements of our Revolution. It is not for nothing that it is called Great. But this very greatness obliges us to see the problems that have accumulated in society and to see the new demands of present-day life.

It is precisely the lofty responsibility of the Party, for the

destiny of the people, for the destiny of socialism, that suggested the need for restructuring, and the need to speed up the
country's social and economic development.

We now have to do many things all at once, to make up for
the opportunities lost over the past decade. But we have to do
this. We cannot avoid this work. No one will do it for us.

Revolutionary construction, the implementation of the great
ideals and goals of the October Revolution, now continues at a
qualitatively new stage, in cardinally changed internal and ex-
ternal conditions.

What can be said about the restructuring now taking place
in society?

First of all, there have undoubtedly been positive changes
not only as regards awareness of its tasks and problems, but
also concerning practical approaches, concrete actions and
their results.

We are now more fully and deeply aware of many things in
our life than we were in the days of the 1985 April Plenary
Meeting of the CPSU Central Committee and even the 27th
Congress.

The fundamental directions of the work to be done in the
political, economic and social areas have been determined in
the just over two years that have passed since the April Plenary Meeting. The road to changes has thus been fully opened.

We now realize more clearly that in order to implement our
plans and intentions, we all have to put in much work, to
rebuild by joint efforts many things in our society.

We are not satisfied with the housing situation, the quantity
and quality of goods and services, the functioning of the social
sphere, the activity of state and economic organizations, etc.
These issues received priority attention here as well, during
meetings on Murmansk land. But all this is connected with
our work and with our attitude to it. So it turns out that we
must ourselves change if the situation in society is to be
changed the way we want. We know now that the restructuring affects every one of us without exception and that it involves certain difficulties.

We were saying quite recently that we need a new policy—

new decisions and bold approaches. We have such a policy now. There are new ideas and intentions implemented in concrete solutions today in every area of life. A new moral atmosphere without which profound transformations cannot be embarked on is thus emerging.

We all study now. We are learning great lessons from life.

We are learning lessons of truthfulness and openness.

We are learning lessons of responsibility and discipline.

We are learning lessons of wider democracy.

We are learning lessons of internationalism and patriotism.

The first results of the restructuring are most felt in the political climate of our society. It can now be said that the new way of thinking and conduct is emerging step by step in conflicts of opinion and sometimes in heated debates. I would say the social well-being of man is improving. This I feel with particular keenness on Murmansk land.

And one of the most noble tasks of the restructuring is precisely that of elevating working people, enhancing their prestige and dignity and expanding their capabilities and talents. This is the lofty aim and meaning of socialism.

The working people have seen for themselves how potent openness, criticism of shortcomings, and the drive for more democracy are as vehicles for renovation and restructuring. They expect restructuring to produce changes in the conditions of their life.

With this aim in view the CPSU Central Committee and the Government, well aware of the fact that the implementation of the restructuring program will take some time and require immense effort, are seeing to it that issues of vital importance for the people are dealt with promptly in the course of the restructuring process.

At the June Plenary Meeting of the CPSU Central Committee we brought to the fore such tasks as the provision of the population with foodstuffs, housing and consumer goods.

What has been done at the initial stage of the implementation of the social program drafted by the Party?

In the past two years the cash incomes of the population have increased by approximately 16 billion rubles in annual average terms. The salaries of physicians and teachers and grants of students at secondary specialized and higher educational establishments have gone up. Pensions to certain categories of working people have been increased.

In the sphere of foodstuffs—during the same period the annual average meat output increased by almost 2 million tons, milk output by 8.5 million tons, and egg output by 7 billion eggs. More grain, sugar beet and some other crops are being harvested. Changes for the better in foodstuff consumption are taking place on that basis. They are more substantial in those regions and republics where collective and state farms are operating better and where the possibilities of personal small holdings are used skillfully. Now the following principle operates: each republic, territory and region has an assignment for a five-year plan on the supply of products to the union and republican fund. And all the rest is kept to meet local needs. This is why everything produced in excess of the assigned plan will be kept for local consumption. This is stimulating not only every collective and state farm, and every work collective; every district and region is interested in it.

The scale of housing construction has increased. Last year 6.8 million square meters of housing more than in 1985 were built through the use of all sources of funding. In January–August 1987 the state alone put into service new houses with an area of 6.7 million square meters more than in the corresponding period of last year.

Investments in the construction of schools and pre-school child-care centers, clubs and cultural centers, hospitals, outpatient clinics and sports structures were substantially increased.

The situation regarding the output of consumer goods is also beginning to change, albeit slowly and with difficulty. The range of services offered to the population is expanding. All sectors of the national economy are increasing their contributions to the output of consumer goods and services. Let us get it straight: this process proceeds with great difficulties. Far from all have understood so far that no one can stay aloof from the problems involved in the accomplishment of this immensely important state task.

Last year the overall turnover of goods grew by nearly 8 billion rubles, while sales of alcoholic beverages dropped by 10.7 billion rubles. This means that we coped with the task of setting off the loss of a substantial portion of "drunken" incomes. However, for the time being we do not meet to the full the growing consumer demand of the population. In the eight months of the current year, despite diminished proceeds from alcohol sales as against the previous years, goods turnover grew by 5.8 billion rubles compared with the corresponding period of last year.

So, there are some positive changes. But when the consumer market situation is evaluated as a whole it must be frankly admitted: we are still very far from a radical change in that sphere. Our efforts must not be slackened either in the center or on the periphery. On the contrary, they should be intensified. This especially applies to quality and variety.

Soviet people ardently support the state course towards improving the health of the people. A document of great social and humanistic significance—the Guidelines for the development of health services in the country—was published for a nationwide discussion. This is a very major national program. Huge resources will be channelled into its realization.

Let me put it straight: we are ready to invest in health care, as in the educational sphere, the maximum possible share of that which we produce over and above plans. Even today additional financial resources to the sum of 5.6 billion rubles were found and devoted to the urgent needs of health care for the remaining three years of the five-year-plan period.

In a word, Comrades, our long-term and short-term plans in the social sphere are important. Our approach is clear—more concern for the people, more concern for their work and life. But these plans are directly linked with the acceleration of economic development, with the better work of every enterprise, collective and state farm, construction site, research establishment, laboratory, design bureau and so forth. And this means that for us the economy is the main area of restructuring.

We have lately boosted performance in industry, in the

agrarian sector and in capital construction. However, along-side certain changes for the better there have been setbacks, notably in machine building, the chemical and light industries. We are concerned about that. The situation in machine build-ing where deep-running modernization is in progress is a source of special concern. And we must surmount existing difficulties by all available means and ensure the success of the undertaking.

Thus, changes do take place in our economy. But there has been no breakthrough so far. It would be unreasonable to be-lieve that these ambitious goals can be attained in some two or three years, that during this period a dramatic change can take place in the fulfillment of these truly revolutionary tasks. We must do much in order to bring it about. There should be no illusions here, for it is a matter of restructuring the building, not merely repainting the walls. The main work lies ahead.

This question is often asked: what should be done? Let me say this: At the first stage we had to clarify the situation in the economy, in its individual sectors and regions, and determine where to start from, to make the necessary structural changes, alter the policy of capital investment and establish priorities. And, of course, we had to decide how we should run economic affairs, what forms of administration and what mechanism of management we needed, what new approaches we should take and what incentives we should provide in order to encourage the initiative of working people, including production workers, scientists and designers.

We completed this work in the main and adopted relevant documents. They were endorsed by the June Plenary Meeting of the Party's Central Committee. The chief among these is the Law on the State Enterprise.

The next stage has set in now. Every decision taken should now be implemented so that practical deeds follow our deci-sions. And, mind you, in strict compliance with what we have decided.

This effort, Comrades, should be started—if it has not been done yet—by setting things in good order, by strengthening discipline and organization in all production collectives, en-

hancing the responsibility of everyone for conscientiously fulfilling his immediate obligations. This is the starting point
from which all of us should travel—doing one's job conscientiously. A simple answer for all of us, for everyone, no matter
what post one holds, no matter what is one's employment position in our society.

In the past, society paid dearly for its failure to solve the
problems of order and organization. This is all the more impermissible now.

Young workers at the Severonikel plant were right when
they said that discipline has become rather loose among all of
us in general. And this is why things should be set in good
order everywhere, both at the top and in the republics, regions,
districts and in work collectives. Everywhere, Comrades. This
is very important now when we are effecting a radical reform
of our economy, when work should be done in a new fashion,
when initiative, self-reliance and a high sense of responsibility
are needed for accomplishing scientific, technological and organizational tasks, for putting new methods of management to
work.

Hence, the first and very important task of all work collectives is decisively to set things in good order, ensure good
organization, stronger discipline and the greater initiative of
the working people. Our senior officials and Party organizations should be pace-setters in this respect.

Until now many of them used to nod at those at the top: let
them straighten things out first. By the way, many Party bodies and managers used to refer very widely to those on high to
justify their own idleness and passivity, especially when working people literally assailed them, demanding that they make
real steps towards restructuring, changing the state of affairs
and solving problems that have piled up in each work collective, in one or another town or region. The decisions adopted
cut the ground from under such officials. The near future will
clarify many things and show who is worth what. It is important to work now. All political directives are here, decisions
have been adopted and tasks set. Everyone should act.

In a word, those who are still "in the trenches" marking

time should rise without delay and go into the offensive against shortcomings, neglect and lagging.

Today we particularly count on initiative and vigor, and on working people's principled attitude. This is how economic bodies should be guided, as well as our leading personnel and Party organizations. Everything is the concern of working people. It is their country, it is their system, it is their society. They are masters. Party organizations and cadres serve the people; the entire Party serves the people. Not the other way round. In production, members of work collectives should feel and behave as real masters. Any attempts—no matter from what quarter—to hinder the exercise of this right or the manifestation of the working people's initiative should be resolutely stopped.

Everything that is being done to improve the state of affairs, to remove all that impedes advance and the introduction of new methods of management, innovations and achievements of scientific and technological progress, is not only legitimate but vitally needed by our society.

The meaning of the decisions of the January and June Plenary Meetings of the CPSU Central Committee is to draw all working people into a real process of introducing order and organization to enterprises and in running the production and social affairs there. This is the main intent also of the Law on the State Enterprise.

That is why, Comrades, I want to say the following: do not wait any longer for instructions from above. You know the political directives. The relevant legal documents have been adopted. Now it is necessary to act, to release grassroots initiative. Officials and Party organizations should do everything for this process to develop faster and gain momentum.

In this connection I have pleasant impressions of my visit to the Murmansk Region and conversations with people. The people's initiative and their desire to be real masters make themselves felt already. As V. N. Ptitsyn, First Secretary of the Regional Committee, noted, in appraising today's situation in the region in general, it should be stressed outright that working people are pressing the managers and the Party organizations hard. They mean good; they want intensification.

If some people in economic, government or Party organizations are scared of that, it is only because they are not used to it. This is how things should be under socialism. Time will pass and you yourselves will look for ways to draw the collective's attention to any question, to resolve any question with its participation. This is the principal means. If a real alliance of leading personnel, Party organizations and work collectives is formed as a result, it will be a decisive force. Technology is a good thing. But if there is no such alliance, nothing will be achieved. People are the chief protagonists. Democracy and new methods of economic management are the chief means to set this force in motion. This is the conclusion the January and June Plenary Meetings of the CPSU Central Committee arrived at.

I would like to dwell particularly on the following. It is very important now to look closely into everything that concerns the Law on the Enterprise, self-supporting and collective contract, which we call the new economic mechanism. This, Comrades, is not at all simple. I recall 1986 when we were preparing for the first stage of introducing the state quality control system. Some took this seriously, others presumptuously. The first coped with their task well from the beginning of this year, though not without difficulties, while the latter found themselves in a flutter. So much so that some of them cannot get rid of it to this day. Comrades, there is nowhere to retreat.

We had a conversation in the port today. Dockers told us: we were given loaders, but they do not work. Why? The quality is bad. That is one example. Here are others: someone bought a TV set. Several days or hours later it was out of order. A tractor was supplied to a collective farm or a combine harvester to a village, but it takes another month to put it in working order. Can we depart from quality requirements, from the state quality control system, Comrades? Why then do we spend our working hours, strength, raw materials and energy on producing a no-good product? I don't want to deride everything. A lot of good things are being done in the country.

Take defenses, for instance. We are not inferior in anything here. So, we can work. Quality control inspectors in the defenses sphere work in a way that makes everybody sweat: workers, designers, engineers and managers. This is the way the state quality control system should operate. Then we will have the technology and commodities we want. If that is not done, why do we need money, what to buy with it? We should think hard. Why then do we go to work every morning? For what? All of us, our entire society, should ponder over this situation. We cannot forego state quality control. I have already spoken about this on behalf of the Central Committee many times and expressed profound gratitude to the working class for its understanding, class understanding of the fact that we cannot retreat from the line towards improving quality. The working class rendered us immense support in this respect. But some managers simply got lost.

We ought to study thoroughly the experience with state quality control and operation of our enterprises in these conditions and draw proper conclusions so as not to find ourselves in a difficult situation when, on January 1, 1988, 60 percent of our economy starts operating on cost-accounting, self-financing and self-repayment principles. This is more far-reaching than state quality control. As in the case of state quality control, we cannot give up cost accounting, self-financing and self-repayment.

We cannot retreat from what we have started. We began a war on drunkenness—we cannot retreat, although many are discontented. We hear about remarks made on account of the Government by people queueing up to buy this poison. That we know. Locally, some find it hard to withstand this pressure. We foresaw that, too, but the biggest mass of people are all for sobriety. If we waver, the frontline of our restructuring will collapse.

Once self-financing is introduced, the situation at enterprises will change, the entire economy will move forward and end results will be favorable. Thus, Comrades, new opportunities will present themselves for solving the entire complex of social problems. Tons of oil and ore, and cubic meters of gas, are not an end in themselves. Cubic meters of timber, tons of pig iron and steel and so forth are not the final result. We need all in order to have a bigger national income, which we would use to improve all aspects of our society's and our people's life. By the way, we have many tons now. But we spend 50 to 100 percent more energy and material resources per unit of national income than other developed countries. So it turns out that our national income could be 50 to 100 percent bigger with the same resources, provided this is done properly, on the basis of new technologies, on the basis of scientific and technological progress. Think how vast these possibilities are, how wasteful our wealth has made us. I've already said this and I repeat and shall repeat myself because that's how it is. We are swimming in resources. It is shameful how we treat them. We already feel what it may come to. Perhaps this sort of talk is not for an occasion such as this. But that's Leninist style.

Speaking of self-financing, work under this system will be rewarded and encouraged properly. This should also be kept in mind. In simple words, without using categories and terms of political economy, this reduces to one thing—encouragement for good performance and a befitting evaluation for a shoddy one.

Intentionally I don't go into the economic substance of cost accounting. But since all this makes the incomes of working people and, hence, their status and well-being dependent on the final results, one burning issue comes to light. What I want to say is that when an enterprise is self-financing, the working people, work collectives, are all extremely interested in having at the head of teams, production sections, shops, technical services and enterprises as a whole, competent, modern, able people to whom they can entrust their fate and on whom they can depend. This means that preparation for work in conditions of cost accounting includes the discussion and solution of personnel problems. Everything should be done in such a way as is demanded by the times and as the working people believe it should be done—democratically.

Industrial headquarters and national economic bodies must assist enterprises during this difficult transitional stage. This is the most important task for them now. These two days, while in Murmansk, I heard with concern many complaints about ministries, primarily, because they are slow in conveying new economic quotas to enterprises. But, without them, one cannot start preparation for and the transfer to self-supporting.

I want to stress once again that we must prepare to work under the new system in all seriousness and understand that this concerns millions of people, that this concerns the most important and decisive sphere of our society—the economy.

The experience which we have accumulated in the past more than two years in all branches using the new methods of management, new approaches, new forms of organizing production, experience which was gained in the course of the nationwide discussion of the Law on the State Enterprise, convinces us that we are on the correct path, that despite the initial difficulties this is a very promising endeavor for all of us, Comrades—for our society, for socialism. And we must solve all problems arising at this stage with a feeling of great responsibility.

Not everything will be achieved at once. Probably there will be miscalculations and some mistakes are possible. We must treat all this calmly, democratically, openly, without panic and demagoguery, and seriously. For everything that has been planned is meant to accelerate the country's socio-economic development, to improve the life of working people. This should be clearly understood. For in the long run every increment in the economy will raise the people's living standard and make itself felt first of all in the social sphere. All these questions are now being widely discussed in the mass media— the press, radio and television. This is a normal process. It helps us understand things better and act consciously, confidently and effectively.

The question of wholesale, purchase and retail prices is now being discussed along with many other problems of restructuring. Many people here ask me: "How will this problem be handled?" I would like to say that this is an important element in the new economic mechanism and it is impossible to fulfill the task of switching to new methods of management without getting to the bottom of the matter of prices, both wholesale and retail prices. The conversations in Murmansk and Monchegorsk, and information reaching the CPSU Central Committee and the Government show that the discussion of prices has given rise to certain apprehensions among working people and the entire population of the country. This is understandable.

These apprehensions boil down to the following: is the present leadership planning to solve all economic problems by lowering the people's living standards? I have already spoken on this matter both at the Congress and the Plenary Meetings of the Central Committee. I want to say once again that we have to deal with the matter of prices just as with other matters of the new economic mechanism.

First, this should be done with the aim of accelerating our economy's development, increasing the output of necessary products and commodities in the country, raising the national income and improving the well-being of working people. This is the aim.

Second. We will act in the same manner as at the early stage of the restructuring, after the April Plenary Meeting of the Central Committee; i.e., we will act openly. We will discuss, countrywide, all the main questions of our society's life. And, of course, the question of prices, which concerns the entire society, and every family. When it is ripe it will surely be submitted to the working people for discussion. Everything must be clear and there should be no anxiety.

Do you know the situation with prices? I'll cite several examples. The price that the state pays to the collective and state farms for their farm produce, particularly livestock products, is 50 or 100 percent higher than their retail price. For this reason last year's meat and milk subsidies amounted to 57 billion rubles. Many people do not know this, they are not aware of the situation.

Hence the lack of a proper attitude towards foodstuffs. You know it yourselves. You can see children using a loaf of bread as a football. Tremendous amounts of foodstuffs are wasted. There are examples of a different sort. Ladies' boots cost 120 to 130 rubles, and 62 kilograms of meat, which is today's average per capita quota of meat, costs about the same. In other words, the value of meat consumed by a person annually is equal to that of a pair of boots. This is the present situation. This is why no one thinks carefully about foodstuffs.

However, the main thing is that families with larger incomes consume more meat and milk and, consequently, benefit more from the subsidies. This is another problem we are facing.

We are now thinking how best to approach this question. I should like to quote some figures showing the paradox of the situation in this country. Take food products of equal caloric value. If we take the price of bread in the Soviet Union for one unit, its price in the U.S.A. will be 5.5, in Britain 3.6, France 4.1, West Germany 4.9 and Hungary 1.5. Those figures are for wheat bread. The situation is the same with meat, milk and so on.

The problem does exist, and it must be solved. But first it is necessary to find the approach to it that would not spoil the living standards of the population.

I ask you: are we thinking in the right direction?

Voices: *(Yes, of course.)*

As these problems raise their heads, I would like to say once again that you must not get the impression that the leadership is planning some "secrets of the court of Madrid." No, it is nothing of the sort. This is not our way of solving economic problems, at the expense of the living standards of the working people. As I have stated already, all the economic tasks will be accomplished if we all work better.

Another point I would like to mention at our meeting. Comrades, we must pursue a steady policy of economizing. We must save labor, we must save resources and we must save money. Here many things are wrong. I confirm this with a very important example. Since over a period of many decades the emphasis in managing the economy, and in fact the whole of society, was on centralization, command and injunction, the governmental and managerial apparatus (as well as the apparatus of public and, to some extent, Party organizations) has swelled too much.

Some 18 million people are now employed in our sphere of administration; 2.5 million of them are in the apparatus of administrative and law enforcement bodies; and some 15 million in the managing bodies of associations, enterprises and organizations. All this amounts to 15 percent of the country's manpower resources, with one manager for every 6 or 7 employees.

Now as we are advancing along the road of extensive democratization, development of initiative and responsibility of work collectives, of increasing their independence, and as we are introducing methods of management by economic encouragement rather than injunction, it is only natural that we should give serious thought to ways of simplifying the bloated administrative apparatus. Earlier, when any problem arose in the sphere of economy or in society in general, it was immediately suggested that an organization be set up for attending to it, as though it could help. But it did not help.

We shall tackle this problem with a sense of responsibility and in a well-considered manner, showing concern for every person, his future and the future of his family. In each case we should decide everything in a socialist manner. There is much work in this country, and work will be found for everyone, a lot of work.

On the managerial staff we can economize a great deal. Right now we spend more than 40 billion rubles a year on this apparatus (I've mentioned its size), while our national income has only increased in recent years by some 20 billion rubles.

The CPSU Central Committee and the Government decided to put scientific institutions on a pay-your-own-way system. This is being done to increase returns from the research potential accumulated in the country, as well as to make another saving. These measures are more than vital. They are just.

Yesterday, Comrade Yermakov, Director of the Severonikel plant, said: Now that we have adopted a cost-accounting system, we shall pay science for the real effect it has given us. Until now, because the state paid for it, we signed a treaty irrespective of what science gave us. Today we cannot do it. It is our money. We should follow the cost-accounting and self-financing principles. Therefore, the employees of research institutions should also think how to bring more honey into our socialist hive. Let those who fail to bring profit disband themselves. This is also democratic. For socialism means payment for the results of the work done. And if there are no results, there should be no pay. By the way, in keeping with a decision passed by the Council of Ministers, we have already closed two branch institutes which produced nothing essential for the economy over the last years. A decision has now been taken to switch science to the self-supporting basis. This is in the interests of society and the research workers themselves. Frankly speaking, talented research workers insist that real work, real contribution, should be paid for. The principle of socialism—from each according to his abilities, to each according to his work—should be strictly observed.

We shall continue to take decisions and adopt measures that make everyone employed in the economy more thrifty and cost conscious. This is the purpose of the planning and management reform and one of the goals of the restructuring. We should also appeal to the conscience of everyone to combat mismanagement mercilessly. There still remains a lot of it to be cleared up in every sector of the national economy and, indeed, in every collective and at every workplace. Think of all the losses incurred in harvesting and the storage of farm produce, in lumber and construction. All of you sitting here can apparently cite without a moment's hesitation scores of examples proving that mismanagement is widespread. It is our enemy. We still are impermissibly wasteful and extravagant. We should realize this and change absolutely everything in the country for the better.

When we learn to be thrifty and achieve proper economic order in the way things are done in the workplace, the economy will benefit tremendously. It will no longer be necessary to build dozens of new enterprises costing billions of rubles, and the results of the restructuring will be more tangible. Remember that waste has a most adverse effect on morality. Ending waste will make the moral climate in which we live, work and rest, still healthier.

It ought to be stressed, Comrades, that having implemented radical economic reform, our society will enter the decisive phase of its restructuring. Talking yesterday with managers from the mining complex in the Murmansk Region, I said: The Political Bureau believes that the restructuring process has reached a crucial stage. The success of this tremendous historic undertaking depends on competent political and economic leadership and the working people's high sense of responsibility. These are the two main factors. Let us act together, with such an understanding of our crucial situation.

If something goes wrong and produces an unexpected, unforeseen or undesirable effect anywhere, it is not reason enough to be disappointed or give up further efforts.

This is reason for something else, for posing the question the Marxist, socialist and scientific way: what has prevented the plans from being realized? Why do apathy, inertia and wait-and-see attitudes still persist? After finding the causes, decisive action should be taken to remedy the situation.

It will, of course, take a long time to overcome the consequences of stagnation. We have, in a way, become accustomed to it. Our psychology has adapted to its conditions, requirements and manifestations. Egalitarian tendencies and parasitic attitudes have become widespread. I would even say that, psychologically, stagnation suited many. Some people are still nostalgic for that time. This must be seen and understood. This is reality and we should act with due account of it.

Knowing this does not mean putting up with it and letting things slide. For us, seeing and understanding is only a first step, an indispensable prerequisite for changing the situation. It is only by introducing economic and social measures and by raising general political and cultural standards that we shall be able to cope with all our problems—and do that in an atmosphere of openness. This will tell most appreciably on the people's morality and their civic stand. Oblomovshchina* and so-

---

*Oblomov, a play by Goncharov, dealt with an aristocrat (named Oblomov) who managed his estates from his bed.

—Ed.

cialism go different ways—this we should clearly and firmly say to ourselves.

On the whole, the restructuring is gaining both speed and scope and taking firmer hold. It is our common task to make this drive consistent and ensure it the required speed. I would like to repeat once more: everything that we have planned can only be accomplished by our own effort. There will be and can be no miracle. It is only with our own hands that we can improve our life, something we are vitally interested in. This is what we have to say.

Comrades, it is through the prism of the common effort, the restructuring tasks as a whole, that you should look at the situation in your region, too. I have already spoken of your contribution. We highly appreciate it. But all the same I have criticisms to make concerning your work.

First of all, let me say this. You live in the Far North. The composition of the population here is quite specific, the tasks are specific and the conditions in which they are handled are specific. Many of the city residents work at sea, thousands of miles away from home. Extra concern should be shown for these people; social and cultural services should be available to them.

Looking at the issue from this standpoint, I would like to call attention to the low rates of housing construction which have made housing an acute problem, especially for fishermen. The situation has now changed somewhat. However, the calculations made by regional organizations on the basis of data supplied by work collectives show that these rates do not measure up to the task of solving the housing problem by the year 2000. The situation must be changed and the rates stepped up.

There are some problems with child-care centers, schools, medical, cultural and sports facilities.

It pained us to hear the grievances expressed by workers yesterday. The capacity of the Severonikel plant has doubled over the past 6 to 7 years, but neither heads of the enterprise nor heads of the industry have shown enough concern, party approach or conscience, while handling these immense tasks, to take care of the people coping with these production assignments. Once again, the approach to the social sphere rested on the take-what-remains principle. Whatever does remain. As a result, Vladimir N. Yermakov and I, and other comrades, were embarrassed to hear yesterday such just complaints as: there is nowhere to leave children, there is a shortage of pre-school centers. This is outrageous and shortsighted. It is utter irresponsibility.

Of course, Comrades, these are no easy tasks that I mention. Resolute measures are needed, the capacities of pre-fabricated house building should be better used. The region should get down to developing building material production. It has unique opportunities for that, rarely found elsewhere. They could have everything here. But cement is brought into the Murmansk Region. Building materials are in short supply. The output of the Kildin brickworks, built in 1936, is falling, due to dilapidated fixed assets.

Does it not indicate how local regional organizations treat these matters and show the ministries' attitude to the solution of questions concerning social restructuring in the region? And yet enterprises of our major ministries are operating here in the North. Can they not see to it that normal conditions be created for the inhabitants of this harsh region? We will be recommending that all these questions be considered in their entirety. But I ought to say that the Regional Party Committee and the Regional Executive Committee should also act more resolutely. No pains, no gains.

In per capita consumer goods production, you are 36 percent below the average for the Russian Federation. I understand that the economic structure here is rather special—you produce raw materials. But it is possible to produce cement out of local raw materials and supply it to the national economy as a consumer commodity for retail trade, for the development of individual construction, for gardeners. Can the question be solved? It can. But it isn't being solved. By the way, there is a surplus workforce emerging now in the Murmansk Region. It must be employed. Can't women be engaged in production? Especially women from the families of servicemen. They are, as a rule, educated people. Is it not possible to get in touch with such centers as Leningrad and Riga and organize here branches of radio engineering and electronics? This would add to the potential.

The Minister of Shipbuilding, I. S. Belousov, is present here. The ministry manufactures for itself a large quantity of automatic devices and instruments. Could this not be produced here? But no, Igor Sergeyevich says: In Murmansk, not only must wages be paid, but there must also be wage differentials. Is it right to talk like that?

One-quarter of the industrial enterprises of the region and of Murmansk itself has not as yet been involved in the manufacture of consumer goods. This won't do, Comrades.

The population is having problems with repairing flats, domestic appliances and tailoring. Cooperatives are keeping a very low profile.

Take your neighbors in the Arkhangelsk Region. Two to three times less fruit, vegetables and potatoes are marketed through cooperatives in the Murmansk Region than in the Arkhangelsk Region. This means that passive, inert people are heading the cooperatives. I must praise as a real accomplishment the increase in the local production of broilers, pork and milk in recent years. This is good. Ways and reserves should be sought to develop that further and reduce the importation of produce. This would be more reliable, more profitable and stable. It is far from clear why there should be only 18 hectares of greenhouses in the region. There is one principle: one square meter per capita. There are 1,100,000 people living in your region. So, there should be 100 hectares of greenhouses. Greenhouses are assembled from prefabricated units. The State Agro-Industrial Committee can assemble as many units as are ordered. We assemble them in many countries. The capacities are great. Everything has been mastered here. The majority of Northern and Siberian cities have long since solved the problem of vegetable supplies from greenhouses.

In the specific conditions of the North, it is an important task to preserve and use everything that is brought in. Look, in 1986 you lost during storage and wrote off as livestock fodder 40,000 tons of potatoes and other vegetables and fruit. This,

Comrades, amounts to 22 percent of the volume marketed. I understand that this might depend on quality as well, but, probably, on storage, too. Is it not possible to have dependable facilities so as to solve this problem once and for all in large towns and cities? Where are the regional and city organizations looking? It means that their approach is based on the take-what-remains principle, too.

What concerns us are the unfavorable tendencies observed in the development of the fishing industry, your major economic sector. The set targets are not being met. There are a lot of problems here: vessels standing idle in port for longer than necessary and shortcomings in processing. Today we heard some interesting ideas and proposals on that score. It's good that they were corroborated by concrete findings by amalgamations producing equipment for fish processing. I believe that we should help the region tackle that problem. But fishermen themselves should give the matter some thought, too. They should act more decisively at the local level, and Party organizations should keep these questions in the focus of attention. I believe that the Ministry of Fisheries and the Minister, Comrade Kotlyar, who is present now, will also take measures.

The problem of the comprehensive utilization of resources and natural riches of the Kola Peninsula has acquired great importance now. I'm speaking first of all of apatite-nepheline ores. Many approaches have been found here. Researchers have made concrete suggestions. It requires huge investments. I heard figures of three and more billion rubles mentioned. But I think that yesterday's talk will benefit both the center and all those who are associated with that problem. In the coming days the comrades here will think these problems over and the Ministry, the State Planning Committee and the local bodies will draft proposals for the Central Committee and the Government. We shall consider these matters at a Politburo meeting. The interests of the entire country are involved and they must be thoroughly considered.

Comrades, I would like to express the hope that the working people of Murmansk and the Murmansk Region will persistently tackle the tasks facing the region and the country. And I believe that you have sufficient skill both to tackle the most difficult tasks and to uphold the Party line. You don't have to borrow patriotism from anyone. I wish you every success.

Comrades, millions of people throughout the world are watching the restructuring process in our country with immense interest. Our bold embarking on large-scale constructive work and revolutionary change demanding consolidation of all of the country's efforts is convincing evidence of our confidence that peace can be preserved, that mankind does have a future.

Indeed, the international situation is still complicated. The dangers to which we have no right to turn a blind eye remain. There has been some change, however, or, at least, change is starting. Certainly, judging the situation only from the speeches made by top Western leaders, including their "program" statements, everything would seem to be as it was before: the same anti-Soviet attacks, the same demands that we show our commitment to peace by renouncing our order and principles, the same confrontational language: "totalitarianism," "communist expansion," and so on.

Within a few days, however, these speeches are often forgotten, and, at any rate, the theses contained in them do not figure during businesslike political negotiations and contacts. This is a very interesting point, an interesting phenomenon. It confirms that we are dealing with yesterday's rhetoric, while real-life processes have been set into motion. This means that something is indeed changing. One of the elements of the change is that it is now difficult to convince people that our foreign policy, our initiatives, our nuclear-free world program are mere "propaganda."

A new, democratic philosophy of international relations, of world politics, is breaking through. The new mode of thinking with its humane, universal criteria and values is penetrating diverse strata. Its strength lies in the fact that it accords with people's common sense. Considering that world public opinion and the peoples of the world are very concerned about the situation in the world, our policy is an invitation to dialogue, to a search, to a better world, to normalization of international relations. This is why despite all attempts to besmirch and belittle our foreign policy initiatives, they are making their way in the world, because they are consonant with the moods of the broad masses of working people and realistically minded political circles in the West.

Favorable tendencies are gaining ground in international relations as well. The substantive and frank East-West dialogue, far from proving fruitless for both sides, has become a distinguishing feature of contemporary world politics. Just recently the entire world welcomed the accord reached at the talks in Washington to complete promptly drafting an agreement on medium- and shorter-range missiles to be later signed at the top level. Thus, we are close to a major breakthrough in the field of actual nuclear disarmament. If it happens, it will be the first such breakthrough to be achieved in the postwar years. So far, the arms race has proceeded either unimpeded or with some limitations, but no concrete move has as yet been made towards disarmament, towards eliminating nuclear weapons.

The road to the mutual Soviet-American decision was hard. Reykjavik was a crucial event along that road. Life has confirmed the correctness of our assessment of the meeting in the Icelandic capital. Contrary to panic-wavering of all sorts, skeptical declarations and the propaganda talk about the "failure," developments have started moving along the path paved by Reykjavik. They have borne out the correctness of the assessment we made, as you remember, just 40 minutes after the dramatic end of the meeting.

Reykjavik indeed became a turning point in world history. It showed a possibility of improving the international situation. A different situation has developed, and no one could act after Reykjavik as if nothing had happened. It was for us an event that confirmed the correctness of our course, the need for and constructiveness of new political thinking.

Full use of the potential created in Reykjavik is yet to be made. Gleams of hope have emerged, however, not only in the field of medium- and shorter-range missiles. Things have started moving in the field of banning nuclear testing. Full-scale talks on these problems will soon be held. It is obvious that our moratorium was not in vain. This was not an easy step for us, either. It engendered and intensified worldwide demands for an end to the tests.

I can't undertake to predict the course of events. By no means everything depends on us. There is no doubt that the first results achieved in Washington recently and the forthcoming meeting with the President of the United States may cause a kind of peaceful "chain reaction" in the field of strategic offensive arms and nonlaunching of weapons into outer space as well as in many other issues which insistently call for international dialogue.

So, there are signs of an improvement in the international situation but, I repeat, there are also disquieting factors that threaten to aggravate sharply the world situation.

It would be irresponsible on our part to underestimate the forces of resistance to change. Those are influential and very aggressive forces, blinded by hatred for everything progressive. They exist in various quarters of the Western world, but the largest concentration of them is observed among those who cater directly for the military-industrial complex, both ideologically and politically, and who live on it.

Here is a recent and fine example. A series of hearings on the subject of "Gorbachev's Economic Reforms" began at the Joint Economic Committee of the U.S. Congress on September 10, with Senators and Congressmen participating. The hearings are both open- and closed-door ones. Speakers include representatives of the Administration and Sovietologists from the Central Intelligence Agency, the U.S. Defense Department and from various scientific centers. In general, it is quite normal and even good that in America officials of such a level should want to gain a thorough understanding of what is taking place in the Soviet Union and what our restructuring means for the rest of the world and for the United States itself.

Various views are being expressed, including diametrically opposed ones. There is a good deal that is sensible and objective in them. Some can be debated in earnest and it would not be bad, I would say, to pay attention to some of the things in them. The committee members also heard an opinion that the United States "should welcome the restructuring" because it will reduce a risk of a nuclear clash.

But different kinds of recommendations are also being made at these hearings before the Administration and before Congress. Here is one such, almost word for word: if the Soviet Union attains the targets planned by the 27th Congress of the CPSU, that will, first of all, raise its prestige in the international arena and heighten the CPSU authority in the country and abroad and . . . thereby, increase the threat to U.S. national security. Who would ever have thought of such a conclusion? Moreover, success of the restructuring may weaken the political and economic unity of Western Europe, for the USSR will reach its market. The USSR will exert greater political influence on the developing countries, since Soviet military and other aid to them may be increased, and some of them will want to adopt the model of the Soviet economy if it proves competitive vis-à-vis the U.S. economy.

And still further: the restructuring is dangerous because it will strengthen the Soviet Union's positions in international financial and economic organizations. Those analysts see a particular threat in the Soviet Union's increased influence in the world arena due to its initiatives in the field of arms control and the prospect of signing a treaty on medium-range missiles.

Just listen what conclusion they draw as a result: the failure of the socio-economic policy being pursued by the Soviet Union under the leadership of the CPSU and the Soviet Government would accord with U.S. national interests.

In order to "facilitate" such a failure the following is recommended: to speed up the programs of costly ABM systems under SDI and draw the USSR into the arms race in order to hinder its restructuring; to allocate still more funds for the development of expensive high-accuracy weapons and space-based military systems; for the same purpose, to increase the amount of military and other aid to groups and regimes which are actively fighting against the governments of the countries supported by the Soviet Union; to hinder the establishment of

economic and trade contacts by the USSR with other countries and international organizations; fully to rule out the possibility of the transfer of advanced technology to the USSR
and other socialist countries, and to tighten control over the
activities of COCOM and of its member countries.

Such are the views expressed overtly and cynically. We cannot but take into account such stances. The more so as assur-
ances of peace intentions, which we often hear from U.S. officials, are immediately accompanied, at one go, so to speak, by
the lauding of "power politics" and by arguments very similar
to those being used by the authors of the recommendations
which I just mentioned.

Militarist and anti-Soviet forces are clearly concerned lest
the interest among the people and political quarters of the
West in what is happening in the Soviet Union today and the
growing understanding of its foreign policy erase the artificially created "image of the enemy," an image which they
have been exploiting shamelessly for years. Well, it's their business after all. But we shall firmly follow the road of restructuring and new thinking.

Comrades, speaking in Murmansk, the capital of the Soviet
Polar Region, it is appropriate to examine the idea of cooperation between all people also from the standpoint of the situation in the northern part of this planet. In our opinion, there
are several weighty reasons for this.

The Arctic is not only the Arctic Ocean, but also the northern tips of three continents: Europe, Asia and America. It is
the place where the Euro-Asian, North American and Asian
Pacific regions meet, where the frontiers come close to one
another and the interests of states belonging to mutually opposed military blocs and nonaligned ones cross.

The North is also a problem of security of the Soviet
Union's northern frontiers. We have had some historical experience which cost us dearly. The people of Murmansk remember well the years 1918–1919 and 1941–1945.

The wars fought during this century were severe trials for
the countries of Northern Europe. It seems to us they have
drawn some serious conclusions for themselves. And this is

probably why the public climate in these countries is more receptive to the new political thinking.

It is significant that the historic Conference on Security and Cooperation in Europe was held in one of the northern capitals—Helsinki. It is significant that another major step in the development of that process—the first accord ever on confidence-building measures—was achieved in another northern capital—Stockholm. Reykjavik has become a symbol of hope that nuclear weapons are not an eternal evil and that mankind is not doomed to live under that sword of Damocles.

Major initiatives in the sphere of international security and disarmament are associated with the names of famous political figures of Northern Europe. One is Urho Kekkonen. Another is Olof Palme, whose death at the hand of a vile assassin shocked Soviet people. Then there is Kalevi Sorsa, who has headed the Socialist International Advisory Council for many years now. And we applaud the activities of the authoritative World Commission on Environment and Development headed by Prime Minister Gro Harlem Brundtland of Norway.

The Soviet Union duly appreciates the fact that Denmark and Norway, while being members of NATO, unilaterally refused to station foreign military bases and deploy nuclear weapons on their territory in peacetime. This stance, if consistently adhered to, is important for lessening tensions in Europe.

However, this is only part of the picture.

The community and interrelationship of the interests of our entire world is felt in the northern part of the globe, in the Arctic, perhaps more than anywhere else. For the Arctic and the North Atlantic are not just the "weather kitchen," the point where cyclones and anticyclones are born to influence the climate in Europe, the U.S.A. and Canada, and even in South Asia and Africa. One can feel here the freezing breath of the "Arctic strategy" of the Pentagon. An immense potential of nuclear destruction concentrated aboard submarines and surface ships affects the political climate of the entire world and can be detonated by an accidental political-military conflict in any other region of the world.

The militarization of this part of the world is assuming threatening dimensions. One cannot but feel concern over the fact that NATO, anticipating an agreement on medium- and shorter-range missiles being reached, is preparing to train military personnel in the use of sea- and air-based cruise missiles from the North Atlantic. This would mean an additional threat to us and to all the countries of Northern Europe.

A new radar station, one of the Star Wars elements, has been made operational in Greenland in violation of the ABM Treaty. U.S. cruise missiles are being tested in the north of Canada. The Canadian Government has recently developed a vast program for a build-up of forces in the Arctic. The U.S. and NATO military activity in areas adjoining the Soviet Polar Region is being stepped up. The level of NATO's military presence in Norway and Denmark is being built up.

Therefore, while in Murmansk, and standing on the threshold of the Arctic and the North Atlantic, I would like to invite, first of all, the countries of the region to a discussion on the burning security issues.

How do we visualize this? It is possible to take simultaneously the roads of bilateral and multilateral cooperation. I have had the opportunity to speak on the subject of "our common European home" on more than one occasion. The potential of contemporary civilization could permit us to make the Arctic habitable for the benefit of the national economies and other human interests of the near-Arctic states, for Europe and the entire international community. To achieve this, security problems that have accumulated in the area should be resolved above all.

The Soviet Union is in favor of a radical lowering of the level of military confrontation in the region. Let the North of the globe, the Arctic, become a zone of peace. Let the North Pole be a pole of peace. We suggest that all interested states start talks on the limitation and scaling down of military activity in the North as a whole, in both the Eastern and Western Hemispheres.

What, specifically, do we mean?

First, a nuclear-free zone in Northern Europe. If such a decision were adopted, the Soviet Union, as has already been declared, would be prepared to act as a guarantor. It would depend on the participating countries how to formalize this guarantee: by multilateral or bilateral agreements, governmental statements or in some other way.

The Soviet Union simultaneously reaffirms its readiness to discuss with each of the interested states, or with a group of states, all the problems related to the creation of a nuclear-free zone, including possible measures applicable to the Soviet territory. We could go so far as to remove submarines equipped with ballistic missiles from the Soviet Baltic Fleet.

As is known, the Soviet Union earlier unilaterally dismantled launchers of medium-range missiles in the Kola Peninsula and the greater part of launchers of such missiles on the remaining territory of the Leningrad and Baltic military areas. A considerable number of shorter-range missiles was removed from those districts. The holding of military exercises was restricted in areas close to the borders of Scandinavian countries. Additional opportunities for military détente in the region will open up after the conclusion of the agreement on "global double zero."

Second, we welcome the initiative of Finland's President Mauno Koivisto on restricting naval activity in the seas washing the shores of Northern Europe. For its part, the Soviet Union proposes consultations between the Warsaw Treaty Organization and NATO on restricting military activity and scaling down naval and airforce activities in the Baltic, Northern, Norwegian and Greenland Seas, and on the extension of confidence-building measures to these areas.

These measures could include arrangements on the limitation of rivalry in antisubmarine weapons, on the notification of large naval and airforce exercises, and on inviting observers from all countries participating in the European process to large naval and airforce exercises. This could be an initial step in the extension of confidence-building measures to the entire Arctic and to the northern areas of both hemispheres.

At the same time we propose considering the question of banning naval activity in mutually agreed-upon zones of international straits and in intensive shipping lanes in general. A meeting of representatives of interested states could be held for this purpose, for instance, in Leningrad.

The following thought suggests itself in connection with the idea of a nuclear-free zone. At present the Northern countries, that is Iceland, Denmark, Norway, Sweden and Finland, have no nuclear weapons. We are aware of their concern over the fact that we have a testing range for nuclear explosions on Novaya Zemlya.

We are thinking how to solve this problem, which is a difficult one for us because so much money has been invested in the testing range. But, frankly speaking, the problem could be solved once and for all if the United States agreed to stop nuclear tests or, as a beginning, to reduce their number and yield to the minimum.

Third, the Soviet Union attaches much importance to peaceful cooperation in developing the resources of the North, the Arctic. Here an exchange of experience and knowledge is extremely important. Through joint efforts it could be possible to work out an overall concept of rational development of northern areas. We propose, for instance, reaching agreement on drafting an integral energy program for the north of Europe. According to existing data, the reserves there of such energy sources as oil and gas are truly boundless. But their extraction entails immense difficulties and the need to create unique technical installations capable of withstanding the polar elements. It would be more reasonable to pool efforts in this endeavor, which would cut both material and other outlays. We have an interest in inviting, for instance, Canada and Norway to form mixed firms and enterprises for developing the oil and gas deposits of the shelf of our northern seas. We are prepared for relevant talks with other states as well.

We are also prepared for cooperation in utilizing the resources of the Kola Peninsula, and in implementing other major projects in various forms, including joint enterprises.

Fourth, the scientific exploration of the Arctic is of immense importance for the whole of mankind. We have a wealth of experience here and are prepared to share it. In turn, we are interested in the studies conducted in other sub-Arctic and northern countries. We already have a program of scientific exchanges with Canada.

We propose holding in 1988 a conference of sub-Arctic states on coordinating research in the Arctic. The conference could consider the possibility of setting up a joint Arctic Research Council. Should the partners agree, Murmansk could host the conference.

Questions bearing on the interests of the indigenous population of the North, the study of its ethnic distinctions and the development of cultural ties between northern peoples require special attention.

Fifth, we attach special importance to the cooperation of the northern countries in environmental protection. The urgency of this is obvious. It would be well to extend joint measures for protecting the marine environment of the Baltic, now being carried out by a commission of seven maritime states, to the entire oceanic and sea surface of the globe's North.

The Soviet Union proposes drawing up jointly an integrated, comprehensive plan for protecting the natural environment of the North. The North European countries could set an example to others by reaching an agreement on establishing a system to monitor the state of the natural environment and radiation safety in the region. We must hurry to protect the nature of the tundra, forest tundra, and the northern forest areas.

Sixth, the shortest sea route from Europe to the Far East and the Pacific Ocean passes through the Arctic. I think that, depending on progress in the normalization of international relations, we could open the North Sea route to foreign ships, with ourselves providing the services of ice-breakers.

Such are our proposals. Such is the concrete meaning of Soviet foreign policy with regard to the North. Such are our intentions and plans for the future. Of course, safeguarding security and developing cooperation in the North is an international matter and by no means depends on us alone. We are ready to discuss any counterproposals and ideas. The main thing is to conduct affairs so that the climate here is determined by the warm Gulfstream of the European process and

not by the Polar chill of accumulated suspicions and prejudices.

What everybody can be absolutely certain of is the Soviet
Union's profound and certain interest in preventing the North
of the planet, its Polar and sub-Polar regions and all northern countries from ever again becoming an arena of war, and
in forming there a genuine zone of peace and fruitful
cooperation.

* * *

This is how, Comrades, we approach internal and international issues, how we understand the connection between the
former and the latter. In both, our policy has proved its viability and constructive spirit. We are convinced that there is no
other way to security and social progress but creative labor in
the name of happiness and freedom of man inside the country
and the development of equal cooperation between states on
the world scene.

We are legitimately proud of the fact that our country has
always stood at the sources of socialist practice and new thinking. In the last 70 years the world has changed beyond recognition—materially, spiritually and politically. The impact
made by the Great October Revolution on the social and ideological progress of mankind is the greatest contribution to contemporary and future civilization. It is within our powers and
in our interests to multiply this contribution by the practical
results of restructuring.

May I wish you, your families and all working people of the
region success in all your efforts to transform our country, in
studies and life, and congratulate you once again on the 70th
anniversary of the Great October Revolution, which you are
celebrating in your Hero City.

II

THE WASHINGTON SUMMIT

December 2–14, 1987

4

Interview with NBC

Pravda, December 2, 1987

Tom BROKAW, NBC correspondent: Mr. General Secretary, your trip to the United States is widely anticipated. As General Secretary, do you have a better feel for Americans now than you did when you were serving in other posts in this country?

Mikhail GORBACHEV: Well, you know, Mr. Brokaw, I'll respond to that question. But I would like first of all, right at the outset, to avail myself of this favorable opportunity through NBC to say a few words of sincere greetings to all the television viewers who are watching and listening to us and to all the American people. I would like to address them with words of sincere greetings from the Soviet people.

Before responding to your question, let me say that this year already I have received about eighty thousand letters from Americans, and that is a third of all the foreign mail that has been coming into the Central Committee of the Party. The letters cover a broad range of issues. There are letters from Congressmen, from businessmen; there've been a lot of letters

This conversation with Tom Brokaw took place in the Kremlin on November 30, 1987.

from scientists and scholars, from people working in the field of culture and very many young people.

And, you know, a lot in those letters has stirred me, and, you know, many of the thoughts of those letters are similar; they revolve around several simple and yet very important questions and problems which obviously are of concern to the American people. In those letters I read that they are worried about the situation in the world, that there's a lot of tension, a lot of alarm, that regional conflicts are still ablaze, unabated. There is a lot of concern, and that, I guess, takes first place, a lot of concern about the state of Soviet-American relations.

And I felt in those letters and through those letters an immense desire of the American people, a very strong desire to change the situation in the world for the better and, of course, the pride of place is taken by the need for change in relations between us, between our peoples.

And these letters have given me a great deal and have helped me a great deal to understand the American people better. And this certainly adds to the immense political information I receive through other channels, through my contacts with American political figures at all levels, and of course I do now have a better understanding, as I feel, of American society than I did before I took up this job.

But you know what the important thing is, and I'd like to tell you this: what the Americans say in their letters addressed to me and to the Government of the Soviet Union, to our people, all this is very close to our hearts and very easily understood by all of us, by the Soviet people. And I see in this the emergence of a new situation and one which makes it possible, perhaps even makes it incumbent upon the politicians and the Governments of our two vast nations to try and understand better the mood of our peoples and to give expression to the will of our peoples in our policies.

I shall leave other questions aside for the moment, but let me just address the topic of our relationship. I shall be going to Washington with a desire to discuss this problem as well, and I think it's a leading problem. How can we change relations between our peoples for the better? The Americans say in their letters: Why can't we be allies? We were allies at one time, why can't we be allies now? There are so many problems in the world. Can't we join our efforts, can't we pool the enormous might of our countries, the economic, intellectual capacities to resolve all these problems? And that is very important, very important indeed.

We need mutual understanding. And I believe that we must display greater respect for each other, try and understand the history of our nations better.

The Soviet Union is a unique phenomenon. It's a whole conglomeration of over a hundred nations and nationalities. And just try and imagine what is behind every one of those peoples and nationalities which now make up the Soviet Union. Next year the millennium of Christianity in Russia will be marked. But even before that, broad ties existed with a dynamically developing people, an original culture and wide ties with other nations. Or take the peoples of Transcaucasia, of Central Asia. Their history goes way back into the depths of history. A unique history, an original and significant history belongs to the peoples of the Baltic region. But all these nations now make up the Soviet Union. There is a lot in our history that was not simple. There was a lot of struggle. We had to fight back many invasions, starting from Genghis Khan and Batu Khan and others, in order to stand up for our independence. And, you know, that led to a forging of a national character and our values were thus formed. All of these peoples value their language, their culture. They are patriots, they have a feeling of dignity.

And without all that you cannot understand us or our actions if you don't know that history.

We are dedicated to peace, and you can travel far and wide throughout the Soviet Union anywhere, and everywhere you will see and hear testimony of that. And that's why I say that we regard my visit next week as a very important phase in our relations. It will be our third meeting with President Reagan. And we'll be signing a treaty on medium-range and shorter-range missiles. We must address ourselves to strategic offensive arms, we will be discussing other world problems. So, on the whole, we will have a lot of things to talk about.

BROKAW: And we have a lot to talk about during the course of this hour, Mr. General Secretary. Can we begin with some of those now? For example, there is anticipation about your visit to the United States and I think there is general excitement about the signing of the intermediate-range nuclear treaty. But there is apprehension on the part of a lot of people that it will leave the Soviets in a superior position in Europe. Are you prepared now to reduce the number of men, tanks and attack helicopters that you have in Europe?

GORBACHEV: Well, first, the Americans and the Europeans and the others should know that the Soviet Union has no intention whatsoever of attacking anybody. That's number one. Second. There are realities which have taken shape within the framework of the two opposing military blocs. There is a certain asymmetry both in forces and armaments. We are prepared to address ourselves to that without delay. We've made our proposals and we are awaiting a more active position, a more active response from NATO. And therefore we are prepared to deal in practical terms, we are ready to sit down at the negotiating table and tackle these problems in practice.

BROKAW: Well, I think that NATO and the United States especially would be encouraged if you unilaterally would rearrange your forces into a more defensive position rather than an offensive position.

GORBACHEV: We have made known the content of our military doctrine. It is a defensive one. And let me repeat, we are ready to sit down at the negotiating table and, just as we dealt with the medium-range and shorter-range missiles, to tackle the question of conventional forces and conventional arms. We will be acting in a constructive way.

BROKAW: What are the chances do you think that by next summer you and President Reagan can sign a treaty to reduce by half, 50 percent, the long-range nuclear missiles, the really dangerous missiles?

GORBACHEV: Well, I believe that in this matter, which

really constitutes the very core of Soviet-American relations, there are real prospects ahead of us.

I believe it is hard perhaps at this very moment to foresee how our talks will go and what results we will achieve as a result of an exchange of views on this matter during the forthcoming visit in my talks with President Reagan. But in any event, we certainly have a lot to discuss.

And I would repeat what I've said previously. We believe that it is possible to do a lot of work with the present Administration, yes, with this Administration, to make headway on this major direction in the area of nuclear disarmament.

We will act constructively, and I guess the Americans and the world at large have seen with their own eyes that we can act thus and that we are indeed acting constructively.

BROKAW: Your chief arms negotiator said the other day that he thought there could be a 50-percent reduction in the ICBMs and that SDI and "Star Wars" would be a matter for the American people to decide. Has SDI been slightly diminished in your judgment as a condition for the reduction of ICBMs?

GORBACHEV: I believe that the question of SDI is not a subject for negotiations; we shall be talking about the strategic offensive arms, about levels and sublevels. And here we have some steps that we could take to meet the American position halfway; in fact, some of these steps we've already taken. We shall be talking about the strict compliance with the ABM Treaty. That's what we are going to talk about.

BROKAW: Am I clear in understanding that you believe that you can reduce ICBMs, the long-range missiles, by 50 percent next summer and that you would deal with SDI separately?

GORBACHEV: We formulate our position in a very clear-cut way. We are prepared to accept a 50-percent reduction at the first stage with strict observance of the ABM Treaty. In whatever way SDI does not run counter to the ABM Treaty, let America act, let America indulge in research—insofar as SDI does not run counter to the ABM Treaty.

BROKAW: Isn't the easiest way, Mr. General Secretary, to deal with "Star Wars" or SDI, isn't the easiest way to eliminate the need for SDI just to eliminate the threat, to negotiate a great reduction in these long-range missiles first and then you wouldn't have the political or technical need for something like SDI?

GORBACHEV: Well, that is precisely what I suggested to President Reagan in Reykjavik.

And we were just about two paces away from signing an agreement on that score, but SDI came and stood between us.

If we reduce our medium-range missiles and shorter-range missiles and if we agree at the first stage to make 50-percent cuts in our strategic offensive arms and then to go on and fully eliminate nuclear weapons, then the question arises: what is SDI for and what is the militarization of outer space for? You know, this is an attempt, yet another illusion of the American defense planners through, as they think, some kind of technological superiority, through the superiority, as they see it, in computers, somehow through outer space to forge ahead, to achieve superiority.

But look, tell me, Mr. Brokaw, if you and I were to start trying to count how many attempts there were after the war on both sides to try and forge ahead, to gain superiority, we would see that nothing came of them. We're simply wasting the funds of our nations, and we are creating a very acute situation in the world.

Ninety-five percent of all nuclear weapons, or maybe even more, belong to the Soviet Union and the United States. So, what must we do now, take weapons into outer space? That would certainly lead to a destabilization with unforeseeable consequences.

Just think how much time it took to find criteria for comparing the present nuclear capabilities of the sides. This is a very complex question, how to compare them, how to assess those potentials, and yet we found, over the decades, we found a way to do that.

But if we go into outer space with our weapons, if we start having an arms race in space, what will be the criteria there? There'll be a fever: who will beat whom? What is more, what if one side sees that it's being overtaken? What then? That's my first question.

And then, secondly, placing all your stakes on technology, which simply overrules the possibility of taking timely political decisions, is a very dangerous game.

And then, look, if our peoples express a certain wish, why should we orient ourselves on the will or the desires of just one limited group or perhaps one segment in this or that country? That is not democratic, surely. You cannot impose the minority's will on the majority. Democracy is after all the rule of the majority.

BROKAW: But the President feels strongly that he has made a commitment and I am not prepared here, obviously, to negotiate "Star Wars" on behalf of the United States. I would just like the record to show, however, Mr. General Secretary, that there are a great many people in the United States who believe that the Soviets as well are involved in efforts to militarize space and to develop their own SDI program. And, well, I don't believe that we can resolve that here today. I think that we ought to move on to new thinking, which is a subject we've been reading a great deal about in the Soviet Union; in your book *Perestroika* you say that new thinking means that security can no longer be assured by military means. What better way to demonstrate that than by getting the Soviet troops out of Afghanistan? Can you tell us tonight when are you prepared to do that?

GORBACHEV: Well, before I respond to that question, let me just react to your remark that the Soviet Union is engaged in things similar to SDI.

Well, it's really hard to say what the Soviet Union is not doing; the Soviet Union is practically doing everything that the United States is doing.

I'd say we are engaged in research, basic research, which relates to these aspects which are covered by SDI in the United States. But we will not build an SDI, we will not deploy SDI and we call on the United States to act similarly. If the Americans fail to heed this call, we will find a response that will be ten or a hundred times cheaper, but then the guilt, the blame will be with the Americans, with the U.S. Administration.

BROKAW: But that's the whole point. SDI cannot be deployed probably until the next century. There have already been cutbacks. Wouldn't the thing to do in order to send a signal to the American people be to reduce the long-range missiles in the meantime? There have already been delays and questions raised in the United States about the wisdom of the Strategic Defense Initiative. It seems to me that you could move along much more rapidly by agreeing to reduce long-range missiles in the meantime. And then you would still have time to respond, if you needed to.

GORBACHEV: Yes, provided that the ABM Treaty is intact. Now, on Afghanistan. This is our neighbor country. Under all the regimes, we were always good neighbors. It is a state which was one of the first to recognize Soviet power in Russia. There were kings and other rulers. They had their own processes under way, but whatever happened there, we were always friends. And, in fact, that's the way we try to build our relations with all of our neighbors.

After the well-known revolution in Afghanistan, an attempt was made to make some internal reforms and to bring that society out of its ancient system. A new government was established there. But that was a purely domestic process.

At the same time certain processes were building up connected first and foremost with interference from outside designed to undermine that new regime.

And the Afghans appealed to us as neighbors—some say 11 times, others say 13 times. They appealed to us for help in that very difficult period. And at one of these very acute moments, when the situation really became very exacerbated, we met the request of the Afghan Government and introduced our limited troop contingent, which does not run counter to the United Nations Charter.

But we see that today the situation requires a solution. We are looking for ways to bring about a prompt solution to that problem. And I believe that if the U.S. Administration really does sincerely want that problem to be resolved, to be closed by political means, it could be done very quickly.

BROKAW: What is very quickly: within 3 months, 6 months?

GORBACHEV: I think we can talk with the President about that.

BROKAW: Will that be high on your agenda in Washington next week—the withdrawal of troops from Afghanistan and a guarantee that the Government there will not be a threat to the Soviet Union?

GORBACHEV: Well, I guess we will talk about regional conflicts in Central America, in Southern Africa, in the Middle East, in the Persian Gulf and in Afghanistan.

BROKAW: Are you prepared to support Cuba and Nicaragua at the same level that you have been in the past, Mr. General Secretary?

GORBACHEV: Well, we must not only support and maintain the relations we have with those states, we must develop and improve those relations. But I think you meant something quite different when you asked that question.

BROKAW: More arms, more advisers to Cuba and to Nicaragua?

GORBACHEV: Well, I think that there's more talk about that in order to keep up the tensions in that area and to have excuses for intervention. I have to smile when I hear that the security of the United States is being threatened by the Sandinista regime. That's not serious. The country has been turned into the backyard of America, where the people couldn't live the way they did. They couldn't stand the dictatorship anymore. And they rose up against it.

And we feel that those who supported that just indignation of a people which took power into its own hands are morally right. Why shouldn't that suit the Administration of the United States? I think now even in Congress they have understood that, to say nothing of the fact that many Americans have realized that Nicaragua cannot pose a threat to the United States.

BROKAW: But under new thinking, as you have defined it,

wouldn't it be time to reduce the military assistance to places like Nicaragua and Cuba and let those regimes begin to stand on their own?

GORBACHEV: Well, since you keep talking about the new thinking, let me teach you a little lesson. I'm sure you won't have any complaints about what I'm going to say.

BROKAW: You are the teacher of the new thinking . . .

GORBACHEV: *(Laughs.)* I think that the situation in the world is such that it differs fundamentally from what it was 30 or 40 years ago, not to mention, say, 50 or 70 years ago. The empires are gone, they are no more. Dozens of nations emerged and are now developing independently. And all of them want not only political independence and autonomy, they want to live a better life, they want to live as human beings. They need food, they need clothing, they need medicines.

And now just try to imagine two and a half billion people in Asia, Africa and Latin America who dispose of vast natural resources, vast manpower resources, and yet they are in debt, they have a very low standard of living. So the question arises: Can this situation be left without attention? No, it calls for a solution.

Or take ecology. Is it not a common, global problem? Or the struggle against disease? Isn't that a common problem? What about mastering the scientific and technological revolution? Can we resolve all the problems involved without cooperation? Isn't that a common, global problem?

If the Soviet Union has interests, if the United States has interests, I guess other countries and peoples have interests, too. If, previously, international relations were built upon the right of the strong, according to the motto "might is right," that won't work today. However strong we might be, we cannot dictate our values or impose our way of life upon others, impose our social choice on others. It is up to them to decide. Unless we recognize the right to choose and recognize the interests of every nation, nothing will come of international relations.

And those relations are fraught with serious explosions. A

new thinking presupposes respect for the choice of every nation. We not only respect that choice. We try morally, and, where we believe it necessary, economically, militarily and defensively, to support that choice, so that the people can defend what they have taken into their own hands. This is where you have to get to the bottom of the situation. You have to change your approach. You cannot order the world around, you have to change your approach.

BROKAW: You know how important symbols are in politics, Mr. General Secretary. There is no uglier symbol in the world than the division between East and West, than the Berlin Wall. Why won't you use your considerable influence with the East Germans just to have them take it down? What purpose does it serve anymore?

GORBACHEV: You know, I think that's a question that has already been exhausted. That is the sovereign right of a sovereign state, the German Democratic Republic, to defend and protect its choice and not to allow any interference in its domestic affairs. Through West Berlin much was done that caused great harm, both political and economic, to that country, to that people. So, these are all the realities which arose out of concrete situations.

I can say to you what I once said to a West German. He said to me: "Now, Mr. Gorbachev, Stalin used to say that Hitlers come and go, but the German people, the German state remains. But you have divided Germany into two states." I told him: "All right, let's remember the facts of history." And I reminded him of those facts; he, it turned out, knew them all. The division of Germany ran counter to the decisions reached in Yalta and Potsdam. So, that Wall appeared before you think it did. It's another matter that it was made out of a different material. But the result of what happened is what we have just now. Those are the realities and we have to treat them as such.

BROKAW: Well, I don't think we can get all the way over the Wall here this evening, but maybe we can do something about human rights. How can you persuade the world that there is new thinking and a new sensitivity on the part of the Soviet Union if you simply do not let the people who live in this country come and go as they please, without risking their citizenship?

GORBACHEV: Mr. Brokaw, you will not be offended if I'm forthright and say that I assume that I have a very educated man sitting across the table in front of me and a very well-informed one. But when we come to a very important topic you take only a speculative aspect.

I'm ready to talk about human rights with any representative of the United States, with you too, if you are ready. And I can show you how things go in terms of human rights in this country and in your country, and in other parts of the world. We are in favor of rights, in favor of the broad rights of citizens. We are so dedicated to this that it was, in fact, the purpose of our Revolution. Do you know what we did during the Revolution? We took power away from the landowners and gave it to the people. We took away the factories, the plants and private property, and gave them to the working people, and on that basis we eliminated exploitation of man by man. We built up a planned economy, we guaranteed each individual the right to work. And look, for how many years, for 50-odd years we have had no unemployment. There's free education, guaranteed by the state, free medical care, guaranteed by the state, by society. The state has largely taken upon itself care for the provision of homes for the working people.

Why is this interesting? The national income in our country is lower, on a per capita basis as well, than in the United States, but in terms of social guarantees our society is much better than yours. When were you born?

BROKAW: I was born in 1940, Mr. General Secretary, but I know that you know what I am talking about . . .

GORBACHEV: Just a moment, we'll come to that.

In 1944 Franklin Delano Roosevelt introduced his bill on social and economic rights believing that there cannot be any real rights unless these problems are resolved. That was a very interesting bill. But it has remained in Congressional archives.

Taking into account that America is criticized throughout the world for not recognizing social and economic rights, that it is not signing or ratifying international covenants relating to that subject, this last July Mr. Reagan introduced once again another version of that bill on social and economic rights, although it was different from the one that Roosevelt had. And yet I think that a lot of water will flow down the Mississippi and the Volga before the U.S. Congress and the Administration recognize the American people's right to economic and social protection. But all that has been guaranteed in the Soviet Union.

As regards the question that you've touched upon—exit and entry—you know, I understand the concern of the American side to some extent since it's your nation that was formed as a result of immigration. And therefore our views are different. But you know, in the United States or in Canada, they really don't want to allow people in from Mexico or from other countries. Those who don't have the skills. In the 1970s, when there was an especially big flow of those who wanted to emigrate from the Soviet Union, there was a highly placed representative of the Administration who declared that the U.S. resolved its problem of mathematicians by 50 percent at the Soviet Union's expense. Thus the United States wants, through these channels, while making out that it is a champion of human rights, to resolve its own problems by organizing a braindrain. And of course we are protecting ourselves. That's number one. Then, secondly, we will never allow people to be lured out of our country.

BROKAW: There are many cases . . .

GORBACHEV: All these cases will with time become more and more clear. All the individual cases we consider very thoroughly, and this is well known by the Congress, by the President. And we'll continue in a humane spirit to resolve every individual case, but within the framework of our laws. You should not, as we say, try to go into another man's monastery with your own charter. We have our democratic state based on a Constitution and our laws. As for goodwill, we have it. Family reunification, we believe that it is a problem. And we shall do our best to have this problem resolved. There are other problems connected with emigration and we shall always consider them with attention. But let us not inject any political speculations into this problem.

BROKAW: What do you think, Mr. General Secretary, do you think that the law moves too slowly in this country? What about those 4,000 Soviet Jews whose visas have been delayed for a long time? Some of them are now cancer victims who want to leave the Soviet Union so that they could be with their families in their closing days. What do you think about them, just man to man?

GORBACHEV: I think that right now we have only those who have not been given permission to leave because of state security reasons. There are no other reasons. And we will continue to act in that way.

BROKAW: Mr. General Secretary, I'd like to ask you something about perestroika and the reorganization of your economy. There's no greater need in the Soviet Union than in reorganizing how you produce food in this country. This great power has to import food. Two percent of your small farms produce a huge proportion of agricultural output. Are you going to greatly expand the private holdings of farm land and put them more on the incentive basis?

GORBACHEV: This question is one that was posed by President Reagan. I guess perhaps he may have asked you to ask me that question, too. The wording was precisely the same.

BROKAW: No, this information is widely available in America to Presidents and humble reporters alike.

GORBACHEV: Well, let me say this. The food problem is one that does exist in this country, yet we eat 3,400 calories per person per day. The question is thus one of the structure of the diet. Now, as to how much the individual small holdings produce. Those approximately 2 percent of the individual households produce up to one-third of certain agricultural products. But they could not have done this if they did not get their grain, livestock, technical assistance, fertilizers, expert consultations, transport services, seeds from the collective and state farms. They are really integrated with the collective and state farms. There is the practice of contracts. They sign contracts, a collective farm, let's say, and an individual holding. Usually they are members of a state farm or a collective farm. And they participate in the process of increasing agricultural production.

BROKAW: Are you going to expand that?

GORBACHEV: In all of this there is one very interesting side, one very interesting aspect. We are right now, on a long-term basis, suggesting that families and groups of people take a plot of land or hire some implements or machinery and show what their initiative is worth. And we have been able to combine the possibilities of the large-scale farms and the individual interests of these small groups. Now, that is an area where we will lend further support. And already this is yielding good results.

But this does not mean that we're abolishing the collective farm system. No, this is a flexible combination of the possibilities of large-scale farms which assume a great deal, and the initiative and the personal and material interests of a family or of a small group of persons that want to grow a certain crop or to produce meat and dairy products. We'll promote it in every possible way.

BROKAW: Are you going to allow individual enterprises to set prices? Are you going to allow unemployment to rise in this country? Are you going to run the risk of a recession and inflation as part of perestroika? That would be a fundamental overturning of the Soviet way of having an economy.

GORBACHEV: No, we will resolve this within the framework of socialism and by our own methods. It is in the West that the structural policy and modernization are accompanied by growing unemployment. We want to avoid this, and this will be done in that very way. Such opportunities are inherent in a planned economy. Already now, we are elaborating our plans for organizing new jobs in new territories and in other areas, especially in the area of services and trade. And thus, on a planned basis and with due assistance from the state, we'll transfer people from one sphere to another and retrain them. And I believe that this will be done in such a way as not to affect the incomes of the working people. In other words, this adaptation of the economy to scientific and technological progress will be achieved within the framework of socialist approaches, so as not to allow any unemployment. That is our pivotal task.

BROKAW: And no other party besides the Communist Party in the foreseeable future for the Soviet Union?

GORBACHEV: I see no need for any other party, and that is the view of our society. And today's changes which are taking place, the deep-going changes embracing the economy, politics, the sphere of democracy, the spiritual sphere, the social sphere—all this is taking place on the initiative of the Communist Party of the Soviet Union.

We have built up a new atmosphere in the country, an atmosphere of glasnost, openness, and we have plans to move forward the process of democratization and glasnost. All this is being done on the initiative of the Communist Party. The Party has drawn upon its own self the fire of criticism. This is democracy at work.

BROKAW: Well, let me bring you to that point. In your book you say the truth is the main thing. You quote Lenin as saying there should be more light, and yet when one of your colleagues in the Central Committee, Boris Yeltsin, who was the Party chief of Moscow, spoke in favor of faster reforms, his speech was not even published. And yet when he was fired it was done in a very public fashion. To some American observers it had the echo of Stalinism. Was that a mistake?

GORBACHEV: No, there was no mistake. You know, we will follow the path of perestroika firmly and consistently. We will follow the path of democracy and reforms firmly and consistently. But we will not jump over stages. We will not allow any adventurism. We have studied well the experience of all other countries in that respect, and our own experience, too. But we will not allow conservatism to be rampant either. And we shall wage our struggle without allowing adventurism, and at the same time resolutely combatting conservatism. We shall be very thorough, very careful. There is a huge country behind us, a great people. We cannot allow playing with politics. As to what happened to Boris Yeltsin, well, look, in fact it's a normal process for any democracy. I don't want to count how many ministers or secretaries were replaced even recently in the United States, under President Reagan's Administration . . .

BROKAW: Yes, but when they are replaced they get to speak out about why they were replaced. We get to hear from them.

GORBACHEV: Well, you know, by the way, Comrade Yeltsin spoke twice at the Plenary Meeting of the Central Committee and addressed the Plenary Meeting of the City Party Committee. His speech at the City Party Committee was published verbatim. Yeltsin himself posed the question of his being relieved from his post. So please, trust us to resolve such questions. I'm sure there will be other problems in perestroika. They'll have to be resolved. We will continue our political line aimed at perestroika, we will be insistent in pursuing that line.

BROKAW: We have only a few moments left, and I'd like to know more about Mikhail Gorbachev, the man. Recently, there was much talk in the Soviet Union about a possibility for women to return to a purely womanly mission. What does that mean? Do you think women should be spending more time at home in the traditional role of mother and housemaker?

GORBACHEV: No, I think that a woman should take part in all spheres of life, in all of the processes taking place in society. But this must be done in such a way that one should not interfere with the other and we should think about how to help our women combine active participation in social and cultural processes with their predestination, that of keeper of the homefires, the family guardian, for a strong family means a strong society. So, we will not restrict the participation of women in public affairs. We will rather help women so that it is easier for them to combine the functions of motherhood, the role of the mother and the role of an active citizen of the country.

BROKAW: We have all noticed the conspicuous presence of Mrs. Gorbachev in your travels. Do you go home in the evening and discuss with her questions of public life and so on?

GORBACHEV: We discuss everything.

BROKAW: I accept your answer. Where do you learn about the United States? Do you read American newspapers, do you watch television programs, do you have special people who tell you about what is happening in the United States? How do you satisfy your own curiosity about our country?

GORBACHEV: I have access to a lot of information, not only on the basis of the press, but also through other channels. We have many translations of political and Sovietological literature from the United States as well as American fiction. So, in this country anyone who is interested in the United States has a great many possibilities to get to know America.

BROKAW: Have you read any American books?

GORBACHEV: Well, I have to say that, of course, in my reading first place belongs to Russian and Soviet literature. But American literature certainly enjoys great popularity in this country. If we were to start trying to compare the number of translations, the number of authors that are translated and read in this country, the figures would be enormous. Mostly I've read American classics, but I know some of the very important modern writers. Only let the Americans not consider their achievements to be the ultimate truth in all spheres of human thought. And then they will find amongst us many people who'd like to exchange views and discuss a lot of problems with them.

BROKAW: Do you follow the 1988 Presidential campaign in America, and, if you do, who do you think will win next fall? That's a question all the Americans ask themselves.

GORBACHEV: You know, we proceed from the assumption that we will be working constructively with any Administration, regardless of party affiliation—whether Republican or Democratic, or another party perhaps. We will cooperate, provided there is the appropriate desire and effort on the other side. As for the election campaign, well, I just want to say that even after the campaign we will be prepared to actively cooperate with whoever becomes the successor to the present President. As for forecasts about who will win and who will become the next President, I think that's an irresponsible exercise. The

Americans will come to the conclusion of who they need best and they'll do it themselves.

BROKAW: Finally, Mr. General Secretary, very briefly: how would you like to be remembered by Americans ten years from now, about the Gorbachev era?

GORBACHEV: Well, I don't want that in ten years' time everything should be relegated to memory. I think by that time there will only be a real upsurge in what we have begun to develop today. So I hope and believe that this will not simply be something belonging to the old past, it'll be part of the dynamic present. And it is for the sake of that goal that, together with my colleagues, together with our working people, I am today, we are, all of us, working. I think that today we are sowing some good seeds, and they will give a good yield, good results. If that were not so, it would be senseless to do what we are trying to do now, and doing it with enthusiasm, intensively, with a great desire to change everything for the better in the interests of socialism, in the interests of the Soviet people. And I believe that what is now happening in this country will be a certain contribution to the progress of human civilization.

BROKAW: Mr. General Secretary, thank you very much for this time.

GORBACHEV: And, once again, let me avail myself of this opportunity to say to my American viewers: "Until we meet on American soil."

5

Speech at the Welcoming Ceremony at the White House

December 8, 1987

Esteemed Mr. President,
Esteemed Mrs. Reagan,
Ladies and gentlemen,
Comrades,

Thank you very much, Mr. President, for the cordial welcome and kind words of greeting.

History has charged the governments of our countries, and the two of us, Mr. President, with a solemn duty to justify the hopes of Americans and Soviet people, and of people the world over, to undo the logic of the arms race by working together in good faith.

In the world's development, much will depend upon the choice that we are to make, upon what is to triumph: fears and prejudice, inherited from the Cold War and leading to confrontation, or common sense which calls for action to ensure the survival of civilization.

We in the Soviet Union have made our choice. We realize that we are divided not only by the oceans, but also by profound historical, ideological, socio-economic and cultural differences.

But the wisdom of politics today lies in not using those differences as a pretext for confrontation, enmity and the arms race.

We are beginning our visit 46 years after the days when the United States entered the Second World War. And it was in those same days—in 1941—that the rout of Nazi forces began near Moscow. That is symbolic. Those days marked the beginning of our common path to victory over the forces of evil in a war which we fought as allies.

History is thus reminding us both of our opportunities, and of our responsibility.

Indeed, the very fact that we are about to sign a treaty eliminating Soviet and U.S. intermediate- and shorter-range nuclear missiles, which are now going to be scrapped, shows that at crucial phases in history our two nations are capable of shouldering their high responsibility.

This will, of course, be the first step down the road leading to a nuclear-free world, whose construction you, Mr. President, and I discussed at Reykjavik. Yet it is a great step into the future—the future to which our two peoples and the peoples of all countries aspire.

I have come to Washington with the intention of advancing the next, and more important, goal of reaching agreement to reduce by half strategic offensive arms in the context of a firm guarantee of strategic stability.

We are also looking forward to a most serious and frank dialogue on other issues of Soviet-American relations.

Soviet foreign policy today is most intimately linked with perestroika, the domestic restructuring of Soviet society. The Soviet people have boldly taken the path of radical reforms and development in all spheres—economic, social, political and intellectual.

Democratization and glasnost are the decisive prerequisites for the success of those reforms. They also provide the guarantee that we shall go a long way and that the course we are pursuing is irreversible. Such is the will of our people.

In charting these ambitious plans, the Soviet people have a vital stake in preserving and strengthening peace everywhere on Earth.

Mr. President, Ladies and gentlemen,

May I express the hope that the Soviet Union and the United States, working together with all nations, will take their place in the history of the outgoing 20th century not only as allies in the battle against Nazism but also as nations paving mankind's way to a safe world, free from the threat of nuclear annihilation.

On behalf of the Soviet people, I declare that we are prepared to go all the way down our part of the road with the sincerity and responsibility that befit a great and peaceful power.

Thank you.

6

Address to the Soviet and American Peoples

December 8, 1987

I am addressing my fellow countrymen, the citizens of the Soviet Union, and I am addressing the American people.

President Reagan and I have just signed a Treaty which for the first time in history envisages the most strictly verified destruction of two entire classes of nuclear arms.

The Treaty on the total elimination of Soviet and U.S. inter-mediate- and shorter-range missiles will, I am sure, become a historic milestone in the chronicle of man's eternal quest for a world without wars.

On this occasion, I would like to refer for a moment to history.

Not all Americans may know that at the height of a world war, the very first step taken by the Soviet Republic born in Russia in 1917 was to promulgate a Decree on Peace.

Its author, Vladimir Lenin, the founder of our state, said: We are willing to consider any proposals leading to peace on a just and solid basis.

This has been the cornerstone of Soviet foreign policy ever since.

We also remember another concept of his: disarmament, a world without arms. A world without violence is our ideal.

Today, regrettably, the risk of a nuclear catastrophe persists. It is still formidable. But we believe in mankind's ability to get rid of the threat of self-annihilation.

We are encouraged by the growing awareness in the world of the nature of the existing peril which has confronted mankind with the question of its very survival.

The sacred human right to live has now taken on a new, global dimension. And this is what must always be in the minds of, above all, political and state leaders invested with power by the will of their peoples.

The people is no abstract notion. It is made up of individuals and each one of them has the right to life and pursuit of happiness.

The Treaty just signed in Washington is a major watershed in international development. Its significance and implications go far beyond what has actually been agreed upon.

Our road towards this watershed was a difficult one. It involved lengthy and heated arguments and debate, the overcoming of accumulated emotions and ingrained stereotypes.

What has been accomplished is only a beginning. It is only the start to nuclear disarmament, although, as we know, even the longest journey begins with a first step.

Moving ahead will require further intensive intellectual endeavor and honest effort, the abandonment of some concepts of security which seem indisputable today, and of all that fuels the arms race.

In November 1985, President Reagan and I declared in Geneva that nuclear war could never be won and should never be fought. We also declared that neither the Soviet Union nor the United States sought nuclear superiority.

This enabled us to take the first step up the platform of a common search.

Geneva was followed by Reykjavik, where a fundamental breakthrough was made in our perception of the process of nuclear disarmament. That is what made possible this Treaty and a substantive discussion of other issues pertaining to the nuclear confrontation.

We give credit to our American partners. Together, we have

been gaining experience that will help seek solutions to even more challenging problems of equal and universal security.

Most important of all is to translate into reality as soon as possible agreements on radical cuts in strategic offensive arms while preserving the ABM Treaty, the elimination of chemical weapons and reductions in conventional armaments.

The Soviet Union has put forward specific proposals on each of these problems. We believe that agreements on them are within reach.

We are hopeful that during next year's return visit of the U.S. President to the Soviet Union, we will achieve a treaty on the elimination of practically one-half of all existing strategic nuclear weapons.

There is also a possibility of reaching an agreement on substantial cuts in conventional troops and arms in Europe, whose build-up and upgrading causes justified concern.

Once all this is accomplished, we shall be able to say, with confidence, that progress towards a secure world has become irreversible.

The elimination of weapons of mass destruction, disarmament for development—that is the principal, and, in fact, the sole effective way to resolve other problems that mankind is having to face, as the 20th century draws to a close. Among those are environmental problems, the problems connected with the implications of the new technological revolution, energy, mass poverty, hunger and diseases, huge foreign debts and failure to balance the diverse interests and needs of scores of peoples and countries.

To cope with these problems, there will have to be, above all, fresh approaches to matters of national and universal security.

I know that with the signing of the Treaty on intermediate- and shorter-range missiles, some politicians and journalists are already speculating as to "who won." I reject this approach. It is a throwback to old thinking.

Common sense has won. True enough, it is not yet the greatest victory, but politically and psychologically it is very important. It meets the aspirations and interests of hundreds of millions of people throughout the world.

People want to live in a world in which they would not be haunted by the fear of nuclear catastrophe.

People want to live in a world in which American and Soviet spacecraft would come together for docking and joint voyages, not for "Star Wars."

People want to live in a world in which they would not have to spend millions of dollars a day on weapons that they could only use against themselves.

People want to live in a world in which everyone would enjoy the right to life, freedom and happiness, and, of course, other human rights which must be really guaranteed for any developed society to exist normally.

People want to live in a world in which the prosperity of a few is not achieved at the cost of the poverty and suffering of others. They want to have not only military, but economic security.

People want to live in a world which is democratic and free, with equality for all and with every nation enjoying the right to its own social choice without outside interference.

People want to know the truth about each other, and to feel at long last the great universal kinship of nations, ethnic groups, languages and cultures.

Can such a world be built? We in the Soviet Union are convinced that it can. But this requires a most radical restructuring of international relations.

To move towards such a world, there has to be creative courage, new thinking and a correct assessment of, and regard for, not only one's own economic capabilities and interests, but the interests of other nations as well. There has to be political will and a high sense of responsibility.

We in the Soviet Union have initiated a process of reassessing what has been achieved, and of developing a new program of action, and we are implementing it.

This is what we call perestroika. We have undertaken it without hesitation, for we realize that this is what our time demands. We have undertaken it because we want to elevate our society, speed up its development, make it even more democratic and open, and release all of its potential, so as to improve the life of our peoples materially and spiritually.

Our confidence in the future of our country and our conviction that a secure and civilized world can be built are organically interrelated.

On behalf of the Soviet leadership and of our entire people I declare that in international affairs we are acting and will continue to act responsibly and seriously. We know what our interests are, but we seek to accommodate them to the interests of others, and we are ready to meet each other halfway as equals.

The President and I have three days of intensive and important work ahead of us. Our talks are already under way. For our part, we will try to do all we can to achieve results, substantial results.

Thank you.

7

Meeting with American Artists, Intellectuals and Scientists

The Soviet Embassy

December 8, 1987

I'm sincerely glad to have this meeting, and I cordially welcome you to this hall. I appreciate the fact that, as busy as you are, you have responded to our invitation and have put aside other business for a while in order to meet with us here.

If we have made progress towards one another in our hearts, that means a lot. So thank you very much for the emotional effort on your part.

I mentioned in my NBC interview that I had received

The gathering was attended by American community leaders, people prominent in science, culture and the arts, who have for many years influenced politics and public opinion. Mikhail Gorbachev had already met some of them, in particular, at the Moscow Forum For a Nuclear-Free World, for the Survival of Humanity.

Among the visitors to the Soviet Embassy were Thomas Gittins, President of Sister City International; George Kennan, former U.S. Ambassador to the Soviet Union; Gene LaRocque, head of Defense Information Center; Patricia Montandon, President of Children as Peacemakers; John Randolph, President of the National Council of American-Soviet Friendship; James William Fulbright, former head of the Senate Committee on Foreign Relations; Gus Hall, General Secretary of the Communist

80,000 letters from Americans. That doesn't count those that have arrived here at this Embassy. By the way, I get between 70,000 and 120,000 letters a month from my own fellow countrymen. So that's a lot of mail.

This is what Emily Holders, age 17, writes:

"Many Americans mistrust the Russians. Many Russians mistrust the Americans. We have many reasons for not trusting them, and they, the Russians, have many reasons for not trusting us. But I feel there's something wrong about all this, there's something missing."

This is the question posed by someone who is just 17 years old. And then the letter continues:

"We must have a sense of common responsibility for our survival. Therefore, what we must do is to try and build a world of responsibility as if our entire lives depended upon it. And if we, one human family, do not learn to cooperate as one humankind, then we will inevitably be destroyed by what we ourselves have created. But if we do learn to cooperate, just think of the wonderful future that will open up before us."

This is a budding philosopher who has some very good, optimistic views. So I think the young people who will replace us are a good generation. In another letter, addressed both to myself and President Reagan, the following question is raised, "Mr. President, Mr. General Secretary, you've lived your lives. And you are going to meet and discuss questions on which human lives depend. Please see to it that we can live our own lives too, and preserve the future."

Now I feel something very serious is happening, something very profound, something that embraces broad sectors of the

---

Party of the United States; Susan Eisenhower, granddaughter of the late President Dwight D. Eisenhower, prominent in the peace movement; Robert M. Adams, President of the Smithsonian Institution; John Kenneth Galbraith, notable economist; Professor Bernard Lown, American co-chairman of the movement International Physicians for the Prevention of Nuclear War; Carl Sagan, the astrophysicist; Marshall D. Shulman, Professor of Columbia University; Sidney Drell, Director of the Strategic Research Center, Stanford University; the singer John Denver; film stars Robert De Niro and Paul Newman, the singer and community leader Yoko Ono, and other celebrities.

population both in the United States and in the Soviet Union —an awareness that we cannot leave our relations as they are, relations between our peoples, between our two nations. And it occurred to me that anytime this kind of ferment takes place in the minds of people, it begins with the intellectuals—with intellectual ferment. They are the yeast of society, as it were—it is they who trigger off new processes in society.

At the same time, I have a question which I ask myself and you: Aren't we, the representatives of political and intellectual circles, lagging behind what the people have already come to realize?

We should really ponder about whether we might not be lagging behind the sentiments and feelings of our peoples; those sentiments are clearly in favor of the two countries and peoples drawing closer together.

Academician Velikhov has shown initiative and organized an exchange for schoolchildren. A group of American kids spent their summer vacation in the Soviet Union in a place not far from Moscow—Pereslavl-Zalessky. They wrote some marvellous letters and had them recorded on tape.

Back in the United States, they put out a newsletter. One of its headlines was, "The Russians Are Coming." *(Laughter.)* And then they explained what kind of Russian "invasion" they were talking about and what the consequences would be.

I'm really thrilled by the fact that our kids—12, 13, 14 years old—the oldest were just 17—are so deeply aware that something needs to be done. And they certainly lay big demands on us.

I feel that we have approached a crucial point in history when we, especially politicians, have come to bear a special responsibility, that of expressing in full the sentiment of the people in favor of rapprochement between our two countries, in favor of an improvement in relations.

At the Moscow forum, and at a meeting with a group of prominent Americans, including Mr. Vance, Dr. Kissinger, Mrs. Kirkpatrick, Mr. Peterson and others, we talked about the fact that a confident, realistic policy is not possible nowadays unless politicians, scientists and artistic people join their efforts.

There are many former ministers, secretaries and ambassadors present here. It was only later that they realized it is possible to uphold the interests of one's own country only if the interests of others are also taken into account. Only if there is a balance of interests.

The Soviet Union has its own interests, and the United States has its own interests. And so do India, Kampuchea, and Bangladesh . . . Every country has its own interests. And I think it is important that precisely this understanding underlie the building of new relationships.

What I want to say is this. We are all children of our time, but there are new realities, and they have dictated new imperatives—what we call the challenge of the time.

The experience we have acquired is our wealth—if we dispose of that wealth properly, if we don't just lump it all together but rather draw lessons and compare how we acted before, in past situations, when the world was different, with what we have today, and determine whether in today's world we can still act as we did 10, or 20, or 30 years ago.

I see here representatives of very many theories, such as "balancing on the brink of war," "containment," "rolling back communism" . . . But this has all become a thing of the past. And unless we realize this—we and you in the United States—it'll be hard, indeed, for the world to switch to another track, to take a new path, the path of improving international relations, of cooperation.

And you know how strongly this need is felt by those around us. It is knocking at the doors—Soviet doors and American doors—and we cannot under any circumstances turn a deaf ear to something whose time has come.

Such are the new realities. It seems that we have perceived them but, perhaps, we have not yet come to understand everything fully. Yet we have endeavored to perceive them and put them at the basis of our analysis, our vision of the world today. So, while in the past we emphasized only the fact that we are different—and we are saying so today, and this should be realized, but not overdramatized—today we emphasize that we are all part of one and the same civilization. We are interconnected—through science and technology, through the environment, through the challenges that are growing and dictating to us that we must be united in our thoughts and actions. Isn't it the duty of intellectuals to communicate this perception to the peoples? I think this is the duty of all intellectuals. I told the President today it was desirable that there should be a scientific element in the elaboration of the policies of each nation, both domestic and foreign, and that people in the arts should make their ethical contribution to politics. For that purpose we are prepared not only to hold exchanges, but also to maintain cooperation, hold meetings in order to perceive the situation together from the viewpoint of universal human values.

I don't see any grounds for getting upset simply because we are different. Take any family, there are always different people living together in one family. Take the international community—can everyone in it be identical? It's an important fact: we are all different, yet we are one and the same civilization. Everything is interconnected. We will remain different, but we live in one and the same world, so let us all think what intellectual contribution we—the Soviet Union and the United States—can make, above all, from the viewpoint of awareness of the new realities and how we can contribute to a restructuring of relations, first and foremost, between our two nations.

At this point, I would sincerely like to expound my vision of the present-day situation, to share my ideas as to where we stand and what our common responsibility is.

I cannot, for example, understand the people who reacted hostilely to the elements of cooperation and mutual understanding that appeared in the process of drafting the Treaty on Intermediate-Range and Shorter-Range Missiles. I fail to understand them as a human being, although this can be explained—it has to do with interests. Everything is explained by interests. But there are different kinds of interests. There are the interests of the masses of people—including the American and Soviet people—and these are supreme interests. And the task of politicians is to express these interests, and not the narrow, selfish interests of some groups or strata in one or another society.

We do not claim to know the absolute truth on all matters, but we are prepared to make our contribution. We have intellectual resources ready to join in this process of perceiving the world and the process of building up a new relationship. I believe that both our countries have immense potential in this respect.

As for the second part of my address, I can describe—just to keep you informed—the state of the restructuring of Soviet society at the current phase.

We initiated perestroika because we needed it. We could not live any longer in the way we had been living before. Of course, economically, we could have continued to move by the force of inertia. We could have still shown some growth and ensured a 2- or 3-percent rise of the national income. But that is not the point. We tried to take a fresh look at our society as a whole, and the major conclusion we came to was that the potential of the socialist system was not being utilized fully in terms of both the human factor and maneuvering with the help of a planned economy. So we took a look at our society in an attempt to understand it and ourselves, to find out what kind of a society we lived in. Glasnost and democratization were essential for this. These, of course, are complex and extremely deep-going processes. Their purpose is not to shake our society. We want to understand our society. And, on the basis of an objective analysis, to build up a concept and then make our way intelligently through this very complicated period, stage by stage. This is what we have initiated.

The quest is not an easy one, and it is not always easy for us to assess our historical past. We have had to call a spade a spade on many occasions. We have not yet said everything, have not yet sorted everything out, but we have got to the bottom of one thing, the most important thing, which became the basis of the policy of perestroika. In short, over these two and a half years we have formed a view of the society we live in and tried to take a look at the future and the roads we will follow. We are moving ahead. The process is far from simple.

There is no denying this. Comrade Zalygin, Editor of the magazine *Novy Mir,* is sitting here. From the experience of running his magazine, he can tell you how high feelings are running in all spheres of our society—political, economic, intellectual and cultural, moral and social.

We will go along the chosen path. There is simply no alternative other than stagnation and marking time. Our people will simply not agree to this anymore. But while on this road, we will put the conservatives in their place and, at the same time, prevent the skipping of stages and adventurism.

Quite a few meetings have been held in the past one and a half, two years. Yes, they were needed because revolutions have always started in this way. The entire society got into motion. And today, at a new stage, there is a growing need for difficult, serious, profound and responsible practical work. Now that we have started linking the concept with life, millions of people have become affected. The next two or three years will be the most painful. Everything must change—political institutions and the economic situation. Some of you who are present here, have already written that we will not be able to cope with this task because we are trying to solve it on the basis of our socialist values. Let us wait and see. I am convinced that we will make it. We will borrow what is right for us from other economies and will link the interest of the individual with that of the public through relevant mechanisms, through new economic mechanisms, through improved centralism and election of economic managers.

When a person depends on the results of economic performance on the basis of cost accounting, he will no longer tolerate a loafer or an incompetent manager at the head of his enterprise. Now he needs a knowing, intelligent manager, one who is capable of successfully doing his job today and seeing ahead. That is why elections are needed. That is why we are spreading the process of democracy to the economy as well. Economic planning allows us to carry out structural changes less painfully.

I think that we are not using even 50 percent of our system's potential. We are only now beginning to realize what socialism

is and what it can really yield. We are returning to Lenin. In
his concluding years he gave much thought to the future of the
country and saw that something was beginning to happen that
impeded socialism, as a system, from spreading its wings. We
are trying to understand this thought of Lenin's. Of course, we
are not trying to apply his ideas mechanically to present-day
life: the society, the country and the people have changed very
much since then. We are making a big effort to see how to tap
socialism's potential—its economic, democratic, political, intellectual and moral potential.

It should also be remembered that 90-odd percent of the
population are people who were born after the Revolution.
They know no other government and no other system. And we
will remake our society on the basis of this system's mainstays
and values, as we perceive this system. This is our concern. I
do not understand why it should worry Americans. It is only
natural that our new thinking as regards processes inside the
country and our approaches to them are making themselves
felt also in our views on the world as a whole, in our relations
with this world. In our view, international relations also need a
perestroika. We cannot, however, impose it "by decision of the
CPSU." This should be a result of the consent of the entire
human community, of cooperation between all its members.
We are open to dialogue, to a comparison of views and to
exchanges, and we respect the values and choice of each
nation.

We will stick to our path, the path of perestroika, regardless
of the difficulties. It will become easier later on . . .

As for economic relations with America, I simply do not
know how we can tolerate the state they are in any longer. We
have virtually no links with you in this regard. True, this also
shows that in this respect we both can live without one another. But is this the point that we wanted to prove to each
other by our history? No. I think we have many mutual interests. Take our scientists, ask them about the interest with
which they meet and exchange ideas. This is very important to
them, I know. They cannot do without this. It would not be a
normal situation if the scientists of the two biggest countries

didn't have any contacts, were not enriching each other with their ideas. The same goes for other spheres. I know, for example, the opinion of your businessmen.

The time has come when we both really need to think everything over, determine where we are, what stage we have reached, and analyze everything. Perhaps this will require another ten, twenty, thirty or a hundred meetings in order to determine at long last how we should live in this world. This question concerns both our two peoples and all the rest. America and the Soviet Union must find a way to cooperate, to draw closer together and, in the future, to be friends as well. Let us not hurry, let us not get euphoric, and let us take a responsible attitude. We do not need illusions, for stubborn realities exist. At the same time it is necessary to take the first step: everything starts with the first step.

If this visit and the things that have emerged in our relations over the last few years are now drawing energy from public sentiments and these sentiments are moving in this direction, then this means the ice has been broken. Personally, I am an optimist.

8

Meeting with Leaders of the U.S. Congress

December 9, 1987

Due to common effort and meeting each other halfway, we arrived at yesterday's event—a unique event in the history not only of our relations, but of international relations in general. A very big step has been taken. The initial reaction in the world to the act of signing the Treaty shows that it evoked a great response. Proceeding from yesterday's event, I would like to invite you all to ponder over how our two countries—the United States and the Soviet Union—are going to live together in this world of ours. For instance, I can feel there is a great desire among broad sections of the Soviet people for improving our relations. And I feel there is a similar movement among the American public. But if this mood of the people is not really perceived in political institutions, including such authoritative ones as the U.S. Congress, the Supreme Soviet, the United States Administration and the Government of the USSR, this process will not have the necessary impetus.

On the eve of my departure for Washington I had several

Taking part in the meeting were James C. Wright, Thomas S. Foley, Robert H. Michel, Tony Coelho, Trent Lott, Robert C. Byrd, Robert J. Dole, Alan Cranston and Alan K. Simpson.

international meetings, specifically, with the Australian Prime
Minister and the Zambian President. They had come from
opposite corners of the world. And all the conversations
started with them telling me: You are going to the United
States. Do your best to have your relations start to change for
the better. So we all bear a vast responsibility. And it is not
only the responsibility to our peoples. Peoples the world over
want our relations to improve. There is some progress in our
relations on a political plane. More Senators and Congressmen
now come to the Soviet Union. We have always attached much
importance to such visits. And I am sure that you have seen
for yourselves that we all want the dialogue between parlia-
mentarians to be serious, to become broader. That is my first
point.

Now the second. Ahead lies the process of disarmament;
that is by no means an easy process. What we want is to try
and see to it that this burden be lightened as far as possible so
that it should not press heavily on the United States and the
Soviet Union. And when I say this, many of those whom I
would call short-sighted people would start speculating that
Gorbachev is not having an easy time if he has come to the
U.S.A. for talks about easing the burden of the arms race on
the Soviet Union.

But this is not the case, I should say. The point is to have a
true understanding of this problem. The arms race greatly
complicates political dialogue and other ties and is affecting
economic processes in both our countries. We can see how
high are the mountains of arms we have amassed as a result of
the arms race. And we are sitting atop all that. And just consider what would happen if these arms begin to work and we
lose control of them. If we are all aware of that, we should try
to move towards each other. I welcome the fact that through a
difficult dialogue, realistic thought, nevertheless, is making a
way for itself in public and political circles, both in the United
States and in the Soviet Union. We believe the time has come
for our political institutions, the main, supreme institutions, to
become aware of this urgent need and realize it in politics.

Yesterday we took but a first step. Certainly, it relates to no more than 5 percent of the nuclear arsenals, but I think that its political importance is much greater, for the most difficult step has been taken. It seems to me that since the American side and the Soviet side have been very captious towards each other all the time and felt that this is not a simple matter, you should bear in mind that for the first time in our country this matter did not proceed smoothly. I told the President yesterday that many questions are asked in our society, questions are asked of the General Secretary and the Government, openly, in the press, to say nothing of letters, whether the Soviet leadership was right in reducing three to four times greater volumes of nuclear weapons. For that matter, the Gallup Institute and our own institute of public opinion had a poll taken in the United States and the USSR, and it turned out that half of the population of the Soviet Union said that we should carefully consider whether or not the signing of this Treaty will damage the security interests of the Soviet Union. Now, that was news to us, I must tell you. So we feel that we will have to work with our public opinion and with the Supreme Soviet. Perhaps for the first time the process of ratification in our own country will not go through so easily. But insofar as I was deeply involved with the Treaty, including the details of its elaboration, I would like to say that it is a very seriously elaborated Treaty. And the main thing is that we had arrived at quite unprecedented machinery of verification. This is important not only for this Treaty. This also brings hope that when we approach the stage of cutting strategic arms, we can put to good use the experience we have gained. This is an example of how a coincidence of interests can be established and acted upon even in such a delicate matter as verification.

9

Meeting with U.S. Media Executives

The Soviet Embassy

December 9, 1987

Addressing the guests, Mikhail Gorbachev stressed that his visit had been a working one. A Treaty has been signed which for the first time eliminates nuclear weaponry—a major event in itself. "The U.S. President, his advisers and I," said Mikhail Gorbachev, "have been seriously discussing a wide range of problems. We've got enough experience behind us to engage in a constructive dialogue.

"We have reached a stage," Mikhail Gorbachev went on to say, "at which broad strata of the population and representa-

---

Participating were Robert L. Bernstein, Random House Inc.; Cornelia Bessie, Harper & Row Publishers Inc.; Louis D. Boccardi, Associated Press; David Cohen, Collins Publishers; Stanton R. Cook, *Chicago Tribune*; Max Frankel, *The New York Times*; Katharine Graham, *Washington Post Co.*; William Hyland, *Foreign Affairs*; T. Johnson, *The Los Angeles Times*; Jason D. McManus, *Time* Inc.; Gordon Manning, NBC News; Thomas S. Murphy, ABC Inc.; G. Piel, *Scientific American* Inc.; Warren Phillips, *The Wall Street Journal*; John C. Quinn, *U.S.A. Today*; Robert Wright, NBC; Stewart Richardson, Richardson & Steirman; Stephen B. Shepard, *Business Week*; Richard M. Smith, *Newsweek*; Betty Smith, International Publishers Co. Inc.; Howard Stringer, CBS News; Martin E. Tash, Plenum Publishing Corp.; Larry Tisch, CBS; R. E. Turner, WTBS; Alberto Vitale, Bantam-Doubleday-Dell Publishers Inc.; Mortimer B. Zuckerman, *U.S. News & World Report,* and others.

tives of many circles in both countries are eager to see for themselves whether we are doing everything in the area of Soviet-U.S. relations in a way worthy of our two nations and our great powers.

"In the forty-odd years after the war we have proved we can do without each other, without maintaining either trade or other ties. Yet even in that kind of situation we have keenly felt each other's presence. Do we need to prove that we can do without each other? Don't we need to prove something different in politics, in our actions and in our dialogue, and to look for ways to communicate, including through the mass media?

"The question is: Has the arms race made us happier? Someone might say: Yes, I'm happy because I've made money on weapons manufacturing. Someone else might say: I'm happy because my newspaper or magazine has made money on the arms race and the Cold War. But are there many people who are indifferent to the fate of the people, the fate of their country and, in terms of present-day realities, the fate of our civilization, and who are prepared to jeopardize it all as long as they continue making money? At the present level of development, I don't think that such people are in the majority. I am convinced that the feeling of responsibility and concern about the future of humankind prevails in today's world.

"People are straightforwardly asking: When will we learn to live and work normally? We can't always hark back to stereotypes and methods of action. We will be lost and unable to overcome tension.

"I am convinced that we must analyze the current situation in the world and take a realistic view of things. If we do this, we will find solutions in various areas—in dialogue, in disarmament and in the economy."

Other speakers at the meeting stressed the importance of building up confidence and promoting cooperation between the Soviet and American mass media. They also pointed out that scientists of both the United States and the Soviet Union have greatly contributed to the achievement of the agreement on the elimination of the intermediate-range and shorter-range missiles.

Pondering the role of scientists, Mikhail Gorbachev said: "I think a mistake was made when the views of Einstein and his colleagues were not heeded. They warned that the world had obtained a force that required a new approach. At that time people did not take a sufficiently responsible attitude towards it, and now the fruits of their lack of respect for the views of scientists are being reaped. We need the opinions of scientists and their competence. We have seen how the world has listened to the opinion of the movement 'International Physicians for the Prevention of Nuclear War.' Lown and Chazov promoted this idea, and look at the response it has received the world over. This is because knowledgeable people with a clear idea of what the consequences of a nuclear war would be started speaking out. This has had an enormous impact.

"Contacts are now being established between our scientists in physics and mathematics. Scientists have made a number of valuable suggestions, and we used them and found ways to move towards the Treaty on intermediate- and shorter-range missiles. During the talks we proposed forming a committee of Soviet and American scientists. Let them submit their appraisals to the leadership so that we might know the worth of this or that political decision we are in the process of taking."

Representatives of the leading mass media were especially interested in the Soviet Union's policies of perestroika and glasnost.

"As for our problems," Mikhail Gorbachev said, "we have named them, and we have embarked upon the road of renewal, upgrading political institutions, democracy, the form of economic management, and of enriching a spiritual environment. We have termed our plans perestroika. Our pivotal task is to involve the public in all this and make the people real participants in the restructuring drive. This cannot be done without the media, without glasnost. For this reason we will be broadening openness and stimulating constructive criticism and responsibility. It is not sensationalism that is needed. We need reflections that will move people and awaken in them a desire to work hard for the benefit of their country and to find their place in the common endeavor. Of course, such a process involves a clash of opinions, and the press must show this realistically, in a civic-minded spirit, not just in a way to boost sales. The main thing is that society should receive answers to the questions of concern to it through the media.

"We will be broadening constructive criticism and democratic principles in our mass media. They have helped us at the first stage, and we are counting on their help at the next stage, in the realization of our plans. Here we pin our hopes on the press and its energetic involvement. But the press itself cannot be outside the realm of control and criticism. It, too, should be subject to criticism and control from the people.

"I think that the greatest and most reliable guarantee that these processes will be positive and stable is that politicians have come under close public scrutiny and that the scientific community and cultural figures are becoming very actively involved in international politics. Evidently the peoples of our two countries and of the entire world have grown tired of politicians failing to respond to the imperatives of the present-day world. A synthesis of politics, science and culture, and the energetic participation of public movements and their advance to the forefront of the international political scene are the guarantee that no one will be able to manipulate the peoples, as was the case in the past. Everyone has realized that things can't go on as they have been. I see that as the chief guarantee. Politics has come out of the offices and corridors of power. It has now emerged on the expanses of the broad international arena; people who are interested in the preservation of peace are entering this arena."

During the talks the American participants also raised the issue of human rights in the USSR, referring to alleged facts that often figure in the American mass media.

Mikhail Gorbachev said: "Your information has absolutely nothing to do with the real state of things. In fact, we do not even have such a notion as 'political crimes,' we have only the concept of crimes against the state. We will defend our system against those who want to undermine it, just as all other states do. Why should capitalism and capitalist law have the right to defend the capitalist system, and socialism not?

"So it happens that some things recognized as lawful in the U.S. are regarded as unlawful in the Soviet Union.

"The President asked me yesterday: 'Why do you set emigration quotas? Why not allow everyone wishing to leave to do so?'

"I replied: 'And you, Mr. President, why do you set immigration quotas? You have installed barbed-wire fences and placed submachine gunners along your border with Mexico to prevent people from that country from entering the United States. And at the same time you demand unlimited emigration from the Soviet Union. What kind of logic is that?' The President replied that the U.S. cannot take in all the Mexicans.

"But how can you be so sure that all of them will abandon their native land, Mexico, in order to come to the United States?

"We have now let everyone wishing to emigrate to do so. We are not letting out those who have worked at defense enterprises or are associated with computer technology, arms development or control systems, because they hold state secrets. Every state protects its secrets. Why then should we be some sort of fools who don't care about the future of their state and its defense capability?

"Instead of speculating on these issues, we should take a look at a concept that U.S. legislation implements. If we do so we shall see that it ignores social and economic rights. All over the world America is being criticized for that. It does not sign international agreements to this effect. Who then has given it the moral right to adopt the pose of a teacher with respect to the rest of the international community and to preach to us? I told the President yesterday: 'Mr. President, you are not a prosecutor, nor am I a defendant.'

" 'If you want discussions on these and other issues in a broad context, let's have them. And, by the way, let's have them through the press.'

"Our press has now started giving over entire pages to Western correspondents on which they are free to publish their reports and views unabridged. The newspaper *Izvestia*, for example, has printed a complete interview with the U.S. President with his accusations of the Soviet leadership. We are not afraid of criticism. Your criticism is often unconvincing. It is disrespectful towards our people and this also makes us disrespect it. It can only appeal to the groups of extremists who are dissatisfied with society."

Mikhail Gorbachev cited concrete instances of misinformation being spread when various rumors had been picked up by the Russian services of the Voice of America, BBC and other stations. "If," said the General Secretary of the CPSU Central Committee, "the Western mass media are trying to present the Soviet Union in a bad light, that means that we have started something positive and that perestroika is tackling major tasks. If there are such vigorous attempts to kill the interest in that policy, that means that our perestroika is a serious thing, both for us and for the rest of the world."

In the course of the talk concrete proposals were made for an exchange of editors of various publications between the Soviet Union and the U.S.A.

Mikhail Gorbachev supported that idea, saying that the very idea of contacts and closer mutual understanding was very important. He promised that the Soviet side would give careful thought to those questions and consider the organizational forms.

10

Speech by Mikhail Gorbachev at a Luncheon in His Honor

U.S. Department of State

December 9, 1987

Esteemed Mr. Secretary of State and Mrs. Shultz,
Ladies and gentlemen,

Allow me to express gratitude for the invitation to such an authoritative institution as the State Department of the United States of America. A great deal in international politics depends on those who work here. In any case, the event which we witnessed yesterday and in which we participated would not have taken place without their part.

The President of your country and I signed yesterday the Treaty on the elimination of an entire class of nuclear weapons, or, to be more precise, two classes of nuclear weapons.

The world will be rid, as a result, of approximately 2,000 lethal warheads, altogether. This is not a very large number. But the importance of the Treaty goes far beyond the limits of its concrete content.

We assess it as the beginning of the implementation of the program for the construction of a world without nuclear arms, the program which I proposed on behalf of the Soviet leadership and Soviet people nearly two years ago, on January 15, 1986.

I have been asked more than once since then if I continue to believe that the program is realistic. I answer: yes, certainly. The signing of the Treaty on intermediate- and shorter-range missiles shows that the road to this aim is far from easy, but it also shows that it is the right road and that the aim is feasible.

The will of hundreds of millions of people operates in this direction. They come to realize that as the 20th century is running out, civilization has approached the divide between not so much systems and ideologies as common sense, the instinct of self-preservation of humankind, on the one hand, and irresponsibility, national egoism, prejudice, in a word, old thinking, on the other.

Humanity is coming to realize that it has fought enough wars, that wars should be banished forever.

Two world wars and the exhaustive Cold War, along with "local wars" that have taken and continue to take millions of lives, is too high a price to pay for adventurism, conceit, disregard for the interests and rights of others, unwillingness or inability to face the realities, to show consideration for the legitimate right of all peoples to make their own choice and have a place in the sun.

This means that the lofty ideals of humanists of all times—the ideals of peace, freedom, the awareness of the value of every human life—should be the basis of practical policy.

Each new step in world development, given a sound and responsible approach to it, enables us to grasp problems more profoundly and equips us with additional opportunities for their solution.

It is essential not to miss these opportunities, to use them to the utmost for building a more secure world, rid of the trappings and psychology of militarism, a more democratic world.

It won't be an overstatement to say that this step—I mean the Treaty signed—and the preparations for it were truly instructive. They enriched our two countries and world politics with the recognition of the significance of difficult but simple truths. It will be appropriate to mention some of them.

First of all, in meeting each other halfway we came to appreciate still more the role and importance of Soviet-American relations in present-day international development, and at the same time, our great responsibility not only to our peoples but also to the world community.

Second, we have become aware how important the support our allies give our efforts is. Moreover, what a substantial reserve is contained in their ideas, advice, in their real and involved participation, in coordinating our actions with them.

Third, we have tested in practice how important is the understanding of one's intentions, proposals and plans by the allies of one's partners and, certainly, sympathy and solidarity, and even a simple wish of success from many, large and small, developing and nonaligned countries.

All this confirmed convincingly a simple but very important truth that peace today is not a monopoly of a state or a group of states, no matter how powerful. Peace is the concern and lot of many, and is more and more becoming the concern of all. And wherever many interact, reciprocity is indispensable and compromises cannot be avoided.

Peace from the positions of strength is intrinsically fragile, no matter what is said about it. By its very nature it is based on confrontation—covert or overt—on the constant danger of outbreaks, on the temptations to use force.

Over centuries humanity was compelled to put up with such a really lean peace. But we can tolerate this no longer.

Some people think that in drafting the Treaty the Soviet side conceded too much, while others think that it is the U.S. side that made too many concessions.

I think that neither view is right. Each side conceded exactly as much as is necessary in order to balance their interests in the given specific area.

In creating the atmosphere of contacts, of direct communication, getting to know each other better, without which it would be more difficult to achieve the Treaty, we, and I hope

you, too, realized more profoundly that in order to ensure that
we all remain different, live in our homes the way we choose
and have the opportunity to hold disputes with each other and
assert our views, we need more than anything to preserve
peace.

A fundamentally new important step, if a modest one, was
made yesterday towards a more equitable, more humane order
in international relations. One would like to hope that the
subsequent steps will not be long in coming. Besides that, it is
easier to continue a good undertaking, relying on the experience of the work already carried out.

We are all now living through a period of transition from
knowledge as dogma to knowledge as thinking. We have embarked on restoring peacemaking as the center of politics. It
should not be any longer the continuation of war by other
means, as happened in the 20th century after the ending of the
world wars.

As politics change, the predestination of diplomacy changes,
too. It is called upon to seek out seeds of accord even in the sea
of differences and to turn the possible into reality.

The diplomatic services of our two countries had to exert
themselves much in recent years. And marking this truly historic event, the signing of the Treaty, moreover, while here,
within these walls, one should pay tribute to the many who
applied their minds, drive, patience, persistence, knowledge, a
sense of duty to their people and the international community
in order to make this Treaty possible. I would like above all to
commend Comrade Eduard Shevardnadze and Mr. George
Shultz.

I would like to say a kindly word also about diplomats
working abroad. They were not merely conducting negotiations. In the capitals of their host countries they helped people
realize what can be achieved and what cannot, what is promising and what is so far not feasible.

I like the thought expressed in a recent article in an American newspaper that diplomacy is the first line of a country's
defenses and the front line in the struggle for peace.

But foreign policy ceased to be the domain of professionals alone. The practice of accords and agreements deceiving peoples and dooming them to actions and sacrifices running counter to their vital interests becomes a thing of the past. Any falsity, any untruth, becomes revealed one way or another.

In this characteristic feature of the present I see a guarantee of genuine democratization of international relations. In a strong field of human attraction, attention and exacting demands on people authorized to represent their states in other countries, they should constantly account for their steps and explain them.

Beside that, they are at the sensitive point of contact of cultures, and the degree to which peoples understand one another greatly depends on them. And this is extremely important now in politics, too.

The presence in this hall of outstanding representatives of the United States and the Soviet Union is not a mere concession to protocol and etiquette. This is the evidence of the fact that a political course towards better mutual understanding between our countries has an authoritative support.

This support inspired us on the long and arduous road to the agreement on the beginning of real nuclear disarmament. But since we do not intend to halt at the start of the road, this support will be needed also tomorrow, when we continue joint work to eliminate the biggest and the most dangerous part of our nuclear arsenals.

In this connection I would like to mention such a reserve for the relations between our countries as contacts between scientists and workers in the field of culture. It is precisely they who largely shape national awareness and attitude to other nations. And precisely for this reason they find the common language quicker, creating the necessary background also for politics. The role of the intelligentsia of the two countries in relations between our peoples and states is large and important.

In the language of ordinary human communication, in Russian and in English, what we have achieved here means the revival of hope. Force is a variable and unstable category, while truth achieved by honest work is constant, for it is humane.

We are now closer to truth than we were yesterday.

My congratulations to you.

11

Speech at the Dinner in Honor of Ronald Reagan
The Soviet Embassy

December 9, 1987

Esteemed Mr. President,
Esteemed Mrs. Reagan,
Ladies and gentlemen,
Comrades,
The second day of our talks is over. The talks are proceeding in a frank and businesslike atmosphere.

In the center of our attention are major problems both of Soviet-American relations and of world politics.

I have the impression that we have made progress on a number of serious issues, and this instills optimism. There are still areas, however, in which the divergences are great.

I ought to say, Mr. President, that I sense that what we are discussing here is so significant for the entire world that we are constantly aware of the world's keen attention and interest in what is happening here.

This is only natural. The decisions we reach, the results we attain, may become crucial for the destinies of the world. This is the point at issue today. Such is the scope of our responsibility.

Ladies and gentlemen, without confidence in the future, without faith that one's children and grandchildren will enjoy life, the joy of everyday life fades. No benefits of modern civilization and no achievements of the scientific and technological revolution can make up for that.

Our great Russian poet Alexander Pushkin said: The joy of life is the best university.

We would like to be involved in the establishment of a "university" whose curriculum would not include such "subjects" as enmity between nations, suspicion and disrespect of other peoples, disregard for their interests, fear and coercion.

Such a university would teach us how to live together in the present-day complex and multifaceted world.

As for our idea of a nuclear-free future, it is, as we understand, in line with public opinion in America.

Back in 1945, at the time when the first atomic bomb was made, outstanding American scientists who had taken part in its development came out against the production and use of this terrible weapon.

Of course, bombs and missiles are not capable of thinking, although people do equip them with an "electronic brain." This mechanism has no soul or conscience and, therefore, is more dangerous than any madman.

There is no issue—be it conventional arms, regional conflicts or human rights—on which it would be impossible today to reach understanding or make progress, if, naturally, the issue is approached honestly and seriously.

The world is interconnected and interdependent for many reasons, not just because a nuclear catastrophe would spare nobody. The risks arising due to the ever greater distance between the poles of wealth and poverty increase every year. Solving that problem is one of the huge tasks involved in protecting the contemporary world from annihilation.

Investments in disarmament and peace are the most reliable and promising use of capital.

Shortly before my trip here, I was shown a youth newspaper called *Bridge,* which American children who had visited the Soviet Union this year began putting out. Together with Moscow schoolchildren they set up a camp of friendship near the ancient Russian town of Pereslavl Zalessky, which is not far from Moscow.

Their activities there included computers, telecommunications, sports, music, the Russian and English languages, games and excursions—everything they are capable of. The American children are now writing about their impressions.

I am not sure that any of you have held this newspaper in your hands. But it deserves most serious attention. This is a significant phenomenon. This is a school of human contacts in which we adults should learn from our children.

The children are showing us how to get rid of prejudices and boring stereotypes.

It turns out that it is easy and natural to establish the most friendly and close relations, to trust the citizens of another country and to work together to create something useful.

This is very ennobling and makes everyone involved more humane, simple and, I would say, smarter.

The history of relationships between our peoples and states includes various pages. Some of them are inspiring, while others evoke bitter feelings. Much has been spoiled over the past forty years.

Nevertheless, it is my deep conviction that everything positive—and there are a lot of positive things—can be used to the benefit of both peoples. As far as the Soviet people are concerned, they know how to appreciate both goodness and kind words.

We shall never forget the American sea convoys to Murmansk, the sacrifices for the common victory and, of course, the link-up on the Elbe.

We also remember the factories built in the first five-year-plan periods with the assistance of American engineers and workers, the joint work of scientists who have battled the serious ailments of the century, and the joint space flight.

Our confrontation and antagonism have causes which are evaluated in different ways. However, it is much more wise to have peace and cooperation than confrontation and unfriendliness.

Peace to the peoples of the United States of America and the Soviet Union! Peace to the peoples of the planet Earth!

I wish Mr. President and his wife and all guests of our home health and happiness.

Till we meet in Moscow.

12

Meeting with U.S. Businessmen

December 10, 1987

I very much appreciate this opportunity to meet with members of the business community whose activities are connected with the very foundations of the life of peoples and states.

Over the 40 years since the war we have proved that we can get by without each other. We have managed without each other surprisingly well. In so doing, we have spent enormous funds on the arms race and find ourselves together atop a huge powder keg, not knowing what will become of us now. We must break the trend. We must see each other as partners rather than enemies. Now that a major impulse has been given to political dialogue and to the process of disarmament, a favorable situation is emerging for giving joint thought to how we shall trade and develop economic relations.

We could become useful to each other. We are convinced that it would be beneficial to American business to launch

---

Among the businessmen present at the meeting were C. T. Acker, Dwayne Andreas, Armand Hammer, Barron Hilton, James H. Giffen, Donald M. Kendall, David Kearns, Robert D. Kennedy, Leonard Lauder, Richard J. Mahoney, Hamish Maxswell, John J. Murphy, John A. Petti, David Rockefeller, Felix Rohatyn, Edson Spenser, R. E. Turner, Richard D. Wood, and A. W. Clausen as well as the Honorable C. William Verity, U.S. Secretary of Commerce.

operations in the Soviet Union. We are confident that such interaction will to a certain extent—and I don't want to conceal this—make it easier for us to solve our problems. We regard ourselves as a part of the world economy. One doesn't really have to be a specialist to realize the need for cooperation between our vast countries.

We have been thinking about this and have done a great deal in this direction in our legislation. We have adopted political decisions on cooperation. This process is currently picking up speed. I would like you now, using new forms and new approaches, to take a more active part in this joint search. Why? Because I think that logic is such and history is such that there is no way we can escape one another. It could be that you would like to get rid of the Soviet Union so that it would not be an obstacle. It could be that somebody in my country as well would like to get rid of America so that it would not be an obstacle. But I think that these people are unrealistic in their thinking.

America and the Soviet Union are the biggest realities of our time. And since that is so we must live, coexist. And it would be even better if we did not simply live and coexist, but also cooperated. The feelings of our peoples towards one another are changing, and this is very important as well. People want rapprochement, mutual understanding and an atmosphere of trust between our countries for them to get to know each other better. The current Soviet leadership has advanced a course of perestroika and a new policy for our country. It views foreign economic ties as a very important aspect of cooperation with other nations, both from the standpoint of domestic interests and in terms of strengthening international relations and putting them on a real basis, on commercial interests.

All peoples and nations are interrelated. We have a common interest—to rid ourselves of the threat of nuclear weapons, preserve peace and tackle global problems, as well as the consequences of the scientific and technological revolution—ecological problems, backwardness and poverty. We should try to do this by joint effort. This is the first point. Second, we believe that if we become more dependent on each other in the economic sphere, we will act more responsibly towards each other in the political sphere. This is all rather dialectical and interrelated. The Soviet Government and the organizations which are connected with the economy and which are now making use of new economic mechanisms and implementing radical economic reforms, proceed from the premise that economic cooperation and trade between our countries are two factors for domestic development and for a more stable international situation.

You have, of course, taught us some lessons over the past decade and we have become cautious as well. It is no longer so easy to draw us into this cooperation. I told this to the President as well. When we were deprived of 17 million tons of grain in two days—which was in the middle of winter—and we had to look for ways of obtaining that grain (you know that this happened when the embargo was declared), this led us to the conclusion that we cannot be oriented towards the United States alone. It turned out that America could use economic ties in order to take us by the throat. That was one lesson. Here's the other. We tied ourselves to the West through buyback agreements, equipment purchases, licenses and some accessories, and then suddenly the COCOM lists and other impediments emerged. So when the problem arose of how we should go about fulfilling our tasks, strategic, scientific, engineering and technological, we said: No, we won't allow any further underestimation of our own machine building and our own science, which possesses a tremendous potential. We have now doubled investments in machine building and boosted outlays in some areas of computer engineering between five and seven times. We are developing all these advanced technologies, all these advanced areas, in order to overcome our lagging behind. We have already sensed how actively our scientists, technicians, specialists and designers have become involved in the efforts to cope with the problem and have seen how much talent we have in reserve.

We have learned our lessons and shall not allow our national interests to be exposed to another blow. This does not mean, though, that we are against large-scale projects and large-scale

cooperation. No, we are, nevertheless, for that. We shall combine cooperation with the work on the tasks we have outlined
for ourselves. And if there's anybody who wants to be in on
this, help us and receive his benefits, we invite him to do this.
We invite him and will look for approaches and create prerequisite conditions for such cooperation. I am talking to you
plainly and bluntly to make it clear that we don't want to be
cunning with you. It must be clear: we invite you to cooperate.
Everyone willing to join in will get the support of both the
Government and the political leadership, not to mention that
of economic and business quarters.

We should think about how to develop trade, since duties on
our goods are as high as 75 percent. Can one trade in this way?
Is this trade? Can the Soviet Union put up with such a disrespectful attitude? Our people are perplexed by this. Let's think
how to get rid of these trammels. We realize that cooperation
won't develop if you find it unprofitable. But let's also think
about how to make sure that we'll be interested in going to the
American market with our goods. To rearrange political, economic and cultural relations, involve broad popular masses in
exchanges, draw our peoples closer together and create prerequisites for cooperation, we need to start with clearing away the
logjams. I am very supportive, for example, of the consortium
idea which has been suggested by the American side. We are
very interested in it. A consortium of our own has already
been formed. This is why, when the leading centers of these
consortiums have been established, they will be able to make
contacts. And such a meeting is planned for the immediate
future. This is a very interesting idea, because we have projects
that cannot be handled by just one firm. There are very big
projects. This is why it is essential to pool efforts. Think this
over. We would welcome this. Joint ventures are another new
form. As a matter of fact, the President and I have ended our
talks with a concluding document which contains a good pas-
sage on trade between our countries. The business community
could rely on this joint statement. So now you have a political
document which will serve you and help you broaden contacts
and ties.

This is what I would like to wind up my speech here with. I invite you to cooperation. I know that sitting before me are people who can be called realists. They may take a great deal of time thinking and weighing the pros and cons of getting into this or that project. But I also know that they can accept the realities, appreciate them and move towards new approaches and new realities.

13

Address at the Press Conference

December 10, 1987

Ladies and gentlemen,
Comrades,
We can now regard the visit as being over. Our delegation is leaving for home today. We will have a brief stopover in Berlin. We have agreed with the leaders of the Warsaw Treaty countries to meet in order to discuss the results of my visit to Washington and the negotiations that I've had with President Reagan and other political leaders of the United States.

I realize, and that is natural, that you are interested, first of all, in our opinion, our assessment of the results of this visit. And I feel that you want to know as much as possible about those results. So perhaps I will take more time than usual in my introductory remarks.

First of all, I'd like to say that this has been our third summit meeting in the last two and a half years. And this in itself, probably, says a great deal—first of all about the dynamic nature of the political dialogue between the U.S. Administration and the leadership of the Soviet Union.

And, therefore, we can say that Geneva and Reykjavik were not in vain, nor were other steps taken by our side as well as by the U.S. Administration.

Had the third meeting not led to definite results, there would be no grounds for regarding it as an important event.

And now I am completely justified in beginning my assessment of this visit by saying that it has indeed become a major event in world politics. We could even go so far as to say that from the standpoint of both Soviet-American relations and the world situation in general an important new phase has been entered.

Much took place during the negotiations. But I would like to find the right words so as to avoid extremes and successfully convey the character and atmosphere of the talks, and, of course, give a correct assessment of the political results.

What, then, are these results? What can we tell you about them today?

First, we can talk about a deepening political dialogue between the leaders of the Soviet Union and the United States of America. Today the President and I have issued a joint Soviet-American statement at the highest level. This fact alone bears witness to a certain dynamism in our political dialogue.

The importance of that document lies in the fact that it shows both the range and the content of the discussions that we had. In reading this document you will be able to gauge both the degree of mutual understanding and agreement on various questions. At the same time, you will also feel, I trust, that this document indicates that there are still serious differences remaining.

What do we assess on the positive side in that document?

First, the President and I have noted that certain progress has been achieved of late in relations between the U.S. and the USSR.

Second, once again, having looked back on the events of the last few years, we have agreed that what has been achieved so far is based on Geneva and Reykjavik. It was those events that made the steps aimed at improving strategic stability and lessening the danger of conflicts possible.

We have, and I want to draw your attention to this, forcefully reaffirmed the solemn declaration of Geneva. We deemed it necessary to do this once again at this meeting in Washington. We affirmed that nuclear war should never be unleashed and cannot be won, that we are fully determined to prevent any war between our countries, be it nuclear or conventional, and that we shall not seek to achieve military superiority.

This is something that we regard as an undertaking of unlimited duration by the two great nations before the entire world community.

Third, emphasis has been put on the special responsibility of the Soviet Union and the United States for finding realistic ways to prevent military confrontation and building a safer world for mankind as it enters the third millennium.

Fourth, while realistically assessing the fact that differences still exist, and that on some points those differences are very serious indeed, we do not regard them as insurmountable. On the contrary, they only urge us to engage in more active dialogue.

Summing up this conceptual part of our joint statement, I will say that it has been recognized at the highest level of our two countries that they are now emerging from a long, drawn-out period of confrontation and are prepared to leave it behind them.

You will probably agree that this is an important political result and an important political statement, which the joint document contains. It is this that constitutes the essence of the transition to a new phase in Soviet-American relations.

Second, in the course of the visit, work on the Treaty, eliminating all intermediate- and shorter-range missiles in the world, which took many years to prepare, has been completed. As you know, the President and I have signed that agreement.

I have already had occasion to speak about the significance of this first step on the road leading to the elimination of nuclear weapons. Now that this has been done, when our signatures have been affixed to that document on behalf of our two nations, we can speak about a major event, what I would call a history-making event, having occurred. We can speak of a great success having been achieved through joint constructive efforts.

That is probably what makes this document so significant.

The percentages of the cuts don't really matter. What does matter is that we have entered a new phase in the process of real nuclear disarmament by agreeing to eliminate two classes of missiles.

I would say that this is our common success, the success of our two countries. But at the same time, it is a success for our allies who took part at all stages of this long marathon in the quest for compromise, the quest for new approaches and new solutions to these difficult problems. And I would also like to mention the participants in public movements whose actions induced politicians in our countries and political circles around the world to work to ensure that the search for solutions aimed at concluding a treaty on the elimination of nuclear missiles, of these two classes in particular, continues in spite of all the difficulties and obstacles. And difficulties and obstacles did exist. They were not invented, but very real, and many of these problems were new and unique, especially insofar as verification was concerned.

Generally speaking, this Treaty is the net result of joint efforts by all nations. So today we can sincerely congratulate each other on having taken the first step on the path towards a nuclear-free world. And that is our common victory.

Third, our negotiations of the past few days focused on the problem of achieving a real and radical reduction in strategic offensive arms. That problem took up the most time. And some of the questions relating to this part of our discussions were resolved even as the participants in the official farewell ceremony were already waiting for us on the South Lawn of the White House. And I think this is understandable, because such a reduction in strategic armaments is, after all, the centerpiece of Soviet-American relations. It is a question of great concern to the entire world community. And you, as journalists, should know quite well how closely the world has been following the process of negotiations on this particular question.

The idea is to cut strategic offensive arms in half. This is a complex issue. Both sides came to the conclusion that on this road, too, we must make a serious breakthrough, drawing on the experience we accumulated in the preceding phase of negotiations, including the experience gained in preparing the Treaty on intermediate- and shorter-range missiles. This should be done without delay, while there is still a real opportunity to stop the arms race and the build-up of strategic potentials and begin eliminating them.

Now, what kind of a scope can we talk about now with regard to the agreement on these issues? Right after we met and exchanged views on this issue—and this topic became central to our discussions right from the outset—the President and I issued instructions for a group of Soviet and American experts to be set up. And this group was set up. It is headed on our side by Marshal Akhromeyev, Chief of the General Staff of the Soviet Armed Forces, and on the American side by Ambassador Nitze.

Over these three days the group has been working round the clock. It was given the task of preparing an agreed draft of instructions for the Soviet and American delegations in Geneva, on whose basis the delegations are to elaborate a treaty on the reduction and limitation of strategic offensive arms, which would also ensure compliance with the ABM Treaty and nonwithdrawal from it for an agreed period of time, so that this treaty could be signed during the visit of the U.S. President to Moscow in the first half of 1988.

As a result, we have achieved significant progress—and I am saying this after careful consideration—on this problem, which is the major one for the Soviet Union, the United States and all nations in general.

As is known, even before the meeting in Washington, agreement was reached on reducing the strategic offensive arms of the USSR and the U.S.A. by 50 percent, limiting the number of strategic vehicles to 1,600 and of warheads to 6,000. Sublevels on heavy missiles, the rules for counting heavy bombers, etc., were also agreed upon.

Following the work done here in Washington, quite a lot that was new was added to those agreements.

At long last, we worked out the problem of limiting the deployment of long-range sea-launched cruise missiles carrying nuclear warheads. The American side has agreed to establish limits for such missiles over and above the 6,000-warhead level and to conduct a search for mutually acceptable and effective methods of verification of those limitations.

On this score, we had a very interesting exchange of views. We took advantage of the achievements of our science and technology in the area of creating national means for verifying the presence of nuclear weapons on various naval ships—whether surface craft or submarines—without conducting any on-the-spot inspection on board the vessels themselves.

I don't know whether this was accepted, but we suggested that if we reached agreement on this we could share our achievements so that our partners could see for themselves that those national means helped to identify not only the presence, but also the yield, of nuclear warheads. And this problem of verification had been the most difficult one blocking the resolution of the entire problem of sea-launched cruise missiles.

Incidentally, on the subject of scientific and technological achievements, I said to the President that it was very important to involve our scientists in such undertakings, because they can really give expert assessments and realistic recommendations. I suggested that we set up a Soviet-American commission of scientists who could put forward their views and recommendations to the U.S. Administration and the leadership of the Soviet Union.

But let's go back to the results of the negotiations. The question of verification has been elaborated in detail. Previously it presented a big problem. Mutual understanding in this field is a consequence of the successful work done in preparing the INF Treaty.

Limits have been set: a total of 4,900 warheads for ICBMs and SLBMs within the aggregate level of 6,000 warheads. As you can see, that is a new point, and a substantial one at that.

The President and I, with due regard for the preparation of a treaty on strategic offensive arms, have instructed the delegations in Geneva to elaborate an agreement which would commit both the Soviet and American sides to observe the ABM

Treaty, as signed in 1972—and that includes the research, development and, if necessary, testing which are permitted by the ABM Treaty—and not to withdraw from the Treaty for a specified period of time. That is what we inscribed in our joint statement.

We agreed that we would continue intensive discussion of the question of strategic stability.

It has also been defined that if the USSR and the United States fail to come to an agreement before the end of the period of nonwithdrawal from the ABM Treaty, each side will then have the right to determine its mode of action.

As you can see, we have made significant progress on the problem of nuclear and space arms, which is the most important and complex one.

But for us to be able to prepare a treaty on the reduction of strategic offensive arms within several months, there is a great deal of work ahead for our delegations in Geneva, and not just for them, but also for the leaders of the Soviet Union and the United States.

Fourth, now that we have reached agreement on eliminating intermediate-range and shorter-range missiles and are addressing the problems of reducing strategic offensive arms, the questions of conventional arms and of chemical weapons are becoming increasingly important.

It can be said that they have become very acute and have come to the forefront. We don't tend to dramatize the situation and we condemn all attempts to speculate on this issue. I would like to emphasize my last remark so that it sinks in. Perhaps you ought to give it some thought.

There are some very real concerns as regards the questions of conventional arms. They are shared by both us and the West Europeans. Therefore, we're inclined to pay very serious attention to these types of arms right now. And we now have accumulated good experience through preparing the INF Treaty. Those present here may recall the ups and downs that we had to go through in the course of its preparation. I'm sure you remember the question of the French and British nuclear potentials, the question concerning shorter-range missiles, the missiles deployed in Asia, and so on.

And, nonetheless, a readiness to meet each other halfway has brought us to a conclusion of the Treaty. From here stems a simple conclusion: that is also the way we should act in questions pertaining to conventional arms—to address serious questions, to remove existing concerns. The West asserts, for example, that the Warsaw Treaty countries have a superiority, but the East says that NATO and the West Europeans have the edge over it.

And I must say that in a way both sides are right, because they're basing themselves on actual existing data. But these facts confirm one thing—that there are indeed asymmetry and imbalance which have taken shape as a result of specific historical features in the building of armed forces.

We believe it is necessary to begin by elaborating an agreement on a mandate for the conference presently under way in Vienna. We must sit down at the negotiating table and look for solutions to the problems at hand. Negotiations can be meaningful only if we can talk about a mutual and simultaneous reduction and the elimination of imbalances and asymmetries. With that approach, we could surely resolve all the issues.

Some declare, for instance, that the Warsaw Treaty states have an advantage in Central Europe, but those who speak of this, for some reason, are silent about the fact that NATO has a considerable superiority on the southern flank of Europe, next to our borders.

We believe it necessary also to discuss such questions as the creation of a corridor between NATO and the Warsaw Treaty Organization with limited armaments, particularly as concerns those of an offensive nature.

We should also think about the principle of sufficiency, and, in general, thoroughly discuss the problem of comparing military doctrines from the standpoint of transforming them into purely defensive ones.

I must say that the American side treated our proposal seriously and displayed interest, and we have agreed to address this problem directly, in a concrete way, at the level of our military establishments and with the participation of scientists and experts.

In short, in the area of conventional arms and armed forces, I suggested to the President here in Washington that we give that issue a new political impetus, such as the one that was given in Reykjavik on the problems of nuclear disarmament when we saw that the Geneva negotiations on them had virtually reached a deadlock. And that was beneficial then, and now we have the first Treaty eliminating nuclear weapons.

We can take the same approach today to the problem of conventional arms. We believe that is exactly how we should act. We should sit down at the negotiating table and lay our cards out. We should cast aside all altercation. And that will surely show who is trying to be sly and who is in earnest, because both Americans and West Europeans, and we, and allies, all of us are fully aware not only of what there is installed and stored, and how much, but also where. And I think that it's good that both our Western partners and we know it. Knowledge is a great thing.

We should lay our cards on the table, exchange all of the relevant data, assess that data, identify the asymmetry in the arms and armed forces and embark upon a search for solutions. This is our approach.

As far as we are concerned, let me say right out that we are prepared to adjust ourselves to that task immediately, and we shall insist on that being done. That is the opinion of our allies, too. So I am expressing our common view on this matter.

Moreover, we are prepared for most radical reductions. Here, too, we are trying to be realists. Most likely, this is a process that will have to go through certain phases. You can't resolve everything just like that. But we have to start by sitting down at the negotiating table and beginning to eliminate asymmetry and imbalance in order to lessen drastically the confrontation. That would be a significant achievement. And that could be accomplished in the near future.

In other words, we must be very thorough when dealing with the concerns of either side over questions of conventional arms.

During our meetings, the President and I also talked about chemical weapons, in the same spirit. It is obvious how important their elimination is. This question has long since been under consideration and its discussion has recently gained momentum thanks to the constructive cooperation of the sides.

I deemed it necessary, both in my discussion with Mrs. Thatcher and here in my talks with the U.S. President, to note the contribution made by the United Kingdom, the Federal Republic of Germany and some other West European countries to the solution of this problem. And let me say that this contribution stimulated us as well. The Soviet Union has acted in a constructive way, especially on questions of verification and elimination of the stockpiles of chemical weapons. And let me remind you once again that we have ceased production of chemical weapons.

There was also a positive statement issued by the United States. But recently the progress in elaborating the convention has clearly slowed down. We said this directly and frankly to the President and the other American participants in the negotiations. We believe that the process slowed down through the fault of the United States. We felt that the U.S. side wanted to go astray from the objective agreed upon in Geneva—a universal and complete ban on chemical weapons—and wanted to exclude binary types of chemical weapons. In the event the convention is signed, even if there are "holes" in it, the United States would like to limit the facilities subject to verification to state-owned ones.

And what does that mean? For the Soviet Union it means all of them, but for America and Western Europe—practically none. So, what kind of equitable approach is that? What kind of consideration for concerns? What kind of partnership?

The U.S. Administration, all the West Europeans and every participant in the negotiations should understand that the Soviet Union is not looking for any unilateral advantages and is prepared to move along all directions in the process of disarmament, but at each stage there should be a balance and parity. We shall insist on this. If someone starts having doubts and believes that he is being outpaced, it will undermine the process of disarmament, inject nervousness and uncertainty and complicate the atmosphere of the negotiations.

The attention of the American side was drawn to this and we proposed that those imbalances be rectified, and we suggested that this viewpoint be registered in our joint statement. And although our talks on chemical weapons proceeded with difficulty, we did, at long last, manage to agree that the two sides would conduct more active and intensive talks on elaborating a convention. The President and I expressed our dedication to the solution of this extremely important question, and we have instructed our experts to continue active discussion on the question of the non-use and of the nonproliferation of chemical weapons as well.

And now, about one other problem that has always been extremely important, but now, after the signing of the INF Treaty and in connection with the scheduled progress on reducing strategic offensive arms, has become still more topical —the problem of halting nuclear tests. You know that we have begun negotiations with the United States on that question. We asked the President if, given the changed situation, it would not be very desirable (and this would be correctly understood and properly appreciated in our countries and throughout the world) if we took a fresh look at this process as well, at these negotiations, and their content. We said it would be desirable to reach agreement on lessening the yield of nuclear explosions and drastically reducing the number of nuclear tests in the nearest future. But that is the minimal step which must be taken as quickly as possible in order that further progress could be made without delay.

At the same time, in the present, new situation, taking into account and respecting the demands of the world public, we consider it appropriate and possible to establish a mutual moratorium on nuclear tests while the talks are under way.

Unfortunately, so far we have not gotten a positive response from our partners on this very important question which is causing concern throughout the world. Now, if we've started to disarm, this means we must consider any question in that context, and think and act accordingly. That is why we are not losing hope that our very important invitation to the American Administration to introduce a mutual moratorium on nuclear tests while the talks are in progress will still be given serious thought, that it will be carefully weighed. Perhaps, the U.S. Administration might wish to consult with the people. We are told that America is a democratic country. So why not consult with the people on this issue and, perhaps, positively respond to our proposal? We are not losing hope.

Now, what else would I like to say on the military aspects of the negotiations? I would like to point out that a major and extremely important breakthrough has been achieved in the area of verification. I would say that the INF Treaty establishes unprecedented standards of openness, of glasnost. The scope and depth of mutual verification and control are unprecedented.

We have confirmed in practice the position that we have set forth on numerous occasions: when it comes to verification of disarmament, we will be the firmest advocates of the strictest, most effective control possible. For if verification is only talked about while the arms race goes on under cover of such talk, then what is the point of verification? In short, we are in favor of any kind of verification, of the strictest verification, if that verification concerns disarmament and the elimination of armaments and as long as the principle of reciprocity is observed.

This is all the more important today when we are approaching solution of the problems connected with strategic offensive arms, when we have approached the problems of eliminating chemical weapons. Besides, we already have experience and we feel more confident.

We exchanged views with the President on a whole range of other questions as well: regional, humanitarian. The examination of regional problems was not easy. We came here with serious intentions, with proposals to really come to an understanding on the most acute problems. We drew attention to the need to consider our joint approach to the solution of regional conflicts proceeding from the following: we are now witnessing an unquestionable striving of the world community to solve the existing regional conflicts by political means. This is clearly seen in the attitudes of many political quarters and governments, in the actions of the world public.

That's the phenomenon we are now witnessing.

This gives the USSR and the United States—two countries upon which much depends—an opportunity really to do something for resolving these very acute problems of world politics.

I can't say that we have made much headway on this issue. Yet, I and members of our delegation have the feeling that the U.S. Administration has started approaching regional problems somewhat more realistically. Indeed, new approaches are needed here. And most important, both we and the Americans and other countries should unconditionally recognize that all nations have the right to their own choice. That is the crucial point of departure.

Regional solutions cannot be divorced from the question of human rights and humanitarian issues. What can be higher than the right to security, to life, to settling one's national affairs as one sees fit? What can be more favorable for democratic forms and processes than a country's reliable security?

In short, all these things are interconnected, and it is from these positions that we approach the situation in Afghanistan. We are for a settlement which would make it possible to put an end to the bloody conflict, eliminate the possibility of its recurring, and prevent in the process of reaching a political settlement the origination of such a situation that would have serious consequences for the interests of the world community.

We said clearly that we do not want, we do not strive for, a pro-Soviet regime in Afghanistan. But the American side must state just as clearly that it is not striving for a pro-American regime there. In a free, nonaligned and neutral Afghanistan, a government must be established on the basis of reconciliation, on the basis of all political realities being taken into account, on the basis of cooperation and a coalition of various forces and their national reconciliation. And to promote this our two countries can do a lot.

We put the question of Afghanistan as follows: the political decision on the withdrawal of troops has been taken. We've named the time limit—12 months. It could be less. That is the fourth item and it is awaiting its solution under the aegis of the Cordovez Commission. Our position is that the beginning of the withdrawal of troops must, at the same time, become the beginning of the termination of assistance in arms and money to the Dushmans. From the very first day this is declared, our troops will start withdrawing. They will not take part in military operations, except in self-defense. Hostilities will cease and a process of political settlement will begin. We shall facilitate this process as much as our influence allows. But the main effort should be made by the real forces within Afghanistan itself, by all the sides concerned.

It seems that all this could produce a genuine document facilitating the process of political settlement. We have agreed to continue our work in this direction.

We also discussed at the talks in Washington regional conflicts in Central America, the Middle East, Southern Africa, the situation in the Persian Gulf, and so on.

On bilateral Soviet-American relations. The Soviet position was the following: the USSR and the United States are world powers, possessing major economic, intellectual and military potentials. Their weight in international affairs is immense. That determines their role, and that determines their responsibility.

The many years of confrontation and sharp rivalry have produced nothing but harm. We have already proved sufficiently that we can live without one another, without trading, without having any extensive scientific or cultural contacts, without any cooperation in the solution of global issues. But the question arises: do we need to prove this? Is this not reminiscent of the futile labors of Sisyphus? Shouldn't two great nations, two world powers, actually ponder the situation which has arisen as a result of acute confrontation throughout almost all the post-war years? The time has come to think all this over, so I said to the President and his colleagues: Does it not seem to you that politicians are lagging behind the moods of the peoples? We judge by the sentiments in our own country, and we judge by the sentiments of the American people, and feel they both want changes for the better. And they are beginning to act on their own. They are establishing contacts, searching for various forms and means of these contacts and displaying amazing ingenuity, from the children to the wisest people in our countries. Everybody understands that the time has come to turn the last page of confrontation and begin a new stage.

These are very powerful imperatives, I believe, and they should be reflected in the policies of our Governments.

I assure you that the Soviet leadership has but one opinion. A firm decision has been taken about which I am speaking today—we are in favor of a definite improvement in relations with the United States of America. Our peoples need it, the entire world needs it.

I reminded the President that the world already regarded the way in which our two countries have been developing their relations as something laughable and as something to be mocked. There have been many comments along this line; for example, that we approach every problem by galloping towards each other head-on, with our visors down. When we do that we really are on the wrong path and can go much too far unless we stop ourselves.

I feel that everything that went on at the talks and everything that was publicly said by me, the President and other political leaders these past few days confirms that, except for some narrow circles, there are no opponents to a sensible approach and understanding.

If these responsible political declarations are followed by responsible and real steps, then we can look forward to better times, to better years. I believe that not only our peoples, but the whole world will applaud this.

Also this last week, on the eve of my visit to Washington, I had some meetings with foreign statesmen—Kenneth Kaunda, a well-known political figure of Africa, and Prime Minister Hawke of Australia. They were very insistent in advising me, in asking me to tell the U.S. President that both in the West and on all continents people are hoping for an improvement in international relations.

In my discussions with them I encouraged them to make their own contribution. And they responded that they were ready to make their contribution, but that it was most important for the USSR and the U.S.A. to come to terms with each other.

I feel that we must become aware of this and embody it in real politics. The time has come.

I assure you that our actions will proceed from such an understanding of the situation.

I said this to the President at the very first meeting we had, at meetings with leaders of Congress and representatives of the intellectual circles of America. And I said this in my meeting with the U.S. media executives and representatives of the business community. I said this openly in all my speeches.

I hope that our voice will be heard. And it has been heard, I think, by the American people. People are even changing the way they treat one another on the street.

All of a sudden Americans who are in good spirits have appeared in Washington's streets. They wave their hands. At one point today when I was driving around with the Vice-President, we got out of the car and met with a group of Americans. And I could sense their mood. I told them that we are talking with the President about how to come closer to each other, how to improve our cooperation. So go ahead and prod the President towards that. Our Soviet people are solidly prodding us towards that goal. So I've not only been indulging in politics, but also I've been conducting propaganda. But I still think that the best propaganda is a real, progressive and constructive policy.

In our bilateral questions, as soon as we began to think about how to come closer to each other, a great many problems came up for discussion which we could address, and you will see this in the joint statement. There are many concrete questions concerning the environment, the preservation of the ozone layer, a peaceful outer space, a flight to Mars, medicine, a thermonuclear reactor, trade, etc. This opens up possibilities for us to consider joint projects in concrete terms.

So these days were filled with serious discussions, exchanges of opinions and views. And I believe that the substance of this visit allows me to say that it was a significant dialogue and the results, too, are significant. I believe all this will bear fruit if we consistently move ahead step by step, however difficult it might be, and I'm sure that it will be very difficult. We will move ahead in the quest for mutual and acceptable solutions, taking into account each other's interests. A great impetus has been given to that process.

In conclusion, I deem it my duty once again to say a few sincere words about the feelings expressed by Americans on the eve of the visit and during the visit. Just before the press conference I met a group of young Americans and told them that young American and Soviet people seem to come to terms with one another much faster than we politicians. They have no complexes. Before we can come to terms, we have to get rid of the old stereotypes, of the obstacles standing in the way. And that's not all that easy at a ripe age. But the youngsters are open with each other and find a common language very quickly. And this is not a superficial, children's approach, it's not a matter of looking at things through rose-colored glasses. They are serious people. Between fifteen and seventeen years old, they are already giving serious thought not only to their personal problems, not only to what is of interest to themselves, but also to how we should live in this world. It's an amazing phenomenon and, by the way, it should be written about.

In my discussion with the media executives, I explained why I give interviews so rarely, although I like lively exchanges very much. After three, four or five interviews, it becomes clear that the same questions are being asked. Then what are we going to talk about? Are we to talk for the sake of talking? To try and prove that we have not 4,000, not 2,000, not 500, but only 22 individuals who are imprisoned in our country for having broken the law; that there are only 220 persons who have been refused permission to leave because they worked with defense and computer technology, control systems, in short, with state secrets. No matter what you say, no matter what you write, no matter who shouts at us and from where, we will not let them go until these secrets are no longer secrets. This is what the world is like today, and we are forced to take this into account. But then everything in our relations is being reduced to this and interviews are being requested not to find out the truth, not to prompt each other to thought, but simply to expose a politician as quickly as possible, to drive him into a corner.

Is that a dialogue? Is that the purpose of interviews and is that what the media in general is for? People want to live better, people want to understand each other better; they want to communicate and be friends. And how much is being blown out of proportion through the press? And this is done supposedly because it will lead to more openness. I'm not trying to accuse you of something, to say that politicians are such great people and that such bad people are working in the media. No, I'm simply saying that the media, too, need a perestroika and need to master a new way of thinking. Do you agree with this?

Let's think about this together, because we're all in the same boat. Or is everything clear to you? If so, I envy you. But at the same time, if everything is already clear to you, I pity you. Please give thought to this.

Taking advantage of this opportunity, I want to return to the thoughts about the Americans' reaction, the feelings they expressed over these days. And I would like right now, as this visit is drawing to a close, to say thank you for the hospitality, the openheartedness and cordiality. And they can be sure that this will be heard in the Soviet Union, by the Soviet people, and it will be met by the most sincere and lively response. I want them to hear these words. And upon our return home, we will share our impressions of our visit to this country.

The visit was limited to Washington. I would like to come to the U.S. again, when circumstances permit, and communicate with the people. This I would truly like to do.

And I would like to wish the American people success and the realization of their hopes. I wish to assure Americans that, on the part of the Soviet people, they have a reliable partner in all that concerns peace, cooperation and common progress for all.

Thank you.

* * *

After that, Mikhail Gorbachev answered questions put by correspondents.

Question: In your book *Perestroika* and in your speeches, you've talked about a process of democratization in the Soviet Union. Now that you've had at least a fleeting encounter with the American concept of democracy, I wonder if you could tell us what you've learned and what differences you see between American ideas of democracy and your own ideas of democratization?

Answer: I have felt that there is a need, both in your country and in ours, to try and understand what values underlie American society and what values underlie ours.

This problem was a subject of serious dialogue and discussion both with the President in private meetings and in meetings attended by other parties, including a meeting with Congressional leaders.

We have agreed: let us take all these issues—on democracy, on human rights, everything that lies in the humanitarian sphere—out of the plane of political speculations and bring them into the plane of realistic study of and acquaintance with the values that the American people have formed in following the road of their choice and the accomplishments of the Soviet people since they made their choice in 1917.

We agreed that this should be done at the level of the Supreme Soviet and U.S. Congress by organizing workshops, seminars and meetings, holding thorough discussions and making assessments. We are prepared to present and characterize our situation and set forth our view of the situation in America. Similarly, the American side must say in a firm, substantive way what it believes must be said. In other words, we must take this seriously. I think we will find that to be beneficial.

Question: Mr. General Secretary, probably one of the most abnormal conditions in the relations between the U.S. and the Soviet Union is the level of trade. Can you tell us: in this summit meeting, were you able to discuss this problem with President Reagan, or with other leaders on your visit here? And could you give us your thoughts on the potential for economic cooperation between the United States and the Soviet Union?

Answer: This is a very interesting question on a big subject. I think that if we have seriously made a decision to change our relations for the better, we cannot allow a weakening in dynamics in any direction. So far, little has actually been done to expand economic cooperation and trade.

One cannot hope to conduct a political dialogue successfully without restructuring economic ties, economic relations. I had discussions over the past three days with the President and with leaders of Congress—which has made its own "unique contribution" of adopting so many amendments that it will now require a huge bulldozer to remove them all. *(Laughter.)*

I asked them to review this situation. Today, I had a substantial conversation with businessmen, with major representatives of America's business community. One can say that there is an understanding of the need for change for the better in this important sphere. The final document contains a record on this account. It is directed at stimulating trade, economic relations and the implementation of major projects, including the undertaking of joint ventures.

I think that this political message will enable U.S. business and business circles in the Soviet Union to step up cooperation. The possibilities for that, according to those who know the Soviet Union, are enormous.

An American representative said today that, in contrast to ties with China, he has noticed that there's a great purchasing capacity in the Soviet Union, and, accordingly, a tremendous stimulus for undertaking joint ventures.

But that is not competition. We both maintain ties with China, and we will be pleased if you continue developing them further. I think that our relations with the People's Republic of China, our neighbor and friend, will continue developing.

Question: On several occasions during the past week your authorities roughed up nonviolent, peaceful demonstrators outside the Soviet Foreign Ministry. Is that perestroika, is that glasnost?

Answer: Where laws are violated those whose duty it is to confirm that the state and the law exist go into action. Sometimes incidents occur, but only then when the law is violated. In this particular case everything happened as it should, in accordance with the law, and the incident ended there.

Question: There were some hints from some of your colleagues before you arrived here that there could be some progress on offensive weapons without sticking strictly to the ABM Treaty, that there could be some compromise on strategic defense. It seems as though those issues are still linked. We're told by Administration officials that you insisted on that linkage during the talks. Do you see any way that between now and the President's visit to Moscow, a treaty on offense could be reached without first reaching agreement on defense? Or is that linkage permanent?

Answer: Our position was outlined in my opening remarks. We will work hard to make the President's visit to the Soviet Union culminate in the signing of that treaty. We shall be acting constructively on the basis of the principles which were agreed upon and published in the final document.

Question: You recently proposed a reduction of the military forces in the north, in particular naval forces. Somehow later this proposal was not mentioned again, although it is part of NATO–Warsaw Pact relations. Is this proposal still alive? What is the fate of this proposal? Will it be included in further exchanges between East and West?

Answer: At a time when we have embarked on the road of nuclear disarmament and intend to tackle the problem of conventional armaments, it is important to make sure that as we are solving one set of questions we don't allow even bigger problems to pile up in other spheres. That is, as we start removing nuclear arms from Europe and Asia, on a global scale —I refer to the class of intermediate- and shorter-range missiles—there should not be any sudden "compensations" for the purposes of intensifying the military confrontation in other regions.

I think that would be wrong and that is why our proposal to scale down military activity in northern areas is constructive and proceeds from the general idea to reduce military confrontation. It remains in force.

Question: Diego Cordovez, the United Nations Mediator on Afghanistan you mentioned, has proposed to begin a new series of negotiations in January or February to help reach a political settlement—an interim government in Afghanistan that would include the People's Democratic Party of Afghanistan, the seven Mujaheddin factions, or, as you call them, Dushmans, and a group of Afghan elders, perhaps led by the former king. Do you support those efforts to create an interim government in Afghanistan, and if such an effort were to succeed before summer of next year and the United States were willing to cut its arms supplies to the Mujaheddin factions at that time, would you begin troop withdrawals, that is next summer, from Afghanistan?

Answer: It seems to me that I have given a detailed explanation of our approach. But since the question has arisen, I'll tell you that if there is a meeting next January–February, we will welcome it. And, for our part, we are prepared to facilitate this. I believe that if these two questions are linked, as the rest already are—the question of the withdrawal of troops and the question of terminating the assistance in arms and money— then we could reach a positive result even in the coming month. We have agreed with the President to continue consultations and to study in greater detail the positions of the sides on this matter.

Question: What is the most promising field of political dialogue between the Soviet Union and the United States in the immediate future?

Answer: Let's not indulge in guesswork. But at any rate I believe that we have created some assets during this meeting. And if we are consistent in our actions, if we display restraint, we can bring about serious changes in various areas, first and foremost disarmament.

Question: How much did your views and the American views coincide or differ on the issue of the Persian Gulf? In particular, how do you feel about being charged [with] jockeying for position and shielding Iran? And why is the Middle East international conference no longer of importance to you, or at least not a priority?

Answer: Let me start with your second question. I asked the President to give thought again to the U.S. Administration's attitude towards the preparation and holding of an international conference on the Middle East because, as it seems to me, there is broad agreement in the world as to the expediency and possibility of holding it.

It seemed to me that the discussion of this subject would be continued because the preparations for the conference should not give the U.S. Administration reason for concern. Bilateral, trilateral and regional meetings could be held within the framework of this process. So it appears to me that if the conference has such a format it will be possible to take into account the diversity of views many different governments express on this score. I think progress is possible here.

As for your first question, yes, we have been accused of wanting to look good and purposefully acting in a way that makes the Americans look bad. I disagree with these accusations. A side makes this or that impression depending on the way it acts and not on how its actions are characterized by somebody else. You can observe how we act and how the Americans and others act, and form an opinion of your own.

We believe that the great powers, the permanent members of the UN Security Council, have a big responsibility to prevent a situation from arising in that region that would bring about a major conflagration. At all stages, even before the adoption of Resolution 598, and today as well, we have always said that it is necessary to act in such a way that the parties to the conflict would know what is expected of them and that they would be able to realize the impermissibility of aggravating the situation. We also feel that we have not yet exhausted that resolution's possibilities.

I will limit myself to this remark. We did have a more con-

crete discussion on this but have not yet completed it. We will
continue it so as to fulfill the responsible role of the two countries at this very complex stage of the development of the situation in the Persian Gulf and in the Iran-Iraq conflict.

Question: If two or three years ago someone had tried to
forecast the events of these past days, it might have been called
political fantasy. Now it is becoming reality. I would like to
ask you what is the objective basis underlying the current process, the current turn? And why is this turn happening now?

Answer: When we made our statement of January 15 and
set forth our plan for a phase-by-phase elimination of nuclear
arms and the easing of military confrontation in all spheres,
many people said that it was illusory. Now life itself has shown
that such forecasters were wrong.

When we arrived in Reykjavik, the place of a most dramatic
meeting—incidentally, who of you present here were in Reykjavik? *(A lot of hands are raised.)* Good . . .

You will recall the atmosphere in which my press conference began. The expectations were not fulfilled and everything
ended very dramatically. I saw journalists in the hall and
sensed their mood. I saw that I was facing not just professional
journalists, sharp-tongued media people, but people concerned
about what was going on. And that mood was catching.

I remember that press conference. Today I can fully confirm
what I said there—Reykjavik was a dramatic event, but at the
same time it was an important breakthrough in coming to
realize that, in the end, there is something that governs and
determines the actions and behavior of politicians. A dramatic
change has taken place in the sentiments of the world public in
recent years—a change leading people to realize the irreversibility of many troubles that affect the whole of humanity. The
activities of the intelligentsia of all countries brought this
change about. They came to realize what was happening—
physicists and mathematicians, doctors, people in the arts.
And then they passed their apprehension and alarm on to all
other sectors of the population. Without momentous changes
in the minds of people in all countries we would have hardly
seen the transformations that have made it possible to take the

first major step in the sphere of real disarmament—the signing of this major, history-making document.

Question: We know you are planning a trip to Latin America soon. What is the purpose of that trip and what political initiatives can Latin Americans expect from the Soviet Union in the near future?

Answer: And you already know that I'm going there soon? *(Lively response in the hall.)* I have a strong desire to go to the countries of that continent where very serious, deep changes of historic scope are taking place. And I believe that the way things will be developing on that continent, if you add to that what is going on in Asia, will largely determine the course of world politics. This is why dynamic and momentous changes in Latin American countries, in my opinion, make any politician interested in knowing what the reality there is want to go there so as to make his own observations and come up with his own analysis that could be used in political activity. So that's the main motive. I think that the prospects for Latin America are big in terms of embarking on a broad path of development. But the difficulties facing it are also big.

Question: Do you think that you were able to change President Reagan's ideas about the Soviet Union in your meetings with him? Six or seven years ago he used to say that the Soviet Union was an "evil empire."

And the second part of the question. Have you changed any of your ideas about the United States based on these three days in Washington?

Answer: Well, I guess that Mr. Reagan's views have changed for the better, as have mine.

Question: It's nice to hear that you'll be flying to Berlin tonight. How do you assess the contribution made by the allies, the contribution made by the German Democratic Republic, to the treaty you have signed?

Answer: Not a single constructive move made over the past few years was made without the participation of the allies. We considered and discussed everything together. In all things we acted in perfect harmony, on a permanent basis, and this is why I want to say once again that we are grateful to our allies for the major contribution they made to this meeting, to this Treaty on the elimination of intermediate-range and shorter-range missiles. Well, the rest I'll say in Berlin.

Question: It appears that both you and President Reagan are of the opinion that in this three-day summit you have significantly altered the course of relations between the Soviet Union and the United States. It would appear that in these three days the relationship between you, one to the other, was somehow altered. What changed, sir, and how did things change between you and the President?

Answer: I think that the agreements we have achieved in the past three days will be important for the development of relations between our countries. There is one condition: that we remain loyal to our commitments. I would like to assure the American people and the U.S. Administration that we shall act in a responsible manner, proceeding from our agreements. I think we now have a better understanding between the President and myself. Our dialogue has become more businesslike and our approaches have become more constructive. I'd even venture to say that we trust each other more.

Question: In today's remarks at the farewell ceremony at the White House, neither you nor the President mentioned the forthcoming visit by Ronald Reagan to the Soviet Union. Will that visit take place, or does it depend on further progress in your relations?

Answer: It definitely will take place. The joint statement says so.

Question: Would you tell us to what extent the achievement of agreements in the field of disarmament might determine the success of perestroika?

Answer: The notion of a relationship between disarmament and development applies to perestroika as well.

Question: After signing the INF Treaty, what, in your view, is the significance of establishing a nuclear-free corridor in Central Europe?

Answer: This subject is now acquiring greater urgency. I would call it a valuable initiative.

Question: Did you discuss during the talks in Washington a

definite time limit for nonwithdrawal from the ABM Treaty
and the so-called interpretation of the Treaty? Was anything
said by the Soviet or the American side on the SDI program?

Answer: I would put it like this: everything was discussed.

Question: You said that the Soviet Union was also working
in the field of strategic defense . . .

Gorbachev: I did not say that.

Question continued: After your meetings with Ronald Reagan, what will you instruct your experts to do in this field?
Will they speed up their work or slow it down?

Answer: I said that we were conducting basic research
which, in some areas, covers problems that are designated in
America as defense initiative. I did say that. But I also said
that we are strong opponents of SDI. We will not develop it at
home. We call on the U.S. Administration to do likewise.

But if the U.S. Administration does not heed our opinion,
if it continues developing SDI, it will assume all the
responsibility.

Strategic stability will be disrupted. The arms race will acquire new spheres which will have unpredictable consequences. If the Americans have a lot of money, let them waste
it on SDI. We will look for a response along other, asymmetrical lines that will be at least a hundred times less expensive.
This is what I said.

Question: In your recent address in Moscow, you said that
the world and you would not agree to a summit which nothing
came out of except the signing of agreements already reached.
Now, all that has happened, from what you tell us, is that the
INF Treaty was signed. You were turned down on the disarmament corridor, you reached no agreement on the test ban,
and I'm wondering if you are at all disappointed, and if you
think maybe we should be?

Answer: I don't want to repeat my introductory remarks in
which I gave a detailed assessment of the outcome of the visit.
I have nothing to add.

Question: Are the two sides any closer on the question of
how long you both agree to comply with the ABM Treaty?
And do I understand it correctly that without such an agree-

ment the Soviet Union will not go ahead with any deal on strategic missiles?

Answer: We issued instructions to our delegations, and they will continue the talks in Geneva. At the moment, I don't want to go into the specifics of those problems.

Question: You've always said that the most important thing is to stop the extension of the arms race into outer space. Has your meeting here this week made that any less likely?

Answer: I don't think so. I will say once again that preventing the extension of the arms race into outer space remains the goal of our policy.

14

Speech at the Farewell Ceremony at the White House

December 10, 1987

Esteemed Mr. President,
Esteemed Mrs. Reagan,
Ladies and gentlemen,

In these last hours before our departure for home, we note with satisfaction that the visit to Washington has, on the whole, justified our hopes. We have had three days of hard work, of businesslike and frank discussions on the pivotal problems of Soviet-American relations, and on important aspects of the current world situation.

A good deal has been accomplished. I would like to emphasize in particular an unprecedented step in the history of the nuclear age: the signing of a Treaty under which the two military and strategically greatest powers have assumed an obligation actually to scrap a portion of their nuclear weapons, thus, we hope, setting in motion the process of nuclear disarmament.

In our talks with President Ronald Reagan, some headway has been made on the central issues of that process—achieving substantial reductions in strategic offensive arms, which are the most potent weapons in the world. However, we still have a lot of work to do.

We have had a useful exchange of views, which has clarified each other's position concerning regional conflicts, the development of our bilateral ties, and human rights. On some of these aspects, it seems likely that we shall be able to arrive at specific solutions, satisfactory both to us and to other countries.

A useful result of the Washington talks is that we have been able to formulate a kind of agenda for joint efforts in the future. This puts the dialogue between our two countries on a more predictable footing and is undoubtedly constructive.

While this visit has centered on our talks with the President of the United States, I have no intention of minimizing the importance of meetings with members of Congress, with other political leaders, public figures, members of the business and academic communities, cultural personalities and media executives. Such contacts enable us to gain a better and more profound knowledge of each other and provide a wealth of opportunities for checking one's views, assessments and even established stereotypes.

All this is important, both for policy making and for bringing peoples and countries closer together.

These meetings have confirmed the impression that there is a growing desire in American society for improved and more healthy Soviet-American relations. In short, what we have seen here is a movement matching the mood that has long been prevalent among Soviet people.

In bidding farewell to America I am looking forward to a new encounter with it, in the hope that I will then be able to see not only its capital, but also to meet face-to-face with its great people, to chat and to have some lively exchanges with ordinary Americans.

I believe that what we have accomplished during the meeting and the discussions will, with time, help considerably improve the atmosphere in the world at large, and in America itself, in terms of a more correct and tolerant perception by it of my country, the Soviet Union.

Today, the Soviet Union and the United States are closer to the common goals of strengthening international security. But this goal has yet to be reached. There is still much work to be done, and we must get down to it without delay.

Mr. President, esteemed citizens of the United States! We are grateful for your hospitality and we wish success, well-being and peace to all Americans. Thank you.

15

Speech on Soviet Television

Moscow, December 14, 1987

Good-evening, dear Comrades,

The visit to the United States is over. The way to it was far from simple: there was Geneva and Reykjavik, an intensive dialogue between the leaders of the Soviet Union and the United States, and intensive diplomatic negotiations.

We constantly cooperated with our allies and had an active exchange of views with the leaders of other states. We lent a particularly attentive ear to the sentiments of people internationally, workers in science and culture, and representatives of the different political trends advocating peace. All that enriched our idea of the processes taking place in the world and infused us with confidence that we are moving in the right direction.

Thus we went to Washington with the mandate of our people and our allies. We also took into consideration the sentiments and aspirations of millions of people of goodwill the world over.

Our visit to the United States was preceded by thorough preparations and numerous comprehensive discussions at the Politburo of the principles which would guide us when we got there. We once again calculated everything from the military-technical viewpoint. Philosophically and politically, these preparations were based on the decisions of our party's 27th Congress and the program for a nuclear-free world proclaimed on January 15, 1987.

The content and results of our visit are known. The President of the United States and myself have signed a Treaty on the elimination of intermediate-range and shorter-range missiles. The agreement reached on that issue is a major international event, a victory for the new political thinking.

The intensive talks, which took up most of the time, centered on the issues of the reduction of strategic offensive weapons. We have reaffirmed our preparedness for a 50-percent cut in the strategic offensive weapons on condition the ABM Treaty be preserved in the form it was adopted in 1972, which is reflected in the joint statement on the results of the Summit. We again brought into sharp focus the issue of the need for an early conclusion of a treaty to end nuclear tests. We discussed thoroughly the questions of the elimination of chemical weapons and the reduction of conventional arms and armed forces in Europe.

In general, our aspiration was that the issues of disarmament, the elimination of the nuclear threat, lessening of tensions and confrontation in the world, and strengthening of the new approaches in building international relations be brought to the fore. These things actually happened in the course of the talks.

The main outcome of the Washington visit is, certainly, the signing of the Treaty on the elimination of two classes of nuclear missiles. This is the first step towards a real destruction of the nuclear arsenal. Only yesterday that seemed utopian to many people. Today it is becoming fact.

They say that just a modest step has been made—humanity will get rid of only 4 percent of nuclear weapons. Yet, it should not be forgotten that scientists have estimated that it would take only 5 percent to destroy every living thing on Earth.

But this is not all. The Treaty has shown for all to see the possibility of a turn from the arms race to disarmament. Now the point is to preserve the atmosphere which made it possible to conclude the Treaty, and to continue to act constructively and consistently. To this end it is necessary, in the first place, to give the Treaty its legitimate force by ratifying it.

As far as the USSR Supreme Soviet is concerned, I hope that it will support the Treaty, since this is the will of our people. It is also important that many deputies to the USSR Supreme Soviet, its commissions, in the first place foreign affairs commissions, took an active part in examining issues connected with the drafting of the Treaty.

We know that struggle around ratification is under way in the United States. But we also know that the American people support the treaty. We felt this most acutely once again when staying in America.

This is a very important period. And I wish to tell you that awareness of the importance and pivotal character of this moment was manifest in full measure at the meeting in Berlin of leaders of the Warsaw Treaty countries. Having unanimously endorsed the results of the visit in the adopted communiqué, they resolutely declared that at the new stage they will continue acting in concord in the interests of disarmament and international cooperation.

It can be said that there was a very positive response to the results of the Washington meeting in most countries of the world.

But when old views are being changed, the resistance of those who link their political and material well-being with them invariably increases. Scarcely three days have passed since our return home, but already certain circles in the United States and in other Western countries are rallying to prevent changes for the better. Voices calling on the leadership of the United States not to go too far, to halt the process of disarmament, sound ever louder. Demands are being made for urgent measures to "compensate" for the elimination of intermediate-range and shorter-range missiles by bringing new nuclear forces closer to Europe and into Europe and by modernizing the nuclear and other armaments remaining in Europe. Certain persons even try to assert that the talks in Washington have removed differences on such a problem as SDI and under that pretext make calls for speeding up work on that program.

I must say outright that these are dangerous tendencies and that they should not be underestimated. They may undermine the nascent turn in the process of demilitarization of international relations.

We hope that the world community, above all the peoples of the United States and the Soviet Union, and the sound forces in all countries will redouble their efforts to save the first sprout of nuclear disarmament, which has pushed its way through concrete walls of prejudice and stereotypes of hostility. It is now important for all to work together to promote the deepening of positive tendencies and the strengthening of mutual understanding and cooperation. The agreements reached offer a historic chance for all humanity to start getting rid of a heavy burden of militarism and war which has taken a horrible toll in human life and rolled back economic development and material culture, shackled freedom and the spiritual and social creativity of peoples.

At the discussion of each question during the visit, the issue of the role and responsibility of the United States and the Soviet Union as to how they should interact and build their relations came up one way or another, for this is important for both our countries and the whole world. Awareness of this is growing, not only in the Soviet Union but also in the United States. We noticed this when meeting and talking with political leaders and public figures, with representatives of science and culture.

During our talks with the President and other American politicians, we emphasized more than once that the new realities must be grasped and that our two countries must act in accordance with them, coexist and show respect for the choice of each nation.

We said outright that we came to Washington not to engage in altercation and mutual recriminations, as is often the inclination of the U.S. side, but to engage in real politics.

I think that all of you, Comrades, would be interested in learning how the U.S. Administration responded, what its positions and its view of our relations were, whether there were any changes in this respect. Our delegation more than once exchanged views related to this question, a question that was not easy to comprehend. I should tell you: if we firmly adhere to the hard facts and do not indulge in exaggerations, it is too early today to speak about a drastic turn in our relations. It is still too early.

Nevertheless, I want to point out that the dialogue with the President and other political figures of the United States was different than before—it was more constructive. After talking with representatives of intellectual and business circles and the mass media, I formed the impression that changes do take place. What riveted our attention most was the mounting wave of goodwill on the part of ordinary Americans—as they learned through television and the press our objectives, our true views, what we want and how Soviet people really regard America and Americans.

I said to the President: The Soviet leadership is ready for transferring our relations into a channel of mutual understanding, into a channel of constructive interaction in the interests of our countries and the entire world. It is precisely within this context that we raised other issues, inviting the U.S. Administration to join us in the search for solutions to the most acute problems of present-day politics.

We persistently raised before our counterparts the issue of our two countries' possibilities in promoting the political settlement of regional conflicts.

Although we did not move far ahead in this area, the discussion of these issues has clarified the situation and gives us grounds to believe that the dialogue can be continued.

The Joint Soviet-U.S. Summit Statement, as you noticed, gives much place to the development of bilateral relations between the USSR and the United States. Specific agreements were reached on a number of issues—in the sphere of scientific cooperation, cultural exchanges and individual contacts. In the talk, and especially during the meeting with businessmen, we had an interesting discussion of issues relating to expanding economic cooperation and trade. Positive changes in that sphere would be of major importance for an improvement in the entire atmosphere of Soviet-American relations and the situation in the world, for that matter. However, as I have already said, enormous efforts will be required here from both sides, primarily from the American side, through whose fault there appeared a large number of artificial barriers in the way of normal and mutually beneficial economic ties.

I would like, dear Comrades, to make one more point. The visit to the United States has demonstrated very plainly the extent of attention with which the entire world is watching our restructuring drive. Numerous questions of a most diverse character are asked. What is restructuring? Is there resistance to it? How determined are we to carry restructuring through? Won't we stop halfway? Is the nation willing to accept such a profound renewal of Soviet society?

This interest in what is happening in Soviet society along the lines of restructuring is genuine and sincere. It attests to recognition of our country's role in the world today. And for all of us it is a further reminder that the more successful we are in furthering the revolutionary cause of restructuring, the better the state of international affairs will be.

Such is the situation today, such is the dialectics of the world development—one more proof of the interconnection and integrity of the present-day world despite its inherent diversity and contradictory nature. We should understand this well and bear this in mind as we tackle specific practical tasks in every town and village, in every work collective and countrywide.

Let me say words of gratitude to the Soviet people for their growing contribution to the restructuring drive, for their practical deeds in response to the Party's call for a revolutionary renewal of society, for their active participation in the transformations that have begun, for their support of the efforts of the Central Committee and the Government in the work for peace. Without all this there would have been no success in the recent talks, and those talks could have hardly taken place at all.

Thank you, Comrades!

Let us congratulate ourselves on this success and let us keep working.

Good-night.

III

PRE-MOSCOW SUMMIT
STATEMENTS

February 9–April 13, 1988

16

Statement on Afghanistan

Pravda, February 9, 1988

The military conflict in Afghanistan has been going on for a long time now. It is one of the most bitter and painful regional conflicts. Judging by everything, certain prerequisites have now emerged for its political settlement. In this context the Soviet leadership considers it necessary to set forth its views and to make its position totally clear.

In the near future, a new round of talks conducted by Afghanistan and Pakistan through the personal envoy of the United Nations Secretary General will be held in Geneva. There are considerable chances that this round will be the final one.

By now documents covering all aspects of a settlement have been almost fully worked out at the Geneva negotiations. They include agreements between Afghanistan and Pakistan on noninterference in each other's internal affairs and on the return of Afghan refugees from Pakistan; international guarantees of noninterference in Afghanistan's internal affairs; and a document on the interrelationship of all elements to a political settlement. There is also agreement on establishing a verification mechanism.

So what remains to be done? It remains to establish a time frame for the withdrawal of Soviet troops from Afghanistan that would be acceptable to all. Precisely that, a time frame, since the fundamental political decision to withdraw Soviet troops from Afghanistan was adopted by us, in agreement with the Afghan leadership, some while ago, and announced at that same time.

The question of a time frame has a technical and a political aspect to it. As for the technical aspect, it is clear that the actual withdrawal of troops will take a certain amount of time. There is hardly any need to go into the details of that here.

As for the political aspect of the matter, it is that the withdrawal of Soviet troops is, quite naturally, linked with precluding interference in Afghanistan's internal affairs. Prerequisites for that have now been created.

Seeking to facilitate a speedy and successful conclusion of the Geneva talks between Afghanistan and Pakistan, the Governments of the USSR and the Republic of Afghanistan have agreed to set a specific date for beginning the withdrawal of Soviet troops—May 15, 1988—and to complete their withdrawal within ten months. The date is based on an assumption that agreements on the settlement are signed no later than March 15, 1988, and that, accordingly, they would all enter into force simultaneously two months after that. If the agreements are signed before March 15, the withdrawal of troops will, accordingly, begin earlier.

Recently, another question was raised, whether the phasing of the Soviet troop withdrawal could be arranged in such a way to remove, at the very first phase, a relatively greater portion of the Soviet contingent. Well, that, too, could be done. The Afghan leadership and we agree to it.

All of this creates the necessary conditions for signing the settlement agreements in the very near future.

That, of course, does not mean that no one could now obstruct the settlement or push the talks backwards. But we would not like to think that some states or political figures might want to be held accountable by the Afghan nation and other nations for scuttling a settlement. We believe common sense will prevail.

The question of the withdrawal of our troops from Afghanistan was raised at the 27th Congress of the Soviet Communist Party.

That was a reflection of our current political thinking, of our new, modern view of the world. We wanted thereby to reaffirm our commitment to the tradition of good-neighborliness, goodwill and mutual respect which goes back to Vladimir Lenin and the first Soviet-Afghan Treaty signed in 1921. Progressive forces of Afghan society have understood and accepted our sincere desire for peace and tranquillity between our two neighboring countries, which for several decades showed an example of peaceful coexistence and mutually beneficial equitable cooperation.

Any armed conflict, including an internal one, can poison the atmosphere in an entire region and create a situation of anxiety and alarm for a country's neighbors, to say nothing of suffering and losses among its own people. That is why we are against any armed conflicts. We know that the Afghan leadership takes the same attitude.

All of that, as you know, has led the Afghan leadership, headed by President Najibullah, to profoundly rethink its political course, and this has crystallized in the patriotic and realistic policy of national reconciliation. It was an act of great courage and bravery; not merely an appeal to cease armed clashes but a proposal to set up a coalition government and share power with the opposition, including those who wage armed struggle against the Government and even those who, while being abroad, direct the rebels' operations and supply them with weapons and combat equipment obtained from foreign countries. And that proposal was made by a government vested with constitutional authority and wielding real power in the country.

The policy of national reconciliation is a reflection of new political thinking on the Afghan side. It is not a sign of weakness, but rather of the force of spirit, wisdom and dignity of free, honest and responsible political leaders concerned about their country's present and future.

Success for the policy of national reconciliation has already made it possible to begin withdrawing Soviet troops from portions of the Afghan territory. At present there are no Soviet troops in 13 Afghan provinces—because armed clashes have ceased there. It can well be said that the more rapidly peace gains ground in Afghanistan, the easier it will be for Soviet troops to leave.

The policy of national reconciliation has provided a political platform for all those who want peace in Afghanistan. What kind of peace? The kind that the Afghan people choose. The proud, freedom-loving and courageous Afghan people, who have gone through many centuries of struggle for freedom and independence, have been, and will continue to be, the masters of their own country, which, as President Najibullah put it, is built on multi-party politics and a multiple-structure economy.

The Afghans themselves will decide the final status of their country among other nations. Most often it is said that the future peaceful Afghanistan will be an independent, nonaligned and neutral state. Well, we would only be happy to have such a neighbor on our southern borders.

In connection with the question of beginning the withdrawal of Soviet troops, there is a need to make clear our position on yet another aspect—whether the withdrawal is linked with the completion of efforts to set up a new coalition government in Afghanistan, i.e., with bringing the policy of national reconciliation to fruition. We are convinced that it is not.

The withdrawal of Soviet troops, combined with other aspects of the settlement, including guarantees of noninterference, is one thing. Various states are involved in it. Speaking of this, we believe that Iran, a neighboring country, should not stand aside from political settlement.

National reconciliation and establishment of a coalition government is another thing. This is a purely internal Afghan issue. It can only be resolved by the Afghans themselves, though they belong to different and even opposing camps. When, however, it is hinted to us that the Soviet Union should take part in talks on that issue, and even with third countries, our answer is firm and clear: Don't expect us to do it; it is none of our business. Or yours, for that matter.

But could hostilities flare up even more after Soviet troops leave? It would hardly be appropriate to prophesy, but I think that such a course of events could be prevented if those now fighting against their brothers take a responsible attitude and try in deed to get involved in peace building. If, however, they are guided, not by the arguments of reason but by emotions multiplied by fanaticism, then they would be confronted with the greatly increased will of the Afghan people to see their country pacific and with the obligations of states no longer to interfere in its internal affairs. The Geneva obligations will close the channels for outside assistance to those who hope to impose their will on the whole nation by armed force.

And, if necessary, consideration could be given at that stage to using the possibilities available to the United Nations and its Security Council.

And now about our boys, our soldiers in Afghanistan. They have been and are doing their duty honestly, performing acts of self-denial and heroism.

Our people profoundly respect those who were called to serve in Afghanistan. The state provides for them, as a matter of priority, good educational opportunities and a chance to get interesting, worthy work.

The memory of those who have died a hero's death in Afghanistan is sacred to us. It is the duty of Party and Government authorities to make sure that their families and relatives are treated with care, attention and kindness.

And, finally, when the Afghan knot is untied, it will have the most profound impact on other regional conflicts, too.

If the arms build-up, which we are working so hard to stop, and with some success, marks a mad race by humanity to the abyss, then regional conflicts are bleeding wounds which can result in gangrenous growth on the body of mankind.

The earth is literally pocked with such wounds. Each of them means pain not only for the nations directly involved but for all—whether in Afghanistan, the Middle East, taking the Iran-Iraq war, in Southern Africa, Kampuchea or Central America.

Who gains from those conflicts? No one, except the arms merchants and various reactionary expansionist circles who are used to exploiting and turning a profit on people's misfortunes and tragedies.

Implementing political settlement in Afghanistan will be an important rupture in the chain of regional conflicts.

Just as the agreement to eliminate intermediate- and shorter-range missiles is to be followed by a series of further major steps towards disarmament, with negotiations on them already under way or planned, likewise, behind the political settlement in Afghanistan looms the question: which conflict will be settled next? And it is certain that more is to follow.

States and nations have sufficient reserves of responsibility, political will and determination to put an end to all regional conflicts within a few years. This is worth working for. The Soviet Union will spare no effort in this most important cause.

17

Meeting with George Shultz

Pravda, February 23, 1988

On February 22, Mikhail Gorbachev met with U.S. Secretary of State George Shultz in the Kremlin. This is another important link in the Soviet-American dialogue, which is assuming an ever more substantive and regular nature. We firmly steer a course for improvement of Soviet-American relations, Mikhail Gorbachev said. Such is the well-considered decision of the Soviet leadership and it expresses the opinion of the entire Soviet people.

We appraise the summit of December last as a major event on this road. Advancing along it, we live up to the hopes of the international community. Most states rightly hold that the improvement of relations between the USSR and the U.S.A. is in the interests of the whole world.

Personal contacts and personality aspects have played an important role in this process. They have formed a definite potential of mutual understanding. But this process also reflects objective requirements of the world today. This determines the continuity in the policy of the USSR and the U.S.A. with regard to each other, a beginning that was set in Geneva and that has been gaining momentum via Reykjavik and Washington towards the Moscow summit.

During the conversation Mikhail Gorbachev and George

Shultz exchanged opinions on the progress in the implementation of the arrangements reached in December and the state of
the preparation for the coming visit of President Reagan to the
USSR.

We proceed from the premise that the success of this visit
depends on the intensity with which the joint work will proceed on the preparation of the issues and documents that will
determine the content of the new Soviet-American summit
meeting, Mikhail Gorbachev stressed.

It is from these positions that the points comprising the
agenda for the coming months should be viewed.

On the matter of ratification of the INF Treaty. The interlocutors exchanged information and expressed confidence that
it will be ratified, although, naturally, explanations have already been necessary and will yet be necessary to convince
people that the Treaty is reliable and equitable.

The prospects of concluding a treaty on strategic offensive
arms are connected with the ratification. Mikhail Gorbachev
expressed the view that, while there is still time, this treaty
should be thoroughly prepared, although this will require
much work—not only in Geneva but, mostly, on the level of
ministers of foreign affairs. This involves major policy issues
and for this reason the principal moments of translating them
into definite accords should be constantly within the field of
attention of representatives of the leadership of both countries.

Mikhail Gorbachev advanced a number of new ideas on
specific aspects related to reducing various types of strategic
nuclear arms, with a view to imparting greater dynamism to
the ongoing talks and the search for mutually acceptable solutions. In this connection there was a thorough discussion of
the question of verification, which both sides regard as more
complex than in the case of the intermediate-range and
shorter-range missiles. The question of observing the ABM
Treaty in the form in which it was signed in 1972 was also
taken up. The interlocutors confirmed their adherence to the
wording adopted on this score in the joint Soviet-American
statement at summit level, signed in Washington on December 10.

Mikhail Gorbachev expressed amazement at the stand of the U.S.A. at the talks on banning chemical weapons, a stand that hampers the working out of an international convention; and he advanced proposals that could be jointly worked out by the time of the summit in Moscow.

The interlocutors confirmed their assessment of the importance of solving the problem of conventional armaments and armed forces in Europe and agreed to step up efforts to work out a mandate for the conference in Vienna. In this connection Mikhail Gorbachev sharply raised the question of the unacceptability of plans for "compensation," which, if implemented, might devalue the Treaty on the Elimination of Intermediate-Range and Shorter-Range Missiles and everything that has been achieved in the interests of international security of late.

Regional conflicts have been thoroughly discussed. We—the USSR and the U.S.A.—must set the world an example of interaction in this most important area of international life on the basis of balancing the interests of all the parties concerned without exception, Mikhail Gorbachev said. Distrust for our sincere striving finally to stamp out the regional seats of international danger stems from the fact that they in the West continue holding that the Soviet Union is chiefly to blame for their existence.

The situation now favors peaceful settlement of crises. Factors of an internal nature (on the part of those who are directly involved in these crises) and factors of a comprehensive nature (the stands that have become prevalent in the world community) are operating.

That is why the responsibility of the two great powers, the Soviet Union and the United States, is also increasing. For 45 years they were dominated in these and other questions by the concept of confrontation. Is it not time now for us, Mikhail Gorbachev said, to try to exercise our international responsibility on the basis of a search for coinciding interests?

He linked the settlement of regional conflicts with deep-rooted processes taking place in the contemporary world, with the problem of growing interdependence of its various parts. If this is ignored and nothing is done, it will be possible, of course, to hold out for 20 to 30 years, while increasing, however, the risk of missing the moment when the development of events will catch everybody unawares and mankind's common home will start falling apart. Mikhail Gorbachev proposed starting a joint study of these most pressing problems.

On the question of Afghanistan, the interlocutors again declared that the forthcoming round of the Geneva talks should be the last one. Mikhail Gorbachev said that the Soviet Union never had and does not have any secret plans or intentions whatsoever with respect to Afghanistan, like creating some sort of bridgehead there, and so forth. The Soviet Union will firmly and consistently act in accordance with the February 8 statement.

Mikhail Gorbachev invited George Shultz to adhere to existing accords facilitating an end to the conflict in forms ruling out bloodshed and ensuring Afghanistan the position of an independent, nonaligned and neutral state. And this requires that the Afghans themselves settle their affairs without any outside interference.

Concerning the question of the Iran-Iraq war and the Persian Gulf situation, Mikhail Gorbachev promised George Shultz that he would examine some ideas that Shultz advanced.

Mikhail Gorbachev expressed his opinion about the Middle East settlement plan recently proposed by the Americans: the plan is inconsistent and is out of keeping with the principle of considering the interests of all parties involved. It emphasizes intermediate measures and steps to which the USSR does not object in principle, but which, as has already become clear to many, can yield results only in the context of a decision to convene an international conference, in the context of a comprehensive settlement. It was agreed to resume the exchange of opinions following George Shultz's trip to the Middle East.

George Shultz mentioned to Mikhail Gorbachev the interest in the problem of human rights he observed during his current visit.

Eduard   Shevardnadze,   Anatoly   Dobrynin,   Sergei

Akhromeyev, Alexander Bessmertnykh, Colin Powell, Michael Armacost, Rozanne Ridgway, Paul Nitze, and Ambassadors Yuri Dubinin and John Matlock all took part in the conversation.

18

"We Are Building a Long-Term Policy"

Speech Before the U.S.-USSR Trade and Economic Council

Moscow, April 13, 1988

On April 13 General Secretary of the CPSU Central Committee Mikhail Gorbachev received in the Kremlin the delegates to the 11th annual meeting of members of the U.S.-USSR Trade and Economic Council (ASTEC). Present at the reception were: Viktor Nikonov, Nikolai Ryzhkov, Nikolai Slyunkov, Eduard Shevardnadze, Alexander Yakovlev, Yuri Maslyukov, Anatoly Dobrynin, First Deputy Chairman of the USSR Council of Ministers Vsevolod Murakhovsky, deputy chairmen of the USSR Council of Ministers Vladimir Gusev, Vladimir Kamentsev and Ivan Silayev, the heads of a number of ministries and agencies, directors of ASTEC from the Soviet side and other officials. Present from the American side were: U.S. Secretary of Commerce William Verity, Co-Chairman of ASTEC from the U.S. side Dwayne Andreas, President of ASTEC James Giffen, ASTEC directors R. Mahoney, J. Murphy and A. Ozmetel, U.S. Ambassador to the USSR Jack Matlock and representatives of the American business community.

Mikhail Gorbachev spoke at the reception.

Esteemed Secretary William Verity,

Esteemed Mr. Dwayne Andreas, leaders of the U.S.-USSR Trade and Economic Council,

Ladies and gentlemen,

Comrades,

I welcome you to Moscow, and it gives me great pleasure to do so. Your arrival is a good sign for Soviet-American relations and for the atmosphere in the world in general.

We live in interesting times. I think that you have come to Moscow not merely out of business considerations. Although today we are not inclined to underestimate this aspect of your interest, either.

Of late I have been keeping close track of the sentiments in the American business community. I know personally many of its representatives. We have met in Moscow and in Washington. All this allows me to think that your interest in us rests on a basis that is more profound than mere professional interest.

The question as to where the world will go is now being keenly discussed everywhere. All thinking people would like to see Soviet-American relations become, at long last, a constructive factor in the world process.

I'm sure you are interested in our assessment of the present-day international situation. A detailed analysis is probably out of place here, so I will limit myself to general evaluations.

We believe that the situation has changed for the better, that a window of hope has been opened up a little. The opportunities for finding solutions to the complicated issues which arose in the years of the Cold War have become more apparent.

The basic causes of the changes taking place lie in those mighty and ominous objective processes which have sharply intensified their pace as we draw closer to the end of the century—the processes in the scientific and technological sphere, in the arms race, in the world economy, in the Third World, in the fields of ecology, power engineering, information and so on.

This has generated universal anxiety, along with greater responsibility—not only for national affairs, but also for the destinies of the entire world. The fact that we are often slow to understand the course of world developments, which ever more persistently demand the adoption of measures capable of averting baneful consequences, has become more obvious. People have become more acutely aware of the rapidly growing interrelationship and interdependence of today's world.

Many states, public movements and parties have made a contribution to the understanding of the new realities and the ensuing political imperatives. Intellectuals, researchers, outstanding scientists and cultural figures have made an invaluable contribution to this. And I can say that business circles have also made a big contribution. Among those present here there are people known not only for what they have accomplished in the business world, but also for their public and, I would say, political activities. They have placed their energy, business capabilities and art of communication at the service of mutual understanding, and have helped find a practical solution to a number of international issues.

We are pleased to note that Americans are changing their attitude towards the USSR, and I especially sensed this during my visit to Washington. There is now more understanding, less suspicion. Thoughtful interest is taking the place of mere curiosity.

But we don't want to be too modest. We have had something to do with all this, too. I think that perestroika and our new thinking have played a role, which is now generally recognized, in altering the international situation.

You have come to Moscow at a time when perestroika is already three years old. I say "already," but then immediately think: "just three years." For perestroika is a long-term policy. The tasks to be resolved by perestroika are truly historic, truly revolutionary. Nevertheless, we have entered the second stage of perestroika and are approaching a very important point— the 19th National Party Conference.

The first stage, to speak in general terms, was a stage of contemplation, analysis, strict self-criticism and self-analysis of Soviet society. All this involved more than just an armchair analysis, not just scientific study; it involved the whole people.

This is the fundamental, basic distinguishing feature of the entire process of perestroika.

You can see how the Soviet people have squared their shoulders and revealed their potentialities. They have shown so much energy, initiative and readiness to take part in the common cause! And so many original thinkers and talents have appeared in such a brief period. Naturally, an acute confrontation of opinions—and I would even say a clash of views—has begun. Socialist values are being passionately defended, and at the same time there is profound dissatisfaction with the way we have been using those values, the way we have disposed of the gains of our great revolution. The process taking place is not simple; there is a struggle going on, but it is taking place on a socialist platform. I would like to warn those who are watching this struggle on the sidelines against being deluded on this account.

Yes, there is a lack of understanding, there is an unwillingness to change things radically, to give up things that are convenient and customary. But the principal trend of the debate is constructive and dynamic; it is based on our yearning to improve our society, to realize all its potentialities. Debates of this kind are under way in all sections of our society, in all spheres of life—from the economic sphere to the literary and art world. And this is, we believe, good and useful for perestroika. We feel the positive results of true socialist pluralism of opinions. It holds a promise of unprecedented growth in society's intellectual potential.

I know that there is immense interest in our perestroika in the West. We regard this as a desire to understand what the possibilities are for positive development of both Soviet-American and international relations in the immediate future and in the long run. And, as I have already said and written on several occasions, we want to be understood correctly. Quite a lot, by the way, has already been done to ensure this.

True, when I had my first meeting with ASTEC participants two and a half years ago, there was on the record only Geneva and the historic statement made there by the two sides that a nuclear war cannot be won and must never be fought. But today there are Reykjavik and Washington on the record as well, and one and a half months from now there will also be Moscow.

So the past two and a half years have seen three summits and the preparations for a fourth. The U.S. Secretary of State and the Soviet Minister of Foreign Affairs have met 23 times. The first official meeting between the U.S. Defense Secretary and our Defense Minister has taken place.

So the Soviet-American dialogue is becoming more dynamic. The topic of that dialogue has been the major problems of our times. And it is now marked by new attitudes and a gradual overcoming of stereotypes. Just a few years ago it seemed unrealistic to speak about even the possibility of agreements between the USSR and the U.S. on nuclear weapons. Now the INF Treaty has shown to the whole world that the path towards reducing nuclear arsenals, a path leading to their complete elimination, is a real one.

We do not tend to underestimate the difficulties standing in the way of an agreement on 50-percent cuts in strategic offensive arms. The most sensitive aspects of the security of both our countries are involved. At the same time, we are convinced that this goal is attainable in the immediate future if both sides are guided by the fundamental approach agreed upon at the meetings of the U.S. and Soviet leaders rather than by momentary considerations, including political ones.

One of the more urgent tasks is to secure a complete prohibition and destruction of chemical weapons. This, too, is a global task and should be tackled precisely as such rather than from the standpoint of the interests of individual political groups or private companies.

In another highly important issue of world politics—the issue of reducing conventional armaments and armed forces—the time has also come to abandon propaganda stereotypes and move on to practical action. You are aware of our proposals that we exchange relevant date on Europe and hold talks on eliminating asymmetries by lowering the general level of armed forces. This is yet another manifestation of our businesslike approach.

Tomorrow, April 14, an event is to take place which, in terms of its international implications, is perhaps just as important as the INF Treaty. We hope that the signing of the Geneva accords on Afghanistan will promote the process of settling regional conflicts. By participating—as mediators and official guarantors—in the settlement of the Afghanistan problem, the USSR and the U.S. are creating a precedent of constructive interaction, and such interaction is badly needed in order to improve international relations in general. And if it becomes possible for third countries to build their foreign policies, not on the basis of all-out rivalry but on that of reasonable and realistic interaction between Washington and Moscow, the entire nature of international contacts will change. The pluralism of interests in the world around us will then mean diverse possibilities for the peaceful coexistence of states and peoples rather than numerous antagonisms.

Such is the level of responsibility of the USSR and the U.S. before the rest of the world. And so it is all the more absurd to preserve the situation whereby two great countries, each of which possesses a quarter to one-third of the world's scientific and technological potential, continue to realize their potentialities in relations with each other mostly through a race in monstrous weapons.

I think that over the past 40 years we have rather successfully proved to one another that no one can get the upper hand in this baneful competition. So isn't it time to begin converting the economy and changing the political mentality? Isn't it time we began demilitarizing political thought?

New thinking should, at long last, enter the sphere of economic relations. From this point of view, our perestroika is an invitation to work out a new system of coordinates in the economic relations between our socially and ideologically different countries.

There are, and will be, serious differences between our countries. But the times require that these differences should not be a source of enmity and should begin to be used, as far as possible, as a stimulus to mutually advantageous competition.

They can become mutually supplementary components of the world economy in the 21st century.

What we have managed to do with the Soviet economy during the period of perestroika convinces us of this.

We have set the task of overhauling the economic structure on the basis of the latest achievements in science and technology. Along with radical economic reform, the new structural policy will assure an acceleration of our social and economic development.

Already new priorities have been identified for the current five-year-plan period. The output of finished products—machines, equipment and consumer goods—is to grow faster than the output of fuel, raw materials and semifinished products.

Growth rates in the manufacturing industries are to be 2.2 times higher than those in the fuel and raw materials industries.

Another distinctive feature of the acceleration process is the planned pace of development for science-intensive industries, especially mechanical engineering. The output of the latter sector is to grow by 41 to 43 percent, while its basic industries —machine-tool building, instrument making and electrical engineering—are to increase theirs by 55 to 70 percent.

Over the past two years, the mechanical engineering sector has begun manufacturing over 4,500 new types of machinery, equipment and instruments corresponding to world standards, while discontinuing the production of about 6,000 outdated types of machinery and equipment.

Here are just two examples: the Zhdanovtyazhmash production amalgamation has developed a unique combined-blast converter with a holding capacity of 370 tons, which can compete with similar foreign systems.

A 32-bit computer complex of enhanced productivity for computer-aided designing systems and systems of controlling flexible automated production at the most up-to-date level has been developed and its construction has begun.

The transfer of foreign-trade functions to machine builders has also played a positive role. The supply for export of machinery, equipment, instruments, and other products of machine building for freely convertible currency increased in one year by 30 percent. In the current year deliveries will increase by 150 percent.

The re-organization of machine building will make it possible to create a real basis for retooling all production facilities in the country.

The increment in the gross national product over two years added up to 8 percent.

There are positive changes in social development. Average monthly wages went up by 5.9 percent. Some 124.8 million square meters of housing are commissioned a year, an increase of 13 percent as against the previous five-year period. Changes have begun in health services and public education as well.

In agriculture, the gross harvest of grain has gone up by an average of 17 percent a year, the production of meat by 13 percent, and of milk and eggs by 9 percent. All this is a reality.

Foreign economic relations have been assigned a rational place in the solution of the economic tasks of perestroika. Good prospects would open up in this area along the Soviet-American direction, too, if it were still not hoped in the U.S.A. to take advantage of economic ties as a means of interference.

During my visit to the U.S.A., I became convinced that there were opportunities to get our trade and economic relations off the ground. But, speaking in the language of our perestroika, there is a need for breaking through the mechanism of retardation in this area, too. I have already had occasion to mention this.

Speaking of the possibilities for invigorating trade and economic relations, I mean not only their traditional aspect, but also new directions, including joint business ventures, cooperation in major projects for the benefit of all humanity (peaceful uses of outer space, including a joint flight to Mars, ecology, thermonuclear fusion, disease eradication, etc.)

We are radically restructuring our foreign economic activity, are bringing up-to-date the existing mechanism and at times simply changing its composite parts. The number of economic organizations that have been granted the right to do business outside the country is rapidly growing.

Thirty-three joint-enterprises involving foreign firms have already been set up.

They include the first representatives of the U.S. business community—Combustion Engineering Inc. and Management Partnership International. I would like to hail these pioneers in a new form of cooperation with the Soviet Union. Some 50 new projects are next in line. Statements of intent for them have been signed.

I would like to note that as regards the creation of joint ventures with U.S. firms, we bear in mind not only the use of well-tried U.S. technologies and equipment, but the equally great scope for the industrial mastering of Soviet scientific and technological gains as well.

We regard the formation of the American trade consortium and of its partner in the USSR, the Soviet foreign economic consortium, as a major event in our relations. A statement of intent on the creation of joint ventures was signed today.

For our part, we shall render all-round support to the Soviet participants in the consortium and we hope for a similar approach from the U.S. Administration.

We are prepared for active cooperation, not only with large firms but also with medium and small firms. Business with smaller firms has been showing efficiency and profitability at quite a high scientific, technological and commercial level. We are aware of this and are even trying to borrow some of this experience for our own industry.

I am told that at this session you have on the whole approved the basic principles and guidelines for the development of commercial and economic relations between the USSR and the U.S.A. This is a very good undertaking. The task now is to prepare them for signing.

Indeed, it is time to have some basis in the context of international law that would ensure the mutual interests of firms and organizations with due account for the new conditions.

In other words, there is a need to get rid of the legacy of the Cold War in this area, too.

I would like to touch upon another matter.

The USSR and the U.S.A., with their historical responsibility to the world community, cannot avoid their responsibility for radically improving economic relations in the whole world.

I don't know whether or not you will agree with me, but it looks as if the situation in the world economy is getting more complicated; symptoms of growing troubles and instability increase whether the problems of indebtedness or the situation in the world's main stock exchanges is concerned.

Most important, I believe that uncertainty as to what will happen tomorrow has increased over this short period of time. It is not certain whether an avalanche of protectionist measures will not fall on world trade and whether an upheaval in one large country will not set off a chain reaction with unprecedented consequences.

I know that all these matters are discussed in the West at meetings of "sevens" and "nines," at conferences of economics ministers and bankers, etc. But don't you think that the circle of people and countries that discuss problems of the world economy and its future is narrowed to such an extent that quite objective approaches and equitable solutions cannot be found in it?

Indeed, the world market, too, has narrowed to the market of industrial capitalist countries of both Americas, Western Europe, Japan and those directly involved with them. Isn't it time to ponder in earnest on the forming of a real modern world market?

We are prepared to take a fresh look at all these realities, prepared for cooperation. For this is a global problem which can only be resolved by joint efforts.

We are formulating our policy, also our foreign economic policy, to last for a long time. We are making it more predictable for the outside world. And we do this not in order to please someone. We do this for the reason that we need this ourselves and that this is profitable for us. We are striving to take into consideration the international experience of business ties.

Perestroika in the Soviet Union and a foreign policy based on new thinking are not just a long-term program for the development of our society oriented towards the 21st century.

They are an objective reality which starts, as it were, to gain an inertial dynamics of its own, if you please.

And one last thing: with all the importance of business considerations, all of us are citizens of our own countries and representatives of humankind. And we all should be concerned with the quest for the ways to ensure humankind's survival and for a more tranquil and normal life.

Therefore, we are constantly faced with the question: what can each of us do to shape stable, mutually advantageous, demilitarized relations between the USSR and the U.S.A., not for the sake of others but for the sake of ourselves, for the sake of our children and grandchildren?

And, answering this question, let us get down to business. In the beginning was the Word. But if the word were not followed by deeds, there would be neither human history nor civilization.

Ladies and gentlemen, I wish you success in your personal pursuits and business undertakings.

IV

THE MOSCOW SUMMIT

May 18–June 2, 1988

19

Replies to Questions from the *Washington Post* and *Newsweek*

Pravda, May 23, 1988

On May 18 Mikhail Gorbachev met with a group of journalists from the Washington Post Co., talked to them and answered their questions. Participating in the meeting were Katharine Graham, Chairman of the Board of the Washington Post Co., Richard M. Smith, Editor-in-Chief of Newsweek, *Jimmie Hoagland and Meg Greenfield, editors from the* Washington Post, *and Robert G. Kaiser, Assistant Managing Editor for National News of the* Washington Post.

Question: Have the three meetings with President Reagan changed your ideas as to how peaceful competition between capitalist and socialist countries should be regulated in the future? How do you think the forthcoming summit will contribute to stabilizing that competition?

Answer: I am convinced that positive trends are unfolding in the world. There is a turn from confrontation to coexistence. The winds of the cold war are being replaced by the winds of hope. And I see that a significant role in that process is played by the signs of improvement in the relations between the United States and the Soviet Union. All over the world there is an acute need for change or, if you will, a need for restructuring international relations. In that situation it is essential to continue positive contacts between East and West.

As for the dialogue between the United States and the Soviet Union, it is simply vital because of the great role they play in today's world.

What is important is the very fact of that dialogue, not to mention its content, specifically, such exceptionally important joint statements as those regarding the inadmissibility of wars, nuclear or any other, the necessity of resolving problems by political means and of recognizing the realities of today's world.

It is very important that all this is sounded loud and clear for the whole world to hear, and we have seen how the world has responded to it. All this leads to the following conclusion: yes, we are different and will remain so. We will remain loyal to our ideas and our ways of life. But we have a common responsibility, which is especially true of our two great powers, and our every action must measure up to that responsibility.

As for the potential results of the coming fourth meeting with the President and, in particular, the prospects for a detailed agreement on a 50-percent cut in strategic offensive weapons, the part few months and weeks have seen so much speculation that I would like to make the following point: be patient, the meeting is just a few days away, let the President and me work together. Whatever we arrive at will certainly not be concealed from the public.

There are two more points to be made here, though. The very continuation of the Soviet-American dialogue at the summit level is important and substantive. In any case, I hope that our attention will be focussed, as at the previous meetings, on the main international problems and that we will be able to rise to a new level of dialogue and mutual understanding.

And if an agreement on a 50-percent reduction in strategic offensive weapons comes to be drafted under the present U.S. Administration, I see no reason why President Reagan and I should not sign it. I would certainly welcome that.

Question: Many people in the West think that nuclear weapons have been instrumental in maintaining stability in the world over the past few decades. Would it not be more rational for the USSR and the U.S. in those conditions to agree on preserving minimal nuclear deterrents?

Answer: I cannot agree with those who think that there is no point in striving for a nuclear-free world.

I have argued more than once with representatives of the West over their case that without nuclear weapons we would never have managed to escape another world war for 40 years. This is just a conjecture. But what about a sober evaluation of the real role played by the so-called balance of fear? It has given us nothing but an unheard-of militarization of foreign policies, economies and even intellectual life. It has caused damage in the sphere of international morality and ethics and has ruined the atmosphere of mutual trust, friendliness and sincere interest in each other that was generated in Soviet-American relations by the joint fighting against fascism and the common victory over it.

I am convinced that strategic military parity can be maintained at a low level and without nuclear weapons. We have clearly formulated our choice: the arms race must be stopped and then reversed.

As for the so-called minimal nuclear deterrents, I will not argue now with the proponents of this idea. So far, you and we have more than 10,000 warheads each in our strategic arsenals. Let us cut them, for a start, by 50 percent, then, maybe, by another 50 percent and then do so once again. In the meantime, let us come to terms on the elimination of chemical weapons and start reducing conventional armaments in Europe. That process should be open not only for the U.S. and the USSR but for all other nuclear and non-nuclear states as well. That will be an important incentive for the world to move towards a demilitarization of politics, thinking and international relations in general.

And another point: if we start orienting ourselves to a "minimal nuclear deterrence" now, I assure you that nuclear weapons will start spreading around the world, rendering worthless and undermining even what we can achieve at Soviet-American talks and at talks among the existing nuclear states.

A peaceful future for mankind can be guaranteed not by "nuclear deterrence," but by a balance of reason and goodwill and by a system of universal security.

Question: The NATO leaders have announced that even with a balance in the conventional forces in Europe, nuclear weapons will still need to be preserved on the continent as a means of retaliation. If, in keeping with that position, nuclear disarmament is unacceptable for the West, should we not try to reach a joint agreement on the terms of modernization of the tactical nuclear weapons deployed in Europe?

Answer: The talk about nuclear weapons on the continent as a means of retaliation is the same old concept of "limited" nuclear warfare in Europe. It absolutely contradicts what I conferred with the U.S. President about back in Geneva, namely, that nuclear war cannot be won and simply must not be allowed to happen. Isn't the materialization of the formula for modernizing tactical nuclear weapons in Europe fraught with the danger of a nuclear catastrophe in the center of the continent?

I know of the NATO statements concerning nuclear weapons. But I also know that people are thinking not only at NATO headquarters, but also in public, scientific and government circles. There are already a number of ideas which have authoritative supporters in both the East and the West of Europe—on ways of reducing conventional armaments, including dual-purpose systems, from the Atlantic to the Urals. We support the ideas concerning the establishment of nuclear-free zones in Northern Europe and in the Balkans. We are also in favor of setting up a 300-kilometer corridor free of all nuclear and any other heavy weapons in Central Europe. I am naming just some of the ideas but certainly not all of them.

I am positive that it is here, in such interim projects, that we should search for a way of removing the threat of nuclear war, rather than by clinging to nuclear weapons, which do not lead to genuine security in any version. The ideas that you mention in your question are self-delusion.

As for deterrence, isn't the very awareness that a strike at nuclear power stations and chemical plants even with conventional weapons would be lethal for densely populated Europe enough of a deterrent?

Question: NATO has suggested cutting tens of thousands of non-nuclear weapons that could be used for surprise or large-scale offensive operations. Does this approach fall within the boundaries of your stated willingness to negotiate on the basis of asymmetrical reductions?

Answer: On our side, there are no obstacles to that. As for the existing asymmetries in the arsenals of NATO and the Warsaw Treaty Organization, I have already expressed my views on that score many times: asymmetries exist on both sides. We stand for eliminating the asymmetries on the basis of reciprocity. For example, the Warsaw Treaty armies have more tanks. And the NATO armies have more attack planes. The Soviet Union and our allies are ready to eliminate these and other asymmetries without delay but, let me repeat, on the basis of reciprocity. And then it would be possible to balance off armaments on the lowest possible level sufficient for defense alone.

We are not satisfied with the pace of the Vienna consultations of the 23 countries elaborating the objective and format of the future conference. If the work in Vienna proceeds in the same on-again-off-again manner, Europe will have to wait for a long time for those asymmetries to be eliminated.

Quite possibly—I would even say certainly—there are people whom such a situation suits just fine. But I believe that they will be unable to hold their positions for long. The forces realizing that the issue of the dangerous level of armed forces on the European continent should be resolved at all costs are becoming stronger.

Question: In the months remaining of the Reagan presidency, what is required to broaden your personal relationship with the President into an institutional relationship and carry both into the future?

Answer: The experience of present-day international relations shows the paramount importance of meetings between

the leaders of states, especially such as the United States and
the Soviet Union. Since both countries are well aware of the
need for intensifying the dialogue and improving relations, it is
absolutely obvious that it is not only the leaders' personal
views that matter. This is the imperative of our time. This is
the aspiration of our people. Such is the constant in the Soviet-
American dialogue. It remains intact. And if we add to that
the experience we have accumulated, all these factors taken
together give rise to hopes for continuity and even for intensified contacts and improved mutual understanding. However,
let me repeat that everything rests not on the sentiments or
personal motives of individual political figures but on the interests of our countries and peoples. No one can allow their
relations to slide to a point beyond which the unpredictable
may happen. Such is the basis for continuing and developing
the Soviet-American dialogue. It will remain the same in the
future as well.

In a word, we are interested in developing the dialogue, we
will strive to make it more productive, we will try to facilitate
the "adaptation" of the next U.S. Administration to contacts
with us, and we will do everything within our power to keep
the process begun in Geneva in 1985 from stopping. And, naturally enough, we hope for a similar attitude on the American
side.

Question: Do you feel President Reagan is a different kind
of American leader? Which of his qualities and/or ideas would
you most hope to see his successor hold as well? Has he been
able to persuade you that the military-industrial complex does
not determine U.S. policy?

Answer: As is known, I made President Reagan's acquaintance in Geneva less than three years ago. We have maintained
contacts in various forms ever since. There have been three
vis-à-vis meetings. The fourth is approaching.

I'm not particularly fond of giving personal character references. But since you ask, I would like to say that realism is an
important quality in President Reagan as a politician. By this I
mean the ability to adapt one's views to the changing situation,
while remaining faithful to one's convictions.

Who would have thought in the early 1980s, both in the Soviet Union and the U.S.A., that it would be President Reagan who would sign with us the first nuclear arms reduction agreement in history? However, the sober-minded realization that the world has changed and that the interests of our countries are changing enabled the President, while holding to his well-known convictions, to take a fresh look at the existing realities. And indeed, don't the leaders of such powers as the USSR and the U.S.A., who bear a unique responsibility for the destiny of the modern-day world, really need such qualities as the ability to give up dogmas and discard outdated ideas for the sake of making progress? For the goal in question is most noble—ridding our peoples and all humanity of the nuclear nightmare, building new relations and improving the international situation.

As for the military-industrial complex, let me remind you that it wasn't us but one of the predecessors of the incumbent President, Dwight Eisenhower, also a Republican, who came up with that notion.

It seems unlikely that he made a mistake. But is that complex the only force shaping American policy? Hardly so, although, let me repeat, its influence is substantial. And it becomes especially obvious whenever there are signs of positive change in the disarmament sphere, whenever there are prospects for reaching agreements in that field and whenever Congress is about to consider military budgets and other allocations for armaments.

But, to quote the ancient Greek philosophers, all is flux, nothing stays still. If the process of disarmament proceeds actively, if corporations receive fewer military contracts and if the U.S. stops brandishing a "big stick" every time something happens tens of thousands of kilometers away from the U.S.— something pictured as a threat to America's national interests —then we will be able to discuss that matter again.

Question: The Americans are familiar with the rapid erosion that occurred in the situation in Vietnam once they decided to withdraw from that war. What changes, in your view, will take place in Afghanistan in the next year while the Soviet

Union is pulling out its troops? What will the Soviet Union's contribution to bringing about those changes be?

Answer: Any parallel between Vietnam and Afghanistan is artificial. Not to mention how different the nature of the conflicts is. I would only like to remind you of the fact that prior to the Americans' pulling out of Vietnam, that country was divided for 20 years into two nearly equal parts by a border along the 17th parallel. In both sections, there existed governments personifying regimes opposite in nature and incompatible in aim.

There is nothing of the kind in Afghanistan. On the contrary, the Government there has set itself the goal of achieving the Afghan people's national reconciliation and, on this basis, its own reorganization into a coalition government with the participation of all parties to the conflict.

It goes without saying that the future depends in many respects on how honestly and consistently all the signatories to the Geneva agreements will meet the commitments assumed, without trying to get around them in some way or another or deceive their partners.

I can reaffirm once again that the Soviet Union intends to meet its obligations precisely and undeviatingly.

It is the Afghans themselves who are to decide how the settlement will proceed, what changes are to take place in Afghanistan in the future. We adhere firmly to this principle, which means noninterference in internal affairs. The Soviet Union will render assistance to Afghanistan in dealing with the consequences of the war, in strengthening the Afghan economy. In a word, it will act in keeping with the long-standing traditions of good-neighborliness and friendship with this southern neighbor of ours, undoubtedly, respecting its status as an independent, neutral and nonaligned state.

Question: You said that when the Afghan knot is untied, it will have the most profound impact on other regional conflicts, too. Is the Soviet Union prepared to cooperate with the United States and other countries in resolving other conflicts, for example, in Central America, the Persian Gulf and Angola?

Answer: Yes, it is. I have already said that, given constructive cooperation between the Soviet Union and the United States and major emphasis on the prestige and capabilities of the United Nations, its Security Council and other bodies, political settlement of regional conflicts and prevention of new ones will gradually become an international practice, a norm. I would like to confirm this conviction of mine.

The world has ample proof that dragged-out conflicts are the result of politics being exposed to pressure from outdated stereotypes. They are orthodox approaches to national security, with power politics being preferred to sober considerations and political boldness: the old habit of seeking to satisfy one's rights and interests at the expense of others; and a shortage of fairness and humaneness in international relations.

The President and I have discussed this more than once and we will have a chance to take up these matters at the forthcoming meetings, too. Of course, such a talk can be productive only if there is respect for the right of every people to choose their own road.

Question: Recalling her talks with you, Mrs. Thatcher drew a comparison between the criticism and resistance a Western leader faces in bringing change and what you have encountered in pushing perestroika and glasnost. She wished you success. Is the comparison accurate? Or is it fundamentally different? To be more specific, by glasnost you seem to mean something quite different from what we think of as freedom of speech. Could you elaborate on the differences?

Answer: I appreciate the kind words Mrs. Thatcher addresses to us now and then. However, I cannot help saying that I disagree with her views on ways to preserve peace, her dedication to nuclear deterrence and her assessments of socialism.

About the similarities and dissimilarities of economic policy in this country and in the West. Of course, it is possible to find a likeness, formal at least, in anything and such a likeness does exist if you do not go into the essence of one reform or another. However, it is the difference of principle that matters. What is taking place in the USSR is an all-embracing process of revolutionary renovation of socialist society on the basis of the historic choice which we do not doubt and which proved, in principle, the only correct one for our people 70 years ago. Otherwise the country with which you are discussing things that affect the future of the world a a whole would not exist. Of course, combatting stagnation in the course of perestroika and dismantling the mechanism of retardation require that inflexibility and conservatism be overcome. Sometimes we are confronted with hectic impatience. There is also conscious resistance on the part of those whose narrow selfish interests are incompatible with perestroika, socially, economically or morally.

However, this is precisely what we mean by perestroika, in the course of which we want to renovate our society, upgrade it qualitywise. Perestroika is proceeding in width and depth, encompassing all public groups and all our territory. Perestroika is growing and gaining momentum.

As for glasnost, it and freedom of speech are, of course, interconnected. However, these are not identical things. I would put in this way: while freedom of speech is indispensable for glasnost, we see glasnost as a broader phenomenon. For us it is not just the right of every citizen to say openly what he or she thinks about all social and political questions, but also the duty of the ruling Party and all bodies of authority and administration to ensure openness in decision making, be accountable for their actions, act on criticism, and consider advice and recommendations from the shop floor, public organizations and individuals.

Glasnost, as we see it, accentuates an environment allowing citizens to participate effectively in discussing all of the country's affairs, in elaborating and making decisions that affect the interests of society and in monitoring the implementation of these decisions.

Question: Could you discuss what ideas from abroad have had influence in the formation of your political and economic thinking and your mode of action? Conversely, what is the effect of glasnost and perestroika in other socialist countries?

Answer: In my book on perestroika, published by Harper

and Row, I wrote that our new political thinking is a result of our comprehension of the realities of the nuclear age, of deep and self-critical reflections on the past and present of our own country and of the surrounding world.

The new thinking took into account and absorbed the conclusions and demands of the Non-Aligned Movement, of the public and of the scientific community, of the movements of physicians, scientists and ecologists, and of various antiwar organizations. We also take into consideration the experience of other socialist countries just as they take ours into account. The process of mutual enrichment with experience, in which no one tries to impose any models on others, is under way.

Yes, all of us really do understand our dependence on one another better and feel that we live in an interrelated world and that all of us are inseparable parts of the single present-day civilization.

Question: Judging by the President's statements, you disagree with him on human rights. At the same time, your dramatic decision to free Andrei Sakharov and to ease the conditions of emigration for some Soviet Jews who desire to live abroad have attracted attention around the world. What further steps do you plan in this direction?

Answer: Our perestroika, the main factor of which is creative effort, also includes doing away with all distortions of the past years, with everything that hampers manifestation of the humanitarian essence of socialism.

We know our problems and speak honestly and openly about them. The process of democratization does not bypass the sphere of human rights and liberties. We are enhancing the political and public status of the personality. Many issues have already been resolved within the framework of the democratic process, while others will be resolved as Soviet society changes qualitatively in the course of perestroika. But that is our job. We are resolving these issues not because we want to play up to somebody or to please somebody, but because this meets the interests of our society, because perestroika cannot be carried out without it and, last but not least, because it is wanted by the Soviet people, who have long outgrown the restrictions which they put up with in the past and which were to a certain extent an inevitable part of the unusual revolutionary development which we have gone through.

Once I said, and it seems to me, to an American: please show me a country that has no problems. Each country has problems of its own, human rights included. Of course, we are well informed about the situation with political, social, economic and other rights in the United States. We know well the achievements and problems, but also the flaws of American society. But we do not allow interference in your home affairs, though we deem it right to express our views on the processes taking place in American society, on your Administration's policy. But we do not want to make all this a reason for confrontation. We consider such an approach to be correct, fair; we see it as meeting the interests of Soviet-American relations and their future. I want to emphasize once again that we do not try to impose anything on the United States, but at the same time we rebuff attempts by any side to meddle in our affairs, no matter who tries to do so in your country.

Such is, in principle, our approach. At the same time, there are problems in the human rights sphere which require joint consideration. The mechanism of cooperation in that area has begun to take shape of late. Scientists, specialists and public representatives have been widely drawn into it. Specific issues are analyzed at their meetings in a calm atmosphere and businesslike manner.

We also welcome the accord on setting up a permanent body on human rights with the participation of Deputies to the USSR Supreme Soviet and U.S. Congressmen. It is the duty of legislators in both countries to show concern for observance of the citizens' rights.

We are prepared to go on acting in this spirit.

Taking advantage of this opportunity, I would like to say the following. As it seems to me, pragmatism, preparedness to seek new decisions if what has been tested does not work, is the Americans' forte. But they also have a trait—please, do not resent my frankness—which sometimes makes it difficult to deal with them. I mean their confidence that everything

American is the best, while what others have is at least worse if not altogether bad and unfit for use. I am not talking about anticommunism, which has been implanted in the U.S.A. for decades, despite the fact that Albert Einstein called it the greatest lie of the 20th century many years ago.

For the sake of our mutual understanding, please, do not try to teach us to live according to American rules—it is altogether useless. And I repeat that, for our part, we do not intend to suggest our values to the Americans.

Let each side live in its own way, respecting each other's choice and voluntarily exchanging the fruits of our labor in all the spheres of human activity.

I am sure that each nation, each people, does not lose but, conversely, wins if it looks at itself critically and does not ignore others' experience; if it is open to understanding of and respect for a different culture, a different way of thinking, different customs; last, a different political system, of course, if it is not terrorist, fascist or dictatorial.

Question: Does your policy of perestroika require fundamental changes in the way relations among Soviet nationalities are structured? Does this policy offer new ways of promoting their cultural diversity and internationalism?

Answer: The question of changing the socialist principles of relations among the peoples, big and small, in our country is not on the agenda in the USSR. But we will set right the violations of these principles. It is such violations that caused the recent developments in some of our Republics. The West has displayed, I would say, a morbid interest in them, not infrequently with anti-Soviet innuendo and bad intentions. It made lavish use of speculations aimed at weakening our multinational Union.

Problems certainly do exist, and they are linked with the legacy we inherited from the time of the personality cult and the period of stagnation—in the economy, social policy, cultural life and human relations. Internationalism, which is deeply rooted in the hearts and minds of Soviet people of all nationalities, will help us resolve the problems in this sphere, too. And we will resolve them in the spirit of perestroika and in close linkage with the accomplishment of all the main tasks it involves, in the process of radical renewal of society.

* * *

A conversation followed between Mikhail Gorbachev and the *Washington Post* and *Newsweek* publishers.

Mikhail GORBACHEV: I'm glad to greet you here in Moscow on the eve of the summit. What is the mood in Washington?

Katharine GRAHAM: Well, everybody is getting ready for the summit and thousands of people are going to come here. And everybody is looking forward with great expectation and great hopes to this occasion.

Mikhail GORBACHEV: Moscow, too, is looking forward to the summit. And that is good. It's good that the dialogue is continuing. The Soviet-American dialogue can have ups and downs, it may have its evolution, but there's no doubt that since it's proceeding, it promises specific results in the development of our relations. I stated this in the written answers to your questions, handed over to you. We value highly the very fact of constant Soviet-American dialogue. Contacts with the U.S. in different fields—political, scientific and technical, economic and cultural—are very diverse. And yet, they cannot replace the summit.

To this I can add that Moscow, too, is living in an atmosphere of preparations for a visit of a U.S. President after an interval of 14 years.

Katharine GRAHAM: I would like to note that you, together with President Reagan, and with George Shultz and Eduard Shevardnadze, have established an entirely new kind of productive discussion that certainly has been missing for many years.

Mikhail GORBACHEV: I think it really is an important result of our joint work over the past few years. Of course, I highly rate specific agreements reached during these discussions, especially the INF Treaty. And yet, I believe that the most important political achievement is the regular and systematic dialogue.

Well, it sounds like I'm beginning to ask you questions . . .
in order to seize the initiative. But then I've already answered
your written questions and so now it is time to just have a
conversation.

Katharine GRAHAM: I want to begin by thanking you for
answering the written questions. They mean a great deal to us,
and we are grateful for your frankness in them. We would like
to cover as many of the areas of mutual interests as is possible
in this meeting.

In the process of preparing for this meeting, everywhere we
have gone we have been told how many problems you face,
how difficult they will be to resolve. Many people are awed by
the audacity of your undertaking. I wonder if you yourself
sometimes have moments when the task seems overwhelming
or impossible, when you hesitate. I want to ask why will you
reform programs succeed when those of your predecessors, say
like Nikita Khrushchev, have not succeeded?

Mikhail GORBACHEV: Well, you've asked perhaps the
principal question, whose answer our people want to know,
and, I think, Americans do too, because, one way or another,
it is the fate of our two peoples and our two countries, whether
we like it or not, to cooperate and to learn to live together.
And that, naturally, means knowing each other better, and,
particularly, knowing each other's plans. Those plans are truly
grandiose. It is for this reason that we call our perestroika
revolutionary.

Paradoxical as it may seem, now I am more confident in the
political line we've chosen for perestroika, for the renewal for
our society, than at the beginning of this road, although we
now have more difficulties. How can I explain this? Probably
we know better now what we want and how to do it, and this
gives us greater confidence.

At the Central Committee we'll discuss the document for
the coming 19th Party conference. I can say that the conference will give a second wind to all our plans and our work to
implement the concept of perestroika.

But I think I would sound overconfident to you if I just
confined myself to what I've just said. Making decisions at this

turning point in the development of our society is something that carries great responsibility—above all, responsibility to our people. We're not insured against mistakes, but we want to minimize the number we make and we don't want to make major mistakes, because the most expensive mistake are political mistakes. We want to fend them off. Therefore we are preparing all our main and most principal decisions with the active involvement of the whole society, the intellectual forces of our society, within the framework of the democratic process. This is the best way of avoiding political mistakes. This is why we are so persistent in developing the processes of democratization and openness. We shall not backtrack. It is perhaps in this area that perestroika has made the greatest strides.

I've now approached the answer to the second part of your question. Indeed, earlier, too, our society and Party understood the need for reforms, for renewal. Attempts, I would say major attempts, were made at that time to introduce such reforms, including by, as you said, Nikita Khrushchev and the leadership of his time. I would say that in the period of Leonid Brezhnev the leadership of that time, too, conceived and was trying to implement major plans. But they were not fulfilled, and mostly because they did not rely on the decisive force—the involvement of the people in modernizing and restructuring our society. We've learned from the past, which is why we are so persistent in developing the process of democratization.

For us the words that have become popular, "more democracy, more socialism," are not just a slogan or a pretty formulation. This is a well-thought-out guideline: through the development of the democratic process, through the involvement of the people in economic, political, social and cultural reforms, we can reveal the potential of socialism and all that is part of this system.

We now have had three years of hard work under perestroika, of work at the new stage, so we can say confidently that perestroika has become a cause of the entire people, a national cause.

Probably many generations of our people, and certainly my generation, cannot recall a time of such great activity and such interest in the affairs of society as we're witnessing now. People are eagerly discussing the activities of Party, state and economic bodies, and all the developments. There is tremendous interest in everything happening in the country. And that means an end to stagnation, an end to apathy. Our life is turbulent. It's no easy job to steer the ship in this turbulent sea, but we have a compass and the crew, and our ship itself is strong.

Jimmie HOAGLAND: I'd like to ask you a couple of more specific questions on perestroika. As you say, it's a turbulent time and there are more difficulties in some areas now than there were before. Price reform is an awfully important area in perestroika, I think. The system of subsidies operating in your country has been part of the old social contract between the citizens and the Government, meaning that every Soviet customer gets a three-ruble subsidy on a kilogram of meat, a 30-kopeck subsidy on each liter of milk that's sold. Are you persuaded that this has to be changed, these subsidies that cost the Government so much? And, if so, how urgently, and how will you change it?

Mikhail GORBACHEV: We have been discussing this problem and not only in the Government but in society, too. People in Moscow can confirm that there is a vigorous debate on these questions in our press. The people involved in that debate include industrial workers, rank-and-file people, collective farmers, intellectuals, veterans, and experts—because the problem concerns the whole society.

In the whole complex of measures that are covered by the term "radical economic reform," prices and price formation occupy a significant place. They are of great importance. When I speak about prices, I mean wholesale prices, purchasing prices and retail prices. What we think we should do is to formulate the next five-year plan on the basis of new prices.

Now, how should we approach that? The standpoint on this score has already taken shape in both Government and scientific quarters. We've already presented it to the people in the preliminary discussion on this question. While reforming the

prices and changing price formation we will, above all, see to it
that no decline occurs in the actual standard of living.

You may ask, then what is the point? Well, the point is that
the prices should be consistent with actual economic processes, with real costs and work input. That will create a
healthier financial system, and on that basis it will be possible
to organize better cost accounting, and to use economic incentives in every work collective, which will push the economy in
the right direction—towards greater scientific and technological progress and higher labor productivity; to search for ways
of better meeting society's needs for the means of production
and higher-quality goods and services.

Today we're very carefully thinking over a system of compensation for the losses that people may incur in the process of
changing retail prices. When we're ready for this and when the
measures are carefully conceived and balanced, we will submit
them for nationwide discussion. We've promised this to the
people and we'll act in this way. We are not going to do anything without their approval.

Jimmie HOAGLAND: We have just seen in the neighboring
socialist country of Poland that a price reform can create great
civil unrest and serious problems. Do you feel that you can
avoid similar stormy events?

Mikhail GORBACHEV: We have a different situation here.
Our situation is that most of the prices are under very strict
government control. So it is very important to find out how we
can accomplish a release of economic mechanisms while preserving the necessary centralized control. Probably this cannot
be resolved at one go. The shaping of a new price mechanism
will be a process that will pass within the context of our ongoing economic reform.

We are being prodded from the inside and from the outside
towards steps which would be tantamount to a leap. But we
are going to move in a calculated and measured way in contin-
uous consultation with the people through a democratic mechanism.

In any case I think that after hearing this answer the *Wash-*

ington Post will stop advising us to take reckless steps to accelerate the process of perestroika. *(Laughter.)*

Meg GREENFIELD: Mr. Gorbachev, could I ask you about a different kind of perestroika? You've written about perestroika in international relations, and particularly in relations among socialist countries.

You have written and spoken very eloquently about the absolute right of nations to choose their own path: capitalism or socialism or whatever variant of it they wish. And we are curious as to how this will apply to the countries of Eastern Europe, the socialist states. For example, in Poland there are elements in the society arguing for a pluralistic system in which the Communist Party might not play the leading role. Would such an outcome be acceptable, be tolerable, to you?

Mikhail GORBACHEV: I think you should better put that question to the Polish leadership. That would also be more consistent with what you said in the beginning of your question. But still, I wish to say a few words.

We recognize the right of each people, whatever part of the world it lives in, to have its social option, to choose its own way of developing its society. I think the Polish people can better see now what should be done for Poland to gain strength and consolidate so that its development give greater benefits to the people.

What we do in our country is our affair. Perestroika was born out of our conditions, and we need it. We will continue that process, expanding it and also making it deeper. But we will not impose our methods for developing and improving society on any other country. That is everyone's own affair. I think the Polish people will also sort the things out and decide themselves what they should do for Poland's development. I am sure that the bulk of the people, the overwhelming majority of Polish society, favors continuing the path on which they started after the war [World War II].

Meg GREENFIELD: If I could just cite one more statement. In Belgrade, you spoke of there being no circumstances under which an intervention by force in another country would be acceptable. Does this mean—I think people in the

West believe it means—a situation as in 1956 in Hungary or in 1968 in Czechoslovakia could no longer occur?

Mikhail GORBACHEV: Yes, I did speak on that subject in Yugoslavia. I can only reiterate what I said then, and generally speaking, there is nothing I can add to that. I would only point out the following, perhaps: interference from any side is impermissible. When you speak about interference, I can see what you mean. But recalling those situations, I also have in mind something else, namely: before the events you mentioned, there was interference of a different kind.

Look how much time has passed since the war, but even now in some Western countries parliaments or similar bodies find it possible to adopt resolutions which can be regarded only as interference in the affairs of other countries.

The world has changed greatly in the postwar era, and today even very small nations will not tolerate interference or orders from anybody. Our relations with the socialist countries are relations of equality based on independence. They are relations of cooperation and mutual assistance. We share many things, including resources, and depend on one another in the sense that our cooperation allows us, as it did in the past, to expand our economies and to carry out major social changes.

I believe such cooperation is a good basis, and it will play a positive role at the new stage when profound changes in the socialist countries are under way.

Richard SMITH: Mr. Gorbachev, looking ahead to the Party conference, we would like your personal reaction to a number of specific proposals. For example, do you support the idea of fixed terms of office for Party leaders, and, if so, would that include the position of General Secretary itself?

Mikhail GORBACHEV: Well, you'll hear the answers in the coming days to all such questions. But I would say one word—yes.

Richard SMITH: Still we hope that you will say more . . .

Mikhail GORBACHEV: I would have then anticipated what you will read in . . . What day is it now? Is it the eighteenth of May? In five or six days. The *Washington Post* always wants to know more and earlier than others. *(Animation.)*

Someone corrects: This is *Newsweek. (Laughter.)*

Mikhail GORBACHEV: It's all the same. It is your empire. *(Laughter.)*

Meg GREENFIELD: Our empire is competitive within itself also. *(Animation.)*

Katharine GRAHAM: Mr. Gorbachev, from the moment of our arrival here we see immense interest in the forthcoming Party conference. Could you not, perhaps even in more general terms, discuss your hopes for this meeting, which is obviously such an important event?

Mikhail GORBACHEV: My expectations coincide with the expectations of our whole society. We want to take stock of what has happened over these three years, to sort out the history of perestroika. We want to make a critical analysis of this entire period and to draw lessons from it. Perhaps, some corrections will be needed. But the central question is: how to move forward with perestroika and make it irreversible? Therefore, the main questions at the conference will relate to deepening the economic reform and democratizing the Party and society. As for the rest of it, you will soon find out.

(Richard SMITH asked whether the appearance of the articles in *Sovetskaya Rossiva* and *Pravda* newspapers reflected serious differences of opinion in the Soviet leadership.)

Mikhail GORBACHEV: I get the impression that this whole theme of serious differences of opinion in the Soviet leadership about perestroika and the evaluation of the past is prompted by the West, not by Soviet editors. I don't know the motives of those who regularly tout this theme, which is constantly discussed in foreign radio programs in Russian and other languages.It may be a wish to understand what's going on in this country or it may be a wish to make capital of the discussions being conducted here, encourage mistrust and perhaps a real split in our leadership.

The current leadership of the Soviet Union—including the Politburo and the Government—was formed basically after April 1985, when we had already set out on the course of perestroika. All the members of our leadership are deeply

committed to perestroika and are actively involved in designing and implementing its policy.

But now, let's think together and maybe that will make
things clearer. When people take on a task as ambitious as this
and when they have to formulate not only the strategy but also
the tactics of attaining the goals they have set, can they do so
without active debate or dialogue in the leadership and in the
whole society? This is what is happening now. The whole
country is now an enormous debating club. And it is only
natural that in the leadership itself there is lively discussion
within the framework of perestroika seeking answers to those
questions that arise from it. Jesus Christ alone knew answers
to all questions and knew how to feed 20,000 Jews with five
loaves of bread. We don't possess that skill, we have no ready
prescription to solve all our problems quickly. We together
with our society are seeking answers to all questions. And this
is accompanied by discussions and heated debate, and that is
normal. Our problem has been that for many years there was
no such debate in the society, in the Party, in the Central
Committee, in the Government itself or in the Politburo. And
that led to many losses, mistakes and omissions. To present
these discussions—which are a normal part of the democratic
process—as differences within the leadership is a great mistake. Maybe some people want there to be disagreement, even
want the Soviet leadership to quarrel and to be split, but that's
something quite different. That has no connection to the actual
situation within the leadership in our country.

Richard SMITH: It seems to us that some of your own
supporters, people who back perestroika very deeply, are worried about the issue of political division. There was a letter in
Sovetskaya Kultura in which a writer talked about the possibility of a committee plenum "at which M. S. Gorbachev could
be outsted." Then he went on to propose a referendum on your
leadership and on your policy, a referendum for all the people.
Have you heard about that letter and what do you think about
the idea for a referendum?

Mikhail GORBACHEV: That letter is not the only thing
I've heard about. *(Laughter.)* I think those facts are entirely

positive. It means that the society is not indifferent to who is in
the country's leadership. It means that people are taking a
great interest in what is happening. I think the fact you have
mentioned is an interesting symbol which also demonstrates
the achievements of perestroika. It shows that people have
become involved in the political process. They want to participate, to express their opinions and judgments. And that is
wonderful. That may be the most important product of perestroika so far, because in the economic and social sphere a
great deal of work remains to be done. There have been some
positive changes there, too, but for major changes that all of
society can feel, we need more time to work.

Nothing is happening in the Party or in society that would
confirm the anxiety about which you spoke.

Here I am not talking about myself, I am talking about the
question in general. Probably you have to know our political
process to understand that if the General Secretary did not
have the support of the people closest to him and the people he
is working with, then nothing would have happened in our
country after April. Everything that has been born here in our
society, in our Party, in the Central Committee, came with the
participation of the current leadership.

And let me say that perestroika has already pushed forward
a number of new and very interesting people in every sphere:
in politics, in economics, in the cultural sphere. The spreading
of the processes of democratization, and their deepening, will
bring onto the political scene more and more new interesting
people, new, fresh forces. The idea of perestroika is that it
creates mechanisms that could manage and self-regulate our
society within the framework of the democratic process. This
will allow the inclusion of all people, and, of course, the best
part, the intellectual part, the capable, talented part in managing the affairs of society and the state at all levels and in all
echelons.

Our society won't be as it was. It is changing. The mechanisms of change are beginning to work. A great deal remains
to be done, but the train is off and is picking up speed.

Robert KAISER: To me, as an old resident of Moscow,

some of the most startling changes are the changes in the press and on television. Everything has become so interesting. Many political prisoners have been freed. Many of the old refuseniks have been allowed to emigrate. On May 7, you stated that the goal is to create a socialist, legal state. In your very interesting written answers to us, you called freedom of speech "indispensable." Yet some Soviet citizens still get into trouble for what looks to us like attempts to exercise freedom of speech. I mean, in particular, Airikyan in Armenia and Grigoryants in Moscow. Is this because some of your authorities don't get the new thinking or is this because the things that those people have done are not something you consider expression of freedom of speech?

Mikhail GORBACHEV: Interesting question. I will give a short answer. The most substantial thing that perestroika has demonstrated is that our people, while being firmly in favor of the renewal of society, and of change, has firmly expressed the view that changes should happen only within the boundaries of socialism and on the basis of socialist values.

Even such measures in the economy as the development of cooperatives, cost accountability, leasing and individual enterprise have been and are being discussed very seriously and scrupulously in our society also from the following standpoint: is this not a retreat from socialism? Does not this undermine the socialist principles? Today, nine-tenths of our country's population were born and have been raised in the socialist period. And the present leadership is unable to do anything except develop socialism, which opened a great road to us in all spheres of life. We know socialism, we know its achievements and its problems. And we will act within the boundaries of our socialist choice.

That is why, when they try to force other values on us, including in the ideological sphere, this brings a critical reaction from the people. But that is also the democratic process. Democracy is like that.

Our people know that Grigoryants's "organization" is tied not only organizationally but also financially to the West, that his constant visitors and guests are Western correspondents.

Therefore people think of it as some kind of alien phenomenon in our society sponging on the democratic process and on perestroika. This happens—it happens in nature, too: all kinds of parasites attach themselves to a living organism and try to harm it.

Our society is strong enough to cope with this, too. I have said that perestroika is a kind of melting pot which will make our society stronger, which will reveal its democratic, humanitarian potential all in the interest of man. And that which some suggest—that we look for our future in different values and liquidate socialist ownership, etc.—our people reject. This will not be accepted, this is an illusion. And you also should be aware of this.

To conclude, let me express my satisfaction with our meeting and express the hope, a weak hope *(animation in the hall)* that the *Washington Post* and *Newsweek* will illuminate what is going on in the Soviet Union on the basis of objective analysis, serious, responsible analysis. We are not asking for praise, but we invite you to know the truths that perestroika has produced. A respectable publisher must do everything respectably.

Katharine GRAHAM: Could we impose on your goodwill for one really important question that hasn't been asked? We wanted to talk a little about the summit both in terms of substance and atmosphere. In your written answers you say that you would welcome another meeting with President Reagan to sign an agreement on a 50-percent reduction in strategic offensive weapons. Is this agreement on a 50-percent reduction so important and so close to completion now that it could be signed while negotiations on space defenses and on other problems such as sea-launched cruise missiles continue?

Mikhail GORBACHEV: We are confirmed and principled advocates of resolute cuts in nuclear arms, and therefore we are for the signing of the treaty on 50-percent reductions in strategic offensive forces. In our assessments, we have covered together a long road in the search for solutions. But I think you would agree with me if I say that if we sign with one hand a treaty reducing strategic offensive arms in one area and at the same time launch an arms race in space or at sea, what would be the point? That would be senseless.

So our persistence is not a whim; it isn't some kind of a tactical subterfuge or maneuver from the Soviet side, but rather a carefully thought-out and responsible position. It is in the interest of the Soviet people, of the American people and the people of the world. If we just replace one kind of arms race with another, particularly in space, things would take a particularly dramatic turn: we would undermine the trust that has begun to be built; we would depreciate all the experience that we have accumulated at the Geneva negotiations. This new kind of arms race, new sphere for an arms race, new criteria—it would take decades to reach some kind of agreement and come to an agreement.

I think that he who pushes for an arms race in space is committing a crime against the people—his own people, and others. That must be said with all responsibility, and with clarity. Such an approach, such an idea, is a road to destabilization, to unpredictability on matters of security. This must be condemned; the initiators of such an approach must be pilloried.

Sea-launched cruise missiles which they want to leave without limitations and beyond control—this would also be a roundabout maneuver, another avenue for the arms race.

Therefore we are linking all those questions together. I think that this is a fair approach. What is more, we see genuine possibilities to resolve all those questions, to resolve all of them together and arrive at a treaty on a 50-percent reduction of strategic offensive arms and then to continue farther.

Katharine GRAHAM: The reason behind my question is that there has been movement on both sides towards agreement. I thought perhaps that there's been enough movement on the question of SDI and that now the Washington Declaration could perhaps serve to come to the final break problem, it seems to me, on SDI, which is the difference over what happens at the end of the adherence period. Does the Washington Declaration solve the conflict over what happens at the end of the adherence period?

Mikhail GORBACHEV: I believe that what was contained in the statement on the understanding of the ABM Treaty the way it was adopted in 1972 and the way both sides understood it before 1983 provides a basis to move forward towards an agreement on 50-percent reductions in strategic offensive arms. But only that way, no other.

I haven't answered the other part of your question. We will work with any American Administration on this important aspect of Soviet-American relations and, in the framework of the Geneva process, we shall seek ways to reach new agreements to reduce nuclear arms. If that happens during Mr. Reagan's presidency, we would welcome that. If that happens after a new President is elected, then so be it. We are ready to work. We don't want to waste any time. We shall continue to work. It's up to the U.S. side.

I'm going to talk to the President about cooperation in Mars expeditions.

(Mikhail GORBACHEV invites everybody to look at the pictures of the launching of a rocket. He continues:)

This is a model of our Energiya rocket which last year lifted 100 tons into orbit. After certain modernizations it will be able to carry 200 tons. This is a picture of the launching of that rocket sent to me from the cosmodrome in Baikonur, which I visited last year. I will suggest to the President cooperation in organizing a joint flight to Mars. The results expected to be produced by the SDI and ballistic missile defense programs can very well be achieved through peaceful projects for the exploration of space. For instance, as a result of the project to study Halley's Comet, we have been able to develop dozens of new materials, we have been able to make major advances in such areas as electronics, mathematics and so on.

This is a field for work and cooperation that would be worthy of the American and the Soviet people. I will suggest to the President . . .

Jimmie HOAGLAND: As you probably know, we have published an article by Academician Sagdeyev on this issue.

Mikhail GORBACHEV: How interesting! Is it about Halley's Comet?

Jimmie HOAGLAND: About a joint flight to Mars. It is suggested to send an automatic station. As we see it, the flight could be feasible.

Mikhail GORBACHEV: That would be a tremendous breakthrough in science, technology and engineering. In the meantime, you can see what we have been doing. . . . I am very glad to have met you.

(Graham and the others thank Mikhail Gorbachev for the conversation and the interview.)

20

Speech at the Welcoming Ceremony in the Grand Kremlin Palace

May 29, 1988

Esteemed Mr. Ronald Reagan, President of the United States of America,

Esteemed Mrs. Nancy Reagan,

On behalf of the people and Government of the Soviet Union, I extend to you my sincere greetings on the occasion of your visit. Welcome.

It is now almost six months since our meeting in Washington, which has gone down in history as a major milestone in Soviet-American and in international relations.

Now, on this return trip, you, Mr. President, have traversed the great distance that lies between our two capitals to continue our political dialogue. This is a fact we duly appreciate.

As this is our fourth meeting, we can already make some meaningful assessments. As we see it, long-held dislikes have been weakened, habitual stereotypes stemming from "enemy images" have been shaken loose.

The human features of the other nation are now more clearly visible. This in itself is important. For at the turn of the two millennia, history has objectively bound our two countries by a common responsibility for the destinies of mankind.

The peoples of the world, and, in the first place, the Soviet and the American people, welcome the emerging positive changes in our relationship and hope that your visit and talks here will be productive, providing a fresh impetus in all areas of dialogue and interaction between our two great nations.

You and I are conscious of our two peoples' longing for mutual understanding, cooperation and a safe and stable world. This makes it incumbent upon us to discuss constructively the main aspects of disarmament:

—the set of issues related to 50-percent cuts in strategic offensive arms, while preserving the 1972 ABM Treaty;

—problems of eliminating chemical weapons;

—reductions in armed forces and conventional armaments in Europe;

—cessation of nuclear testing.

The world is also looking to us, Mr. President, for responsible judgments on other complex issues of today, such as the settlement of regional conflicts, improving international economic relations, promoting development, overcoming backwardness, poverty and mass diseases, and humanitarian problems.

And, of course, we shall discuss bilateral relations.

Our previous meetings have shown that constructive Soviet-U.S. relations are possible. The Treaty on intermediate- and shorter-range missiles is the most impressive symbol of that. But even more complex and important tasks lie ahead.

And so, Mr. President, you and I still have a lot of work to do, and it is good when there's a lot of work to be done and people need that work. We are ready to do our utmost in these coming days in Moscow.

Mr. President, you and Mrs. Reagan are here on your first visit to the Soviet Union, a country which you have so often mentioned in your public statements. Aware of your interest in Russian proverbs, let me add another one to your collection: "It is better to see once than to hear a hundred times."

Let me assure you that you can look forward to hospitality,

warmth and goodwill. You will have many meetings with Soviet people.

They have a centuries-old history behind them. They love
their land and take pride in their accomplishments.

They resent things that are presently standing in their way
and they are heatedly discussing how their country can best
progress. They are full of plans for the future.

Being ardent patriots, Soviet people are open to friendship
and cooperation with all nations. They harbor sincere respect
for the American people and want good relations with your
country.

Here, within the walls of the ancient Kremlin, where one
feels the touch of history, people cannot help reflecting over
the diversity and greatness of human civilization.

So may this give greater historical depth to the Soviet-
American talks to be held here, infusing them with a sense of
mankind's shared destinies.

Once again, I bid you welcome.

21

Speech at the Dinner in Honor of President Ronald Reagan and Nancy Reagan

Grand Kremlin Palace

May 30, 1988

Esteemed Mr. President,
Esteemed Mrs. Reagan,
Ladies and gentlemen,
Comrades,

I welcome you in the Moscow Kremlin, where for the past five centuries the most important events in this country's history have been celebrated.

It is here that crucial decisions have been taken concerning the nation's destiny. Everything around us calls for a sense of responsibility towards the times and our contemporaries, towards the present and the future.

And it is here that we would like to stress the significance of the truth we have awoken to, namely that it is no longer possible to settle international disputes by force of arms. We have been led to this conclusion by an understanding of the realities of the present-day world.

I like the notion of "realism" and I am pleased to have heard it used more often by you, Mr. President, of late.

Normal, let alone stable, Soviet-American relations, which have so much influence on the world's political climate, are inconceivable without realism.

It is thanks to realism that, in spite of all our disagreements, we have been able to arrive at a very simple but historic conclusion: namely, that a nuclear war cannot be won and must never be fought. Other conclusions have followed from this with inexorable logic.

In particular, we do not need weapons which cannot be used without inevitably endangering our own lives—and the rest of humanity as well, for that matter. I believe this understanding became the pivotal idea of Reykjavik.

Our Warsaw Treaty allies also stand firmly by this view. And this gives us solid support in all our efforts related to nuclear disarmament. Our allies have given the Soviet leadership a clear-cut mandate to press for a decisive limitation and reduction of nuclear weapons in talks with the United States.

I can see from my meetings with leaders of socialist states and authoritative representatives of other countries that we have a common aim in ending military confrontation and the race in both nuclear and conventional weapons.

It must be added that the realistic approach is making headway in all directions, on all continents. The idea of a political solution to present-day problems is particularly gaining influence. The striving of diverse political and social forces towards dialogue, towards exchanges, towards better knowledge of one another and towards mutual understanding is becoming more extensive.

If that is so, if such is the will of the peoples, care should be taken so that the stocks of the ferment of realistic policy increase, rather than diminish.

For that, it is necessary to understand one another better, to take into account specific features of a country's way of life, the historical conditions of its formation, the paths chosen by its people.

I recall you once saying, Mr. President, that the only way to overcome differences is first to understand them. This is true.

I will only add that striving to eliminate differences should not presuppose the elimination of diversity. The diversity of the world is a mighty source of mutual enrichment, both intellectual and material.

Ladies and gentlemen, Comrades,

The word "perestroika" is not out of place even within these ancient walls. The renewal of society, humanization of life and elevation of ideals have always been in the interests of the people and of each individual everywhere.

When this happens, especially in a great country, it is important to understand the essence of what it is living through. We are now observing abroad precisely this wish to understand events in the Soviet Union. And we regard this as a good sign. Because we really want to be understood correctly. This is important for civilized international relations as well.

It is practical for all who want to have business with us to know how the Soviet people view themselves.

We view ourselves as being more and more convinced of the correctness of the socialist choice, and we don't consider our country's development outside socialism, or based on any other principles.

Our program calls for greater democracy and openness, for greater social justice under conditions of prosperity and lofty spirit.

Our aim is to grant maximum freedom to people, to the individual, to society.

In international terms, we see ourselves as part of an integral civilization where everyone has a social and political choice and the right to a worthy and equal place in the community of nations.

In the issues of peace and progress, we proceed from the priority of universal values and regard the preservation of peace as the overriding priority.

This is why we advocate building a comprehensive system of international security as a condition for mankind's survival.

This explains our desire to revive and enhance the role of

the United Nations on the basis of the original aims inscribed in its Charter by the USSR, the U.S. and their respective allies.

Its very name—the United Nations—is symbolic: nations united in their resolve to prevent any further tragedies of war, to remove war from international relations and to ensure fair principles to protect the dignified life of any nation, big or small, strong or weak, poor or rich.

We are keen to broaden contacts among people in every way, to increase the flow of information and improve its quality, and to promote ties in science, culture, education, sport and any form of human activity.

But this must be done without interference in domestic affairs, without lecturing others and foisting one's own views and habits on them, without making family and personal problems a pretext for confrontation among states.

In short, the present era is promoting a wide-ranging program in the humanitarian field. Peoples should understand one another better, know the truth about one another and shed prejudice.

As far as we know, most Americans, just like us, are eager to get rid of the demon of nuclear war. But they are increasingly concerned, just like us and like all the people on Earth, about the danger of an ecological catastrophe. This threat, too, can only be warded off by joint effort.

The truly global problem of the economic state of the world —in the North and South and in the East and West of this planet—is becoming an increasingly acute priority.

The economic foundations of civilization will crumble if the squandering of funds and resources on the purposes of war and destruction is not stopped; if the problem of debts is not settled, and world finances stabilized; if the world market fails to become a truly world one by involving all states and peoples on an equitable basis.

This is the range with which we approach our international ties, including, naturally, those with the United States.

We are driven by an understanding of the realities and imperative of the nuclear and space age, the age of the sweeping waves of technological revolution, when the human race appears to be all-powerful and mortal at the same time.

It is precisely this understanding that has brought forth a new way of thinking, thanks to which a conceptual and practical breakthrough has also become possible in our mutual relations.

Mr. President, the current meeting, in summing up a fundamentally important period in Soviet-American relations, is called upon to consolidate what has been achieved and to create fresh impetus for the future.

Never before have nuclear missiles been destroyed. Now we have an unprecedented Treaty. And for the first time our countries will have to perform this overture of nuclear disarmament. The performance should be faultless.

The Soviet Union and the United States are acting as guarantors of the Afghan political settlement. This is also a precedent of immense significance. The guarantor nations are approaching a crucial period, and we hope that both will pass through it with honor. The entire world is watching how we both will act in this situation.

Elaborating an agreement on cutting strategic offensive weapons by 50 percent, provided the ABM Treaty is observed, remains our principal cause.

In today's conversation, we have paid great attention to discussing the entire range of these problems—justifiably so.

Mr. President,

There are expectations that the Moscow meeting will open up new vistas in Soviet-American dialogue, in Soviet-American relations, and benefit our peoples and the entire world.

For that, one should spare neither strength nor goodwill.

For cooperation between the Soviet Union and the United States of America, for their better mutual knowledge and understanding.

I wish health and happiness to Mr. President, Mrs. Nancy Reagan and all our esteemed guests.

22

Speech at the Dinner in Honor of Mikhail Gorbachev and Raisa Gorbachev

Spaso House

May 31, 1988

Esteemed Mr. President,
Esteemed Mrs. Reagan,
Ladies and gentlemen,
Comrades,

I thank you, Mr. President, for your words of greeting.

Two great nations have given us a sort of mandate: to determine what Soviet-American relations are to be like.

Since the time of our first meeting in Geneva, the relations between our countries have overcome a prolonged period of confrontation and reached an acceptable level from which it is already easier to make further progress.

In Reykjavik, in Washington and in the course of your present visit, we have held an intensive dialogue. The already ratified first Treaty on the reduction of nuclear arms is its biggest result.

The search for the solution of problems is continuing in the course of preparations for the 50-percent reduction of strategic offensive arms.

The Geneva agreement on Afghanistan has entered into force. We already have 47 bilateral agreements on cooperation.

The President of the United States' visit to the USSR is a good opportunity to glance back and, at the same time, to look into the future.

There have been all sorts of things in the history of relations between our two countries. Both good and bad. Of the good, the Soviet-American comradeship-in-arms during World War II is particularly memorable.

The first buds of Soviet-American friendship appeared during those grim years.

And you will not find a single Soviet person who did not feel bitter when this glorious page in the history of our relations was replaced by the Cold War.

That was a grave trial for our peoples. The world found itself in a dangerous situation, when we all sensed the breath of catastrophe. To this day we occasionally feel cold winds.

But if we are to speak of the main tendency of world development, it is turning in the direction of the search for political solutions, cooperation and peace. We have all witnessed significant changes, although considerable efforts have yet to be made to achieve irreversible changes.

Although everything cries out for cooperation and trust, prejudices and stereotypes are still alive and rivalry continues, above all, in the military sphere. That this is senseless and catastrophical has been extensively discussed at this meeting as well. Moreover, we can note a certain advance towards better mutual understanding in this field, too.

Today I would like to mention another crucial world problem—the situation in the developing world, which cannot but also affect our countries.

The problems encountered by the developing states have turned out to be tragically difficult ones.

Terrible backwardness, hunger, poverty and mass epidemics

continue to plague whole nations. Their fantastic debts have become a burning issue that concerns the whole of mankind.

Everybody seems to recognize its complexity and the involvement of extremely different and really vital interests, and to realize that a solution must be found.

We believe that the first and most important thing that can be done here by the international community, most notably the great powers, is to grant unconditional recognition of the freedom of choice.

We insist on justice. We have seriously analyzed the economic situation in developing countries. And we are convinced that a way out is possible through a radical restructuring of the entire system of world economic ties, without any discrimination on political grounds.

This would also assist a political settlement of regional conflicts which not only hinder progress in that part of the world, but disrupt the entire world situation.

Given this kind of approach, our disagreements about which fate awaits the Third World will not take the form of confrontation.

On this issue, as well, our relationship is "doomed" to be of international significance.

Speaking of our bilateral relations, we look at their potentialities and prospects proceeding, first of all, from the domestic development of both countries as well as in the context of the world process.

Many Americans who study us and have visited the USSR —and, I hope, those here now—have had an opportunity to see for themselves the great scope and momentum that the changes have acquired in this country.

They are based on comprehensive democratization and radical economic reform. It is with satisfaction that I can say that the President and I had an in-depth exchange on this topic today. We have also talked about our perestroika with other American representatives more than once. And this is very good. This, too, is a sign of change in our relations.

For our part, we seek to follow closely fundamental processes in the United States. We see the utter dissimilarity be-

tween what is happening here and in your country, in these
very different societies based on different values. But we do not
consider this a hindrance to identifying promising areas for
mutually advantageous contacts, for cooperation in the interests of both nations.

We stand for competition, for comparison.

On more thing. In dialogue with America, with all its ups
and downs, Soviet representatives uphold the interests of the
Soviet state. The same is done by Americans in contact
with us.

The truth is that the Soviet Union and the United States, in
building their relations, can only effectively realize their own
interests by realistically appraising the interests and intentions
of the partner and taking them into account. It is necessary to
master the complex art of not only coexisting with each other
but also building bridges of mutually beneficial cooperation.

The Soviet and American peoples want to live in peace, they
want communication wherever there is mutual interest. And
there is such interest, and it is growing.

We experience neither fear nor prejudice. We regard communication as a good thing.

I envision a future in which the USSR and the United States
build their relations not on the basis of deterrence and perfec-
tion of military potentials, but on the basis of disarmament,
balance of interests and all-round cooperation.

I envision a future when the solution of real problems is not
hindered by problems that are artificially preserved, that are
historically outdated, being the legacy of the Cold War, and
when rivalry gives way to a joint search based on reason, mutual benefit and readiness for compromises.

I envision a future in which our countries, without claiming
special rights in the world, constantly remember their special
responsibility in a community of equitable states.

This will be a world more reliable and safe, a world that is
needed by all people on Earth, their children and grandchildren, so that they can acquire and preserve the basic human
rights—the right to life, to work, to freedom and to the pursuit
of happiness.

The road towards this future is neither easy nor short.

We are, probably, at the start of an exceedingly interesting period in the history of our peoples.

This meeting, Mr. President, confirms that we took the correct decision in Geneva three years ago.

Let the coming years bring about an improvement in the international situation! Let life triumph!

23

Speech at the Exchange of the INF Treaty Documents

June 1, 1988

Esteemed Mr. President,
Esteemed Mrs. Reagan,
Distinguished ladies and gentlemen,
Comrades,

We are approaching the end of the meeting between the leaders of the Soviet Union and the United States of America, the fourth such meeting in three years. The visit of the United States President to our country is drawing to a close.

The President and I have summed up the results of a dialogue between our two countries at the highest level.

We have discussed both the immediate and longer-term prospects for Soviet-U.S. relations. We have signed documents which record what has been achieved and provide guidelines for the future.

Among them, an historic place will belong to the ratification documents which give effect to the Treaty on intermediate- and shorter-range missiles.

The exchange a few minutes ago of the Instruments of Ratification means that the era of nuclear disarmament has begun.

Assessing the work done over these past few days, we can say that what has been happening these days in Moscow is big politics, politics that affects the interests of millions and millions of people.

Each such meeting dealt a blow to the foundations of the Cold War.

Each of them made huge breaches in the Cold War fortress and opened up passages to modern, civilized world politics worthy of the truly new times.

But big politics means difficult politics in which every step is not easy to take.

Weighing carefully each one of our new steps, we measure it against the security interests of our two nations and of the world as a whole.

For that is the only way to achieve truly substantial results with the necessary margin of viability.

Big politics also means big responsibility, and so it cannot be built on pursuing only one's own interest, which is always inherently one sided.

Such politics also needs a great idea.

Humankind has conceived that idea in the pangs of wars and disasters, tragedies and calamities, strivings and discoveries of the 20th century.

This, in our view, is the idea of a nuclear-free and nonviolent world. It is that idea that is inscribed in the mandate which the Soviet people give to their representatives at the start of all negotiations.

This particularly applies to our negotiations with the United States of America.

Addressing the Soviet people and the Americans, addressing all nations from these hallowed steps of the Moscow Kremlin, I hereby declare we have been working honestly and with perseverance, and we shall continue to do so, to fulfill that historic mandate.

The first lines have already been written into the book of a world without wars, violence or nuclear weapons. I believe that no one can now close that book and put it aside.

President Ronald Reagan and I have agreed that the immediate task before us, which is to conclude a treaty on a 50-

percent reduction in strategic offensive arms, can and must be accomplished.

In our joint endeavors and discussions, we have learned to understand each other better, to take into account each other's concerns and to search for solutions.

The atmosphere in our relations is improving. We're working to make it a constant, not only in our official contacts, but also in the day-to-day management of Soviet-U.S. relations. In this, too, we are guided by a mandate from our peoples.

Thanks to the atmosphere of the meetings in Washington and in Moscow, and as a result of the agreements reached, Americans and Soviet people now have more opportunities for communication and for getting to know each other.

I'm convinced that scientists, students, schoolchildren, cultural personalities, ordinary tourists, athletes and, of course, businessmen will continue to enlarge and add new colors to the fabric of cooperative and even friendly relations. Sometimes, they can do that better than politicians.

Historians who will one day describe and evaluate what is now being done have probably not yet been born.

But every day, babies are being born who will live in the 21st century and to whom we must bequeath a safe and humane world.

On behalf of the Soviet leadership and the Soviet people, I wish to tell all those who are concerned and yet hopeful about the future: we shall work to achieve that goal, and we can only do it by working together. Thank you.

24

Statement at the Press Conference

June 1, 1988

Our delegation that took part in the talks is present here, with the exception of Andrei Gromyko. We are at your disposal.

But, apparently in accordance with tradition, I should say a few words as to how we assess the results of the meeting.

The fourth meeting between the General Secretary of the CPSU Central Committee and the President of the United States in three years has ended. This is not just arithmetic. I believe this is a statement full of meaning and big political importance.

Four meetings in three years. This characterizes the intensity of the political dialogue, the level of our relations. And I think that already by itself this is very meaningful.

It is only natural that across the whole world, particularly in the Soviet Union and the United States, and evidently among you journalists, there arises the question—what has the Moscow summit produced? Where has it led to? Has it added anything new to the previous meetings?

I will begin by saying that we all, and I am convinced of this, were participants in a major event. The meeting has really demonstrated once more the importance of the dialogue between the Soviet Union and the United States, confirmed once again the correctness of the choice of road made in Geneva two and a half years ago. By way of Reykjavik and Washington we came to Moscow. This is a unique process in post-war history. It is important that this is realized by all—both politicians and the public, which is displaying a big interest in how relations between our countries are shaping up.

In the three years I have been in the post of General Secretary of the CPSU Central Committee, I have had more than two hundred meetings of an international character. I do not recall virtually a single meeting with friends from socialist countries, with representatives of capitalist and nonaligned countries, in which the thought would not have been expressed and emphasized that everybody is interested in seeing Soviet-American relations directed into a normal, healthy channel.

Such is the reality that is determined by the weight of our countries.

Yet, why has such an intensive dialogue, a process of immense importance, become possible?

I think it is thanks to realism. I mean realism in the policy both of the Soviet Union and of the United States, for the manifestation of this approach by one side alone would not guarantee the possibility of such a process.

I don't want to engage in guesswork as to where confrontation would lead us if it continued, if the Kremlin and the White House lacked the resolve to turn the steering wheel in good time and in the right direction—from confrontation to the search for areas and spheres of cooperation, to the build-up of a political dialogue.

When the realities became clear, we started a dialogue accompanied by negotiations, and these negotiations, in turn, brought about agreements.

Relations that had harbored a dreadful threat to the entire world, to the very existence of mankind, started to change. The two most powerful nations began reforming their relationship in their own interests and the interests of the international community.

That was a hard thing to do. A few minutes ago I mentioned

that as the President and I exchanged the instruments of ratification.

Things are not easy, but, on the whole, an important, productive and positive process is under way.

Each of the four meetings was both a difficult and fruitful search for a balance of interests, each stepped up the efforts for finding solutions to major problems of universal human importance.

To illustrate the point, I will remind you of Reykjavik, the Reykjavik drama. This is but one example of how hard it is for political dialogue between the two world powers to evolve.

What are the results of the fourth summit? The principal outcome is that the dialogue has been continued, now encompassing all vital issues of international politics and bilateral relations. The Moscow meeting has shown again that the dialogue has come to deal with real politics.

I will not say that our meetings got rid of propaganda moves, demarches and attempts to score points through propaganda maneuvering. Nevertheless, these meetings are increasingly characterized by a striving, a desire to make real politics. I'm convinced that this is a correct path; it is precisely in this way that we should act.

When in Washington, at the very first meeting, we felt an attempt at coaching us, we declined this approach and said that we had arrived to engage in real politics. We acted in the same way at this, the fourth summit.

That is why it is characterized by deep-seated, at times keen, debate, up to the last minute of negotiations, not at the table, but when we already stood up—"wall against wall," as we say in Russia.

I would like to emphasize once again the idea of continuity that prevailed throughout the meetings. You will find that in the final document. I regard it as a large-scale document. It embraces the idea that the dialogue of our fourth summit lays bricks building our future relations, and will continue to do so into the 21st century.

What specifically has been accomplished? Following the political dialogue, which I place highest, we have completed the process of agreeing on the elimination of intermediate- and shorter-range missiles. Preparations for the fourth meeting pushed on that process, and we were able to exchange the instruments of ratification. This was not merely a formal act. I'll permit myself to use the following solemn phrasing: the completion of the procedures for putting into effect the INF Treaty has made the Moscow meeting a landmark in Soviet-American dialogue, and in world politics as well.

Not only the peoples of the Soviet Union and the United States but also their allies, the entire world public, the entire world community, can congratulate themselves. This is a joint victory for reason and realism. It has become possible because today on all continents, in all countries irrespective of their social choice and other values which each people chooses and determines itself, there is a common understanding that the world has found itself on a line where one must stop, when it is necessary to open a road in the other direction—the direction towards a nuclear-free, nonviolent world, towards an improvement of international relations.

Many made a real, substantial contribution to the attainment of this major victory. I must also note the role of the press. When it put difficult questions to politicians and to the participants in the talks, this, too, was a necessary contribution, because the questions put by journalists helped to raise the talks to the level at which they were concrete and convincing, helped to find solutions and arguments, helped to work out the forms of verification. So I consider it my duty to note the press as well.

It is now a matter of honor, first of all for the Soviet Union and the United States, and not only for them but for other states as well, for every letter and comma of the Treaty to be observed and implemented.

Further, I must say that the President and I have approved a joint statement. As I have already said, it sums up what has been accomplished after the Washington meeting and what was done here, in Moscow. At the same time the statement confirms a sort of agenda for the Soviet-American dialogue in the future. In short, this is an important political document, heralding a whole stage in our relations. The provisions relating to the importance of continuing and building up the political dialogue between countries and intensifying talks are the most substantial.

I would note the advance also in the sphere of disarmament. This is a very difficult process, especially concerning the question of strategic offensive arms. This, it appears, is the most complex task that we have encountered in post-war world politics. But I must firmly state that we are advancing step by step towards the Treaty on the reduction of these weapons. Today one of the correspondents, maybe of those present here, asked whether after the talks held here I would retain my optimism concerning the conclusion of this Treaty this year, during the present administration. I can say that if the work is conducted effectively, if the present administration and if both sides act effectively, we can achieve the Treaty.

I want to draw attention to our initiative, which has gained much ground, concerning talks on the reduction of armaments and armed forces in Europe. It was published, and I will not be repetitive. Now if something has to be specified, you are free to ask questions.

A whole package of agreements concerning bilateral relations between our countries has been signed. They, too, have been published.

There was an in-depth discussion of the problem of regional conflicts. I was present at all our conversations with the President and at two plenary meetings. It was discussed with particular detail and thoroughness today.

I think that we have come to face a situation in which it is possible to state that at the world's "flash points" real chances have emerged for resolving regional problems and untangling these tight "knots" on the basis of political approaches, on a basis of the balance of interests.

As a matter of fact, we today stated the following: First, there is Afghanistan, and I will talk about that later on. Second, there is a process concerning the Middle East. It is proceeding, position are drawing closer and there is growing understanding of the need for its solution along the lines of an international conference. This has already been recognized. But the point at issue is how to regard this conference. All these issues will be specified in the course of future efforts.

There is a Kampuchean problem. Thanks to the initiative recently displayed by Vietnam and Kampuchea, it is being moved into the plane where it can be resolved in the nearest future.

A real process is under way, and there is a possibility of solutions, in Central America, in Southern Africa and so on.

If some view my considerations as unjustified optimism, as an attempt at wishful thinking, I think they are wrong. Let us compare the situation three or four years ago and today. The situation has substantially changed. There have emerged chances for a political solution of all these conflicts. Formidable forces have been set in motion in these regions and in the world as a whole. I have always stressed in conversations with the President and all American officials the principal idea—we should not lose, nor pass up this chance.

In this connection I directly told the President that the signing of the agreements on Afghanistan creates a precedent that exceeds in its importance the framework of this very problem. This is the first instance when the Soviet Union and the United States, along with parties directly involved in the conflict, have signed an agreement paving the way for a political solution.

We will try our utmost to abide by the agreements, and expect the same attitude from all other parties to the accords, including the United States of America. I think that if we fail this time, if this positive precedent does not materialize, this will have far-reaching consequences and tell upon approaches to similar problems in other regions.

There are grounds for concern. Two worrying events occurred recently: first, in the city of Kabul, the Soviet Embassy and our troops in Kabul were fired upon. Second, comrades of ours perished in the Kandahar area yesterday; several people were reported missing. We promised that Soviet troops would not participate in hostilities from the moment the troop withdrawal began. We did act in this way. But we made a reservation to the effect that such would be their actions if there were no provocations and bandit attacks on our troops. If this happens, we will respond in a proper way. This should be clear, too.

An accord is an accord. We see what Pakistan is doing, and in this connection the USSR Ministry of Foreign Affairs issued a statement. I do not want to go into details. I only want to underscore that there are attempts to torpedo the accords, which would have serious negative consequences. This was stated most candidly to the President and the whole American delegation.

I think that the United States and the Soviet Union can make a constructive contribution to the solution of regional conflicts on the basis of political approaches, taking into account the balance of interests of all the participants in a conflict, on the basis of realism.

I can note a certain advance on humanitarian issues, on human rights. I set the question before the President as follows.

Some concrete problems arise in this sphere from time to time. We have always attentively studied and tackled them. And we shall further study and solve them. But the more thought I give to the situation, the more I come to believe that the American Administration does not have an understanding of the real situation with human rights, with the processes that are taking place in our country in the sphere of democracy. Probably we, too, do not have a clear understanding of the American situation in this sphere of life. I proposed: let us organize a seminar within the framework of interparliamentary exchanges at which the representatives of our parliaments and political and public circles would meet and exchange information and make evaluations as to what is taking place in America and in our society in this sphere. We are prepared for this.

There remains very much speculation regarding the issue of human rights. And I must say that propaganda moves and all sorts of shows prevailed in this part of the fourth summit. So when I learned only today—because I was too busy to read the newspapers—that our press reacted to this accordingly, I arrived at the conclusion that it had acted correctly, within the framework of glasnost. This part of the President's visit had to be shown to our people. The people should know everything.

I am not thrilled by this aspect of the fourth summit. I think that it is necessary to engage in realistic politics. When the President expressed to me his views about human rights in the Soviet Union, I also asked him a lot of questions. And it took him a long time to explain, because he wanted me to change my opinion of the human rights situation in the United States. On hearing him out I said, "Mr. President, your explanations are not convincing. I used facts based on data of the American Congress, not to mention the press, which prints many materials on this question. In my position it is best to proceed from official data."

I think this is the only way to conduct talks. Let us look at one another with open eyes, let us see each other's history, traditions and values, let us respect each other's choice, respect our peoples. For after all, it is they who are making the choice. Incidentally, the peoples always come out for rapprochement, for mutual knowledge, for friendship. The Americans are saying this and Soviet people are openly speaking about this. Much was told to the President on this score yesterday. So let us listen to what our people want. Since they are elected by the people, politicians should detect what the people want and implement this in concrete policies. We should help this process if we are intent on improving Soviet-American relations and the situation in the world as a whole.

I must say that making contact with Soviet people was a substantial fact of the U.S. President's visit to the Soviet Union. This was the first visit by the President and his wife, a first acquaintance to replenish their impressions of the Soviet Union, of Soviet people. There was much within the framework of the program, while in several instances they acted of their own choice, outside the program.

Mrs. Reagan's program, which enabled her to get acquainted with the Soviet Union, was a substantial element. Yesterday, when the President conversed with our people, with me present, somebody asked him, and I think this got into the press, whether he still regarded the Soviet Union as an "evil empire."

No, he replied. Moreover, he said this at a press conference near the Czar Cannon, in the Kremlin, in the center of the "evil empire." We take note of this and it means, as the ancient Greeks used to say, "everything flows and everything changes." This confirms my thought that the President has a sense of realism and that this is a very important quality for a politician. Regardless of what the realities are, one must look them squarely in the eye. It is only a policy based on analysis, on an evaluation of real processes, that merits being termed a policy.

I have got slightly carried away and have begun to speak for the President. I think is best for the President to tell you himself what he thinks about his meetings. But I mentioned only those remarks which I was witness to.

In short, this is how I would sum up the results: The President's visit and the talks will serve the improvement of Soviet-American relations, their development and strengthening, and will raise them to a still higher level.

Could more have been attained? This, naturally, interests both you and us. We have just had a discussion and that is why my colleagues and I were late for the meeting with you. The discussion did not produce any advance; we stopped halfway. I was compelled to say, well, politics is the art of the possible. But I hold that more could have been achieved at this meeting.

For example, I proposed to the President making a big new stride in spelling out the political realities of our time as a platform of intentions and political actions. Here my colleagues in the leadership and I proceeded from the experience that we have accumulated since Geneva. There we stated: Nuclear war is impossible, impermissible, there can be no victors in it and in general no war at all between the Soviet Union and America is permissible.

This did not mean that everything would be solved, and nuclear arms would vanish on the second day or on the second week after the meeting. No, the arms remain, but this joint statement was invested with tremendous meaning, evoking a great response throughout the world. Today we increasingly are arriving at the conclusion that problems should be solved by political means, on the basis of a balance of interests, on the basis of respect for the social choice of peoples. Whether we want it or not, we are all obliged to learn to live in our real world.

If you take the latest book containing the President's speeches and the book of selected articles and speeches by the General Secretary of the CPSU Central Committee, in the first and in the second you will see these statements. So, proceeding from the understanding of lessons that have been drawn from the practice of recent years, we proposed including this political understanding in the present joint statement. Here is the draft that I suggested to the President: Mindful of the existing realities in the modern world, we both believe that no outstanding issues defy solution and that they should not be solved by military means, that we both regard peaceful coexistence as a universal principle of international relations, and that the equality of all states, noninterference in internal affairs and freedom of socio-political choice should be recognized as standards that are inalienable and obligatory for all. I gave the President the Russian and the English texts. I like it, he said, on reading the text.

When we came today to reach agreement on the final text of the joint statement, it turned out that not all in the President's staff liked the idea of such a wording. And this became the subject of a discussion. We felt that there was a dislike for the term "peaceful coexistence" as it had been used in the past in documents which were signed by the Soviet leadership with Nixon and Kissinger. We withdrew this term, since it was unacceptable, although we really want to coexist, and I think nobody will put this to doubt.

There appeared a new variant, and the President himself suggested elements of that formula. Yet it did not appear in such form in the concluding statement, although serious common understandings are stated in it. But they could have been more serious and weightier. This does not mean at all that, were we to state jointly today that we should proceed from the premise of using political methods to solve problems and not to bank on their military solution, the troops and armaments would vanish overnight.

No, nuclear arms did not vanish after we noted in Geneva the unacceptability and impermissibility of nuclear war. But that was a very important political point of reference, both for the Soviet-American dialogue and for dialogue in the world. We regarded that as a very important statement, especially since this view was expressed separately by the leaders both of the Soviet Union and the United States. I think that at the meeting here a chance was lost to make a big step towards forming civilized international relations.

We failed to agree on the subject of the talks on conventional arms in Europe. We suggested using the summit meeting, but, naturally, without replacing the Vienna forum, to make its work easier. For the point at issue is that we, the Soviet Union and the Americans, come to some accord, to some understanding on such an important issue as the subject of the talks, the issue that now restrains the process of preparing a mandate in Vienna.

This position, by the way, was brought forth in Geneva at a meeting between Mr. George Shultz and Soviet Foreign Minister Eduard Shevardnadze. Nonetheless, despite the positive attitude to it from both sides, it has not been included in the statement. Even though the excuse was quite plausible—it was not, purportedly, proper to replace the Vienna dialogue.

That we were not going to do. On the contrary, we wanted to make work on it easier by offering a viewpoint of ours that could be used by the participants in the Vienna meeting. What I think is that there is much talking to the effect that one cannot advance the process of nuclear disarmament, 50-percent reductions, without handling the problem of conventional arms and the reduction of armaments in Europe. But as soon as we come to real proposals in order to advance that process, then incomprehensible maneuvering and departure begin.

The West was alarmed by the Warsaw Pact's alleged superiority in strength. When we said: Let us exchange date to clarify the entire matter, the other side evaded giving an answer.

Now we proposed the following: Let us say that we have reached an understanding on the subject of the negotiations. This will make work easier in Vienna. Nothing has come off.

The Americans have not accepted our bold and quite realistic plan consisting of three stages and integral parts directed at eliminating asymmetry and imbalance in Europe and effecting resolute transition to creating on the continent a situation in which the structure of arms and armed forces is nonoffensive and their level is considerably lower.

I believe that a good chance to impart proper dynamics to the talks on diminishing the danger of confrontation between the two most powerful alliances and, thus, contributing to international security has been passed up.

Politics is the art of the possible. Anyway, I wouldn't draw dramatic conclusions because not everything that could have happened came off. Nevertheless, I ought to share my considerations so that you have a fuller understanding of the content of the talks.

Before concluding my statement, I would like to mention one general impression. I wouldn't be quite honest and truthful with you if I failed to say this. I formed an impression that the American stance was contradictory. This observation is based not only on the results of this meeting. We have already come across this phenomenon before.

What is contradictory about the American approach, about the American stance? On the one hand, we have a joint statement to the effect that war should be prevented, that it is inadmissible. We conduct a businesslike discussion about reducing weapons, about disarmament, talk about the preference of political solutions of problems. On the other hand, we constantly hear, and we heard it this time in Moscow and many times before the President's departure for here, about relying on force.

This means that force—armed force, military might—is proclaimed to be the chief principle of United States policy vis-à-vis the Soviet Union, and not only the Soviet Union. How are we to tally the Geneva statements with this approach? On the one hand, the President and I state that both our peoples want to live in peace, in cooperation and even be friends. This also finds its reflection in what ordinary people say. I have read American press reports. Asked about their vision of our relations in the year 2000, the Americans preferred development of friendly relations and cooperation to rivalry.

It would seem that we should proceed from this, guide ourselves in accordance with the will of our peoples. This does not happen in real politics. This is also noticeable in the sphere of economic ties. The clear interest of an influential part of the American business community to cooperate with us runs up against bans, restrictions and downright intimidation. A most-unfavored-nation status is applied in the United States with regard to the Soviet Union.

The President and I yesterday had a serious discussion on this subject. I said: Why should the dead grip at the coat-tails of the living, referring to the Jackson-Vanik Amendment. One of them is dead, the other is a political corpse. Why should they hold us back? The amendment was adopted in a totally different situation, decades ago.

In today's totally different, changed world, we ought to conceive and shape our policy on the basis of present-day realities.

This reminds me of British legislation under which wrongful actions committed today are judged on the basis of laws adopted in the 13th and 14th centuries.

Traditions do differ. I have nothing against them. This is up to the British people. I don't mean to offend the British correspondents. But in politics, one should proceed from today's realities and even look to the future. I said to the President: We have already proved that we can live without each other economically, now we should prove that we can cooperate, the more so, for we are simply doomed to cooperation. The alternative to that leads to a totally unpredictable situation. One cannot maintain lasting cooperation without it resting on trade, on economic cooperation.

I would even risk raising the question in the following way: The more we depend on each other economically, the more we will be predictable on the political plane.

Do you agree? You need not reply; just give your answers in
your newspaper commentaries.

We see this contradiction in the sphere of propaganda and in
the behavior of officials, especially on issues of human rights.
We say yes, we are independent, each people has the right to
social choice,relies on its values. Yes, we are different, but that
is no reason for confrontation, let alone war. It's good that
there is diversity. This is a ground for comparison, an impetus
to thought, to judgment.

We can remain ourselves and live normally, in a civilized
world.

We have not yet noticed on the part of the Americans a
serious will to orient themselves towards new phenomena, to
take into account the changes in our society. As Mayakovsky
used to say: If stars light up, does it not mean that somebody
needs this? So this must be to somebody's advantage. But I am
sure that our peoples have a different view, and this is the
decisive factor in shaping policy. This contradictoriness in
American policy and the conduct of the U.S. Administration
is disappointing to our people.

And still, returning to the overall appraisal of the fourth
Soviet-American summit, I would like to say that this is a
great event, that the dialogue continues. The continuity has
been given an added impulse, Soviet-American relations have
advanced. I don't know whether by one or by two stages, but
in any case, they were brought to new stages. And this in itself
is a remarkable fact in world politics.

This is what I wanted to tell you.

*   *   *

Then Mikhail Gorbachev answered questions from journalists.

Question (the newspaper *Izvestia*): Mikhail Sergeyevich, you
have held a number of fruitful meetings with President Reagan. He will leave the White House in eight months' time. Do
you think that regular contacts with the next President are
possible? Do you think that there can be a meeting to get

acquainted with the next President of the U.S.A. after he is inaugurated?

Answer: I think this is not just possible, but necessary, and vitally so.

Question (CBS television network, U.S.A.): You have mentioned twice the missed opportunities at the talks on strategic offensive arms. You have also said that politics is the art of the possible. Therefore I would like to ask you if there is an opportunity to conclude a treaty on strategic offensive arms with the current U.S. Administration if the U.S. side continues insisting on preserving the SDI program?

Answer: I am sure there is still an opportunity to conclude the treaty this year. First, I am encouraged in this optimism by the progress that has been achieved over this period between Washington and Moscow and the exchange of opinions that was conducted here almost round-the-clock. It warrants such an optimistic appraisal.

Question (the newspaper *Il Messaggero,* Italy): I would like to ask you if, after your pronouncements, President Reagan said something about the United States' obligations under the Geneva accords on Afghanistan.

Answer: It seemed to me that not only the President but all the members of the United States delegation realize the importance of a successful solution to the Afghan conflict on the principles that have been laid down in Geneva. I think that the exchange of opinions on this theme was sincere and useful.

Question (National Public Radio, U.S.A.): Mr. General Secretary, you have been asked several times in the past few days if a fifth summit with the President of the United States is possible. You have answered as a rule that it is possible, but that everything depends on how matters proceed at the Moscow summit. Has it achieved such a progress as would warrant the holding of a fifth summit with President Reagan this fall?

Answer: I think that the holding of a summit is possible only on one condition—if we have an opportunity to achieve a treaty on strategic offensive arms reductions which takes into consideration the entire range of questions, including the problems of ABM and sea-based cruise missiles. I do not go into details. All this is in the area of talks and exchange of opinions. Since I state the possibility of achieving a treaty, I believe that the possibility of a fifth summit still remains a reality. It is only with this matter that I link the possibility of a fifth meeting.

Question (newspaper *New York Daily News,* U.S.A.): We are all amazed at the degree of openness which exists in your society. Americans were yesterday also amazed at the tone of the speech of President Reagan at Moscow University. We were surprised at the fact that the Soviet press has not contained a word about that speech by the President. What is your reaction to that speech?

Answer: Regrettably, I have not been able so far to familiarize myself either with President Reagan's speech at the meeting with writers or with his speech at the meeting at Moscow University. Nevertheless, I think that these meetings were useful. At any rate, the comrades who are better informed of these meetings said that they had been useful. As to our press, its representatives are present here and if they have not yet managed to publish some reports, I think they will do so.

Question (SANA news agency, Syria): Mikhail Sergeyevich, Arab countries highly appreciate the just words you have said recently about the Palestinian people who have been waging these days a courageous struggle against the Israeli occupants. Tell us please what you have achieved at your meetings with Mr. Reagan on the Palestinian question and on the Middle East settlement in general.

Answer: We noted that there have appeared real aspects related to a political settlement of the Middle East situation.

First, there exists in the world community, also among the permanent members of the Security Council, the awareness of the need for settlement in the framework of an international conference. It is quite a different matter that the question of its content has not yet been elucidated. Then, there is an awareness that there exist the interests of Syria, there exist the interests of the Palestinian people, the interests of Israel, the interests of other countries of the region who are affected by this conflict.

We stand for a political settlement of all issues, with due account for the interests of all sides concerned and, of course, for the fundamental provisions of the relevant UN resolutions. This implies that all the Israeli-occupied lands be returned and the Palestinian people's right be restored. We told President Reagan how we view the role of the United States, but we cannot decide for the Arabs in what form the Palestinians will take part in the international conference. Let the Arabs themselves decide, while the Americans and we should display respect for their choice.

Furthermore, we ought to recognize the right of Israel to security and the right of the Palestinian people to self-determination. In what form—let the Palestinians together with their Arab friends decide that. This opens up prospects for active exchanges, for a real process. Anyway, it seems to me that such an opportunity is emerging.

I will disclose one more thing: we said that following the start of a conference—a normal, effective conference, rather than a front for separate talks—a forum which would be interrelated with bilateral, tripartite and other forms of activity, we would be ready to handle the issue of settling diplomatic relations with Israel.

We are thus introducing one more new element. This shows that we firmly stand on the ground of reality, on the ground of recognition of the balance of interests. Naturally, there are principal issues—the return of the lands, the right of the Palestinian people to self-determination. I should reiterate: We proceed from the premise that the Israeli people and the state of Israel have the right to their security, because there can be no security of one at the expense of the other. A solution that would untie this very tight knot should be found.

Question (newspaper *Trybuna Ludu,* Poland): Comrade General Secretary, you said this morning that issues of conventional arms in Europe would be considered today. Now you have said that the West rejects the Soviet proposal in this area. We know that your initiative also comprises proposals put forward by other socialist countries, Poland included. What, in your view, is the future solution to this issue? What can be expected after Vienna? For your program contains even some replies to the aspirations of Western countries, Social Democratic and other parties.

Answer: To be fully objective, I ought to say the following: The American side does not refuse to consider the subject of the talks on the basis of the accords reached in Geneva at our Foreign Ministers' meeting. It evaded making a statement and jointly recording an attitude to this question at the Moscow meeting.

That is why I should be absolutely objective so as not to cast any aspersions on the American side when such important matters are dealt with. They argue that they have to consult the other participants. But we say that what we have proposed does not contradict the necessity to consult. It appears that something is being withheld. Nevertheless, I believe that the prospects for defining the mandate of the Vienna conference are real.

I must say that the question of this conference's mandate was being linked to a certain extent by the American side with other CSCE issues, especially with the humanitarian sphere. There, too, a live, vigorous process is going on, a collision of views is taking place and they are being compared. I am of the opinion that solutions are possible.

We hold that in its foreign policy the Soviet Union should always take into account the opinion of both Eastern and Western Europe. That is exactly the way we are trying to work with our allies. Now this is being done better and we have a regular exchange of views. With the West European countries, too, we are trying to conduct matters in such a way that there would be full clarity and understanding. We want to build our common European home together.

Question (by a British journalist): There is a widespread view that the differences between the American approach to the SDI program and your position are the main obstacle to the conclusion of the START treaty. Have you succeeded in achieving any progress in removing the differences in respect of the SDI program in the course of this summit? If you have, what concrete progress has been achieved? Do you continue to think as before that this is the biggest obstacle to concluding a treaty on strategic offensive arms?

Answer: I will first answer the last question. Yes, that is what I think, because SDI means destabilization. It defies normal logic—to scale down strategic offensive arms on Earth and at the same time to build bridges for an arms race in outer space. The American side is trying to persuade us that these are only defensive weapons.

We do not think so. And we are competent to pass such a judgment. If the arms race is moved to outer space, this is fraught with a most serious destabilization of the entire situation in the world. I reminded the President: in Geneva we stated that we will not strive for military superiority. You have the impression, I told him, that you have a possibility to surpass us by way of outer space, to achieve an advantage. Thereby you retreat from the Geneva statement. We had a pointed discussion on the philosophical aspect of this "defensive" system.

Then there was yet another moment. In order to convince us to support SDI, the American side stated its readiness to share secrets with us when it achieves any real results in this matter. I told the President: Mr. President, permit me to disagree with you and put this assurance in doubt. The two sides at present are trying in vain to reach agreement on the verification of the presence of sea-launched cruise missiles on two or three classes of ships. You are not prepared for this and refuse to consent. How can we believe that you will suddenly open all secrets related to SDI? This is not serious, this is beyond the framework of real politics.

Yet, while conducting such a philosophical discussion involving military strategy, we nevertheless agreed to act on the basis of the Washington statement, especially since it contains several concrete matters.

I will illustrate this: coming out for strict observance of the ABM Treaty and a commitment not to withdraw from it in the course of an agreed-upon period of time and considering the position taken by the American side, the Soviet side tabled a compromise proposal on this question on which views differ. In particular, we proposed to carry out the following:

First. To exchange data related to work in the ABM field, to hold meetings of experts, to conduct mutual visits of testing sites where work in this field is being conducted.

Second. To exchange information with the aim of avoiding lack of confidence that the commitments adopted by the sides are being observed.

Third. To effect verification of compliance with commitments, up to and including inspections at sites giving rise to concern from the sides.

Fourth. To hold consultations to consider situations which, in the opinion of either side, place its highest interests in jeopardy.

In the course of the consultations the sides shall use all possible means to settle the situations on a mutually acceptable basis.

Therefore the completion of the drafting of the Treaty on a 50-percent reduction of strategic offensive arms in 1988, as you see, will required considerable effort, but we remain confident that this is possible.

This is the first time that I have given such a detailed answer to this question.

Question (*The Guardian,* Great Britain): There are five thousand journalists in Moscow covering the summit. The Soviet Union's internal policy took an unexpected turn for them when in his television interview Mr. Yeltsin suddenly called for the resignation of Mr. Ligachev. Mr. Burlatsky, Mrs. Zaslavskaya as well as Mr. Yuri Afanasyev have suddenly started speaking about difficulties which are encountered in the elections of delegates to the forthcoming Party conference. You call for the proponents of perestroika to be participants and delegates of the conference but at present only some manifestations of perestroika are evident. What is your personal view of the process of political perestroika in the Soviet Union as the Party conference approaches and what do you think of Mr. Yeltsin's call for Mr. Ligachev's resignation?

Answer: The course of perestroika and its prospects are fully outlined in the Theses of the CPSU Central Committee on this question. Sitting before you is one of the compilers of these Theses. Also taking part in this were all the members of the Politburo, the entire leadership. The Theses express our collective opinion concerning the platform for the forthcoming Party conference and the prospects of perestroika. I think that the conference will give mighty second wind to the entire process of perestroika along all the main directions. We will act resolutely but with circumspection. A huge country, a huge responsibility. We should not put either ourselves, our friends or the world community in a difficult situation. In the course of their personal experience of perestroika our people are changing, just as we ourselves. We have emerged from one stage, analyzed it, drawn lessons, elaborated our plans, and are searching for ways.

In the main, we have found them, but there remain many tactical and practical problems. It is not always, maybe, that things are moving successfully. It is not always that we find the correct solution to some matters. Setbacks occur. But if we are to speak of the main thing—perestroika is picking up speed and the people are for perestroika. Society is in motion, the Party is undergoing renewal, all spheres of society are in the process of renewal.

Of course, in our society you can find facts to illustrate any theme and thereby fulfill any assignment that the publishers of your newspapers will give you. Whatever task is set to you, you will confirm by concrete facts. At this summit there were some attempts to use facts out of context. After all, any facts can be selected. The thing to see the tendency of phenomena in generalized form, their direction and their prospective.

As to Comrade Yeltsin's interview with the BBC, I am in total ignorance about it. (*A voice, in the hall:* "and ABC.") I was compelled yesterday to say that I know nothing about this. Of course, this does not do me credit. But you, too, did not do much for me to learn about this in time. I have asked for the full texts of what Comrade Yeltsin said. I want to read them. If the correspondents who interviewed him could provide me with a full recording, without any tape editing, I would be grateful.

Yeltsin is a member of the Central Committee. The things he is speaking about were discussed at last year's October plenary meeting. There were 27 speakers; they spoke without any preparation whatsoever, as here at the press conference. And his speech too came as an absolute surprise. Taking place at the plenary meeting was an exchange of views about the report to be made on the 70th anniversary of the October Revolution. But Yeltsin took the floor and the exchange of views began immediately. All the 27 comrades were unanimous that Comrade Yeltsin's generalizations and conclusions concerning various aspects of the Central Committee's activity, the situation in the Politburo and the work of the Secretariat were wrong. His speech was qualified as politically erroneous. So a discussion took place and a decision was passed. In this particular case it might be that Comrade Yeltsin disagrees with the decision of the Party's Central Committee. Then we in the Central Committee should ask Comrade Yeltsin what this is about and what he is pressing for.

As to Comrade Ligachev resigning, no such problem exists in the Party's Central Committee, in the Politburo. I advise you to proceed from this.

Question (the Soviet magazine *USA: Economics, Politics, Ideology*): Not only journalists but also politologists who consider themselves experts on U.S. affairs have come to Moscow. Many of them say that the conservative forces in the United States, which tried to prevent the ratification of the Treaty, are now closing ranks, believing that the process of developing relations between the USSR and the United States is proceeding too rapidly and that they should take all measures so as to stop this movement or to reverse it regardless of what position is taken by the future Administration. Did you speak about this with President Reagan and what do you think about these forces?

Answer: I think that if you put this question to the President, and he is to appear before you soon, he will give you a better answer. In any case, the views of American conservatives will have little influence on us.

Question (U.S. television company NBC): Concerning your conservatives, Mr. General Secretary. An analysis was conducted in America, and also in your country, and according to it you have only three or five years left in which to ensure the success of perestroika. If you fail, you will be outstripped by conservatives and critics inside the Communist Party of the Soviet Union. What is your personal assessment of what has been achieved to ensure the success of perestroika that is necessary for your great society's survival?

Answer: This is what I will say. The most important thing in our perestroika is that through democracy and openness we have already drawn the people into it. While by way of perfecting our political system we will substantially strengthen this tendency. It may be that there are places and processes that perestroika has not yet influenced but today it is present already everywhere.

The other day, for instance, there was a debate on Sakhalin Island. As a result of it, a plenum of the regional Party committee was convened and discussed the opinions of working people, Communists. The plenum found their remarks and demands to be just, found it necessary to strengthen the Party leadership in the region and adopted decisions that were needed for the process of democratization on Sakhalin to gain momentum. So perestroika has reached Sakhalin. But it also is spreading in depth, penetrating all spheres.

In the course of three years nobody has proposed a convincing alternative to the policy of perestroika, and I am convinced that no such alternative exists. It is necessary to restructure, to renovate the country on the basis of our principles, our ideals, using the tremendous material, spiritual and intellectual potential of society. The Party and the people have the strength to carry out perestroika and accomplish a breakthrough. There is no alternative to perestroika and perestroika will be victorious. It may know occasional retreats, maneuvers, even setbacks, but this will not change the main direction of our society's development. We have embarked on a path of irreversible changes.

Question (Portuguese newspaper *Diario de Noticias*): I would like to hear your views on Angola. Secondly, when speaking of the results of the meeting, you repeated several times the words "missed," "let slip a chance."

Answer: Better "let slip" than "missed." "Missed" is forever, while "let slip" applies only to this meeting and we still have a possibility to go again for this chance in the future.

As to Angola, I must say that we had an interesting, substantive and realistic exchange of views. Both the Americans and we stated the possibility of advancement towards settling that regional conflict, providing, both sides stressed, strict observance of the U.S. Security Council's relevant resolutions, the exclusion of South Africa's interference in Angolan affairs and the granting of independence to Namibia. We are not involved in that process directly, but we supported the talks conducted by the Angolans, Cubans and South Africans through U.S. mediation. If all the parties believe that the Soviet Union should join in more specifically in addition to expressing its considerations, we are prepared for that, too. Anyway, such was the discussion. It was based on the understanding that this process can bring about a positive result.

Question (newspaper *Izvestia*): First of all, I want to say that our newspaper published today a rather detailed account of President Reagan's remarks at the House of Writers and at Moscow State University. This is in reply to the question asked by my American colleagues. We, in watching the Soviet-American dialogue, have always felt that initially the difficulties related to verification and inspection originated from our side. Now we think that the accent has moved to the American side. Has the summit confirmed this reorientation?

Answer: Your observations are correct. And we discussed that, relying on facts. It has turned out that previous statements were largely bluff. Now, on starting to deal with real processes, we are in a very resolute mood. Verification should be real, effective. In the field of verification, thanks to the experience gained in elaborating the Treaty on intermediate- and shorter-range missiles, we now cooperate constructively. We think that solutions will be found on these issues as well.

Question (newspaper *L'Unita,* Italy): President Reagan cited a saying, "It was born, it wasn't rushed." Still, what we are witnessing is a resolute turn for the better in relations between the Soviet Union and the United States. What is Europe's role in that process, and don't you think that Europe should join this process more actively?

Answer: In all the processes so far, Europe was not only present, but actively participated in defining problems that became subjects of discussion at the summit meetings between the U.S. President and the General Secretary. This also applies to our East European allies. So Europe, both East and West, is always there, acting and making its dynamic contribution. We will act precisely in this manner. I know that President Reagan has stated just that. Moreover, today, when the world is looking for answers to burning, hard questions, I see no way for a successful solution of international problems without Europe, which possesses unique historic, intellectual, diplomatic and political experience, without the European contribution.

Question (*Literaturnaya Gazeta*): The previous edition of our weekly published a dispatch by our U.S.-based correspondent Iona Andronov regarding 300 Soviet servicemen in Afghanistan who had been forced across the border inside Pakistan. The publication was immediately followed by letters to the Editorial Board with inquiries about their fate. In discussing regional conflicts, has this question been raised during your conversation with President Reagan?

Answer: I have also received letters from some mothers of these soldiers. We approached the American side in order to consider this question practically. Such discussions have been held. We did not discuss this matter specifically with President Reagan. But it began to be elaborated at working level, at the level of experts. I will add that this problem has also been raised before Pakistan. We will do everything so that our people return home.

Question (*Los Angeles Times*, United States): Presidential elections are held in the United States every four years, no matter whether they are needed or not. But the President is limited to eight years in office. Your term as General Secretary has not been strictly defined. Many Americans would like to know how long you intend to remain in your post.

Answer: This does not depend on my intentions, although your notions of our democracy are such as if the people were not involved. This is another fact showing that we have false notions of each other. Nevertheless, I shall answer your question. This problem, related to Party and other elective bodies, will be referred to the Party Conference, taking into account what has already been stated briefly in the theses. It will be reflected in the new election law. So all this will be put on a basis of law.

Question (the newspaper *Rizospastis,* Greece): Mikhail Sergeyevich, in your opening speech you have mentioned a number of regional conflicts. But you have not touched upon the southern part of Europe, the Mediterranean, the Cyprus problem. Does this mean that these questions have not come up for discussion at the talks, or that the differences were so great that there has been no progress? Do you intend to visit Greece this year?

Answer: As to the first question, I shall say this: We have raised these problems during intensive exchanges of opinions in working groups, but they have not been developed because of the lack of interest on the U.S. part. As to my visits, we plan them, and when there is clarity, we shall surely avail ourselves of the invitation and pay the visit.

Question (NHK TV, Japan): What other regional Asian problems, apart from Kampuchea and Afghanistan, have you discussed with President Reagan? Have you discussed the situation on the Korean Peninsula in connection with the coming Olympic Games?

Answer: We spoke of Afghanistan, Kampuchea and the situation on the Korean Peninsula. I gathered the impression—to tell the truth, we did not have enough time to exchange detailed opinions on the latter question—that the American side is aware that some headway in this respect is needed. Our negotiating partners negatively described the stand of North

Korea. We, on the contrary, described the stand of the DPRK Government to the President as constructive and inviting a dialogue and [said] that the DPRK Government is prepared, both on a bilateral basis and with the participation of the Americans, to conduct an exchange of views on the present-day state of affairs and on prospects for reunification, on the principles of the basis of which the nation should reunite. We said that this was exactly the opportunity which had not been used so far.

Question (*Al Hawadis* magazine, Lebanon): You said that during the summit, the positions on the Middle East problem drew closer together. Could you specify in what exactly the stands of the United States and the Soviet Union on this matter coincide? Will Mr. Shultz take with him some joint position for his trip to the region? And, secondly, yesterday Mr. Reagan did not say anything about the Middle East when addressing students at Moscow State University. Today you did not say anything about the situation in the Persian Gulf area. But today you said that Afghanistan could be used as an example for a settlement of a similar situation in Kampuchea and elsewhere. Could you elaborate?

Answer: About the Middle East, I want to repeat once again that, first, there are elements which make it possible to state that the positions were brought closer together and first of all the recognition that an international conference is needed. Second, there is awareness that within the framework of such a conference, it would be possible to involve other forums. There is awareness that the provisions of appropriate UN resolutions should be utilized. I think there are aspects which will require examination. These are: the essence and content of such a conference, the question of Palestine and of the PLO's participation in the negotiating process. And, finally, the United States of America is aware that the Soviet Union should participate in such a settlement.

We gave the Americans an opportunity to work on that for several years. They did and saw that nothing came out of that. After they saw that, we resumed the dialogue.

For our part, we are ready for constructive cooperation.

As to the Persian Gulf. This question was discussed rather thoroughly. We adhere to the view that the conflict there is very serious and everything should be done for it not to develop in a dangerous direction. This is why we say: It is essential to use to the full the potential inherent in the first resolution of the UN Security Council and to enable the UN Secretary General or his envoy to utilize the potential and to secure cessation of hostilities.

I think we correctly call for restraint and for a display of composure. We advocate settlement of the conflict. The threat of its spread with dangerous consequences is real. We are calling on the Americans: Let us relieve the Persian Gulf of the U.S. military presence. Let us rather introduce a United Nations force so that the process would not be spurred in a wrong, dangerous direction.

Question (The *Washington Post*, U.S.A.): Could you elaborate on the Soviet stand on SDI? Did the American side make it clear that there was an opportunity to resolve the question of a mandate for the Vienna meeting on conventional arms?

Answer: The joint settlement has a point which confirms the Washington statement and the recognition of the need for intensive work in this sphere on the basis of both American proposals, specifically on gauges and sensors, and our proposals. So, it does contain specifics which the negotiators should thoroughly discuss.

Second, I am always for accuracy in wording, but in this case, perhaps, I was inaccurate: I am not a professional diplomat, you know. At Geneva, there was an exchange of views on the questions of the Vienna meeting and on a mandate for the conference and, specifically, the negotiators tackled the subject matter for the talks. Now a few words as to whether mutual understanding of the two sides, American and Soviet, was achieved. There was a formula, which Comrade Eduard Shevardnadze read out at this meeting. Mr. Shultz confirmed that the formula had been really transmitted to the negotiators in Vienna but that the process of discussion was not carried through over there. And here, in Moscow, it was again the subject of a very thorough study, but the work was not completed, for reasons which I already mentioned.

Question (*New York Times*, U.S.A.): Mr. General Secretary, when you were in Washington, you told Mr. Reagan that the Soviet Union was prepared to discontinue the supply of arms to Nicaragua if the United States stopped funding the contras. Then, later on, Mr. Shevardnadze and George Shultz discussed the question, and we were told that the Soviet stand did not change, i.e., if the U.S.A. stops deliveries to Central America, the Soviet Union will discontinue deliveries to Nicaragua. Could you confirm that this is really so and that you discussed this question within the context of consideration of the state of affairs in Central America?

Answer: Today we discussed this problem in a very detailed manner, and made an excursion into history. When we make such an excursion, we reveal different points of view and explanations. I suggested, nevertheless, that one should proceed from today's realities. There is the Contadora process, there are the Guatemala agreements, there is a truce and there is movement in the search for a political settlement. And it is essential, by relying on this process, to support it, giving an opportunity to the opposing forces in Nicaragua to decide this question themselves with the participation of other Latin Americans and representatives of Central America.

I told President Reagan that I was reaffirming what had been said during strolls in the White House: Let us limit ourselves to the delivery of police weapons.

In general, this subject will be examined in future as well. We urged the Americans to take into consideration that the process had reached such a stage when it could be completed positively. Over there a certain colonel of the Somoza Army appeared. He served Somoza well and is now serving America. He makes every effort to frustrate the entire process. I don't know, maybe the colonel should be replaced by a sergeant who will be closer to the people and matters would be settled more speedily.

Question (Soviet television): Speaking of foreign policy aspects of perestroika, it has spread far to the East beyond Sakhalin and far to the West, beyond Brest. I mean the immense attention of the public, of ordinary people, to the goings-on, and the desire to get an insight into the holy of holies of the process. Hundreds of people from among antiwar organizations from all over the world arrived in Moscow and followed the talks. I know that tomorrow you will have a meeting with public and antiwar organizations. Considering all that, what is your opinion about the role of the public and people's diplomacy in the entire process taking place over the past three years?

Answer: I have expressed my opinions on that score more than once, but, summing up, I can say today: We would have made a great error in politics if we did not pay attention to very deep changes in the sentiments of the world public and ordinary people on Earth. They have got sick and tired of wars, tensions, conflicts, and of vast amounts of information which mar the present day and promise a still worse future. People came to feel that not always their will, word and desire, aspiration and interests find reflection in real politics. They have begun to act, uniting into appropriate organizations and bringing into use everything they have available. We see among members of the movements both ordinary people and intellectuals—physicians, scientists, former military officers, veterans, young people and children. I think all this is very serious, and if someone thinks that there is anyone's "hand" in it, I would like to shake that hand, because this is a powerful hand, which has stirred to action vigorous forces.

The world feels that changes are needed. Life itself has raised such questions that people came to feel the need to intervene directly in politics. Only a policy, fertilized by the experience of the masses, their sentiments, their will, and using the competence of scientists and enriched by ethics and by contributions which intellectuals and people of culture can make— only such a policy has a prospect and only such a policy is adequate to the real processes which are under way and has a right to existence nowadays.

Question (Associated Press, U.S.A.): Mr. General Secretary, do you agree with such an evaluation of American-Soviet relations of the past period of détente when the main attention was devoted to economic cooperation and to the observance of political tolerance? To what extent, in your view, can and must both superpowers be interdependent from the economic point of view?

Answer: I think that both today's and tomorrow's realities, if analyzed in earnest, bring us to the view that we must cooperate and this would be in the interests of both our two peoples and of the whole world. I visualize a future world in which the American and Soviet peoples would cooperate in the economic sphere, too, and would exchange the fruits of their labor, complementing each other. This is why I elucidated the idea of a joint space flight to Mars so as to compete not in who gets ahead in the amount of weapons but rather in combining our potentials—scientific, economic and intellectual—and setting an example of cooperation in this direction. This would promote progress very much, never mind affording greater scope to our cooperation and working for greater confidence between our two peoples. Yesterday I was pressuring the President on these matters in public, using forbidden tricks, and he said: "Yes, we shall think it over." And to my mind, his words convey the idea that it is necessary to begin to study the problems.

Now I would like to say good-bye. You should conserve your energies for a meeting with President Reagan. Thank you for your active participation and I must apologize that perhaps I have not been able to answer all the questions. There are so many of you willing to put a question. But I welcome your immense interest in the fourth Soviet-American summit and I thank you for cooperation. Till we meet again.

25

Speech at the Farewell Ceremony in the Grand Kremlin Palace

June 2, 1988

Esteemed Mr. and Mrs. Reagan,

In one hour, you'll be leaving Moscow.

I would first of all like to thank you and your colleagues for your cooperation, openness and businesslike approach to the talks we've had here.

I believe that we both have every reason to regard this meeting and your visit as a useful contribution to the development of the dialogue between the Soviet Union and the United States.

Mr. President, you and I have been dealing with each other for three years now. We've come a long way from the first exchange of letters to the conclusion of this meeting.

Our dialogue has not been easy. But we have mustered enough realism and political will to overcome obstacles and divert the train of Soviet-U.S. relations from a dangerous track to a safer one. It has, however, been moving much more slowly so far than the real situation requires, both in our two countries and in the whole world.

But as I have understood, Mr. President, you're willing to continue our joint endeavors.

For my part, I can assure you that we will do everything in our power to go on moving forward.

Now, given the vast experience of Geneva, Reykjavik, Washington and Moscow, and backed up by their achievements, we are simply duty-bound to display still greater determination and consistency. That is what the Soviet and American peoples, international public opinion and the entire world community are expecting of us.

I hope you will remember your stay here in this country with pleasure.

Mr. President, Mrs. Reagan,

When you return to America, please convey to the American people best wishes from the peoples of the Soviet Union.

Over the past three years our two nations have come to know each other better. They have now taken a really good look at each other's eyes and have a keener sense of the need to learn to live together on this beautiful planet Earth.

I wish you a good journey back home, Mr. President and Mrs. Reagan. To you and to all members of the U.S. delegation I wish good health. Good-bye.

V

POST-MOSCOW SUMMIT SPEECHES

June 28–July 1, 1988

26

Report at the Opening of the 19th All-Union Conference of the CPSU

Moscow, June 28, 1988

Comrade delegates,

The basic question facing us, delegates to the 19th All-Union Party Conference, is how to further the revolutionary restructuring launched in our country upon the initiative and under the leadership of the Party, and to make it irreversible.

That question springs from our very life. It is being widely discussed inside the Party and by the people. And it depends on our answer whether the Party will be able to fulfill the role of political vanguard in the new stage of development that Soviet society has embarked upon.

The past three years of our life may quite legitimately be described as a radical turn. The Party and the working people have managed to halt the country's drift towards economic, social and spiritual crisis. Society is now more aware of its past, present and future. The perestroika policy, as translated into concrete socio-economic programs, is becoming the practical business of millions of people. That is the substance of the political situation in the country.

We can see how society has rallied. The country's spiritual life has become more diverse, more interesting and richer. Many ideas of Karl Marx and Vladimir Lenin previously treated one-sidedly, or totally hushed up, are being rethought. The creative nature of scientific and humane socialism is being revived in the struggle against dogmatism.

People have become aware of their responsibility and are shaking off apathy and estrangement. The winds of change are improving the moral health of the people. Democratization has released a powerful flood of thoughts, emotions and initiatives. Assertion of the truth and glasnost is purifying the social atmosphere, giving people wings, emancipating the consciousness and stimulating activity.

That is striking and impressive process, comrades, and all the honest and forward-looking people in the country have joined it. The forces of revolutionary renewal are consolidating. People have put their faith in perestroika, and they demand that we keep moving forward and only forward.

The working class is displaying a high degree of awareness and good organization. As the unusual, the new and the complicated are invading our lives, the working class is again demonstrating its splendid political and moral qualities, its truly civic, statesmanlike approach to things, and is backing perestroika by its labor. This enables the Party to carry out revolutionary changes with assurance.

The farmers have reacted with deep interest. The Congress of Collective Farmers has demonstrate its powerful charge of energy in favor of perestroika. Perestroika's advocates in agriculture are boldly adopting new ways of working, relying on science, picking effective technologies, and showing that they are ready to try out, search, and even take risks for the sake of progress, to work with complete dedication and with a sense of responsibility, skillfully, for their own benefit and for the good of their country.

Perestroika has confirmed Lenin's well-known idea that the intelligentsia is acutely sensitive socially, and responsive to social change. It has responded eagerly to the Party's appeal to put society's intellectual and spiritual potential completely at the service of perestroika. It has wholeheartedly supported the lesson of truth given by the 27th Congress and shown profound understanding of the Party's decisions of the past three years.

In short, the main political result of the post-April 1985 period has been a change in the entire social climate, a beginning of the materialization of the ideas of renewal and the Soviet people's mounting support for the Party's perestroika policy.

But does this mean that changes for the better are under way everywhere, that they are going on in full gear and that the revolutionary transformations have become irreversible?

No, it does not. If we want to be realists, Comrades, we must admit that this has not yet occurred. We have not yet coped with the underlying reasons for the retarding factors, we have not yet everywhere set in motion mechanisms of renewal, and in some spheres we have not even worked out any such mechanisms. The capability of a large number of Party organizations is no match as yet for the tasks of perestroika. What we need are new, qualitative changes in our development, and that calls for cardinal solutions and for vigorous and imaginative action.

We are facing many intricate questions. But which one of them is the crucial one? As the CPSU Central Committee sees it, the crucial one is that of reforming our political system.

The Central Committee has expounded its platform in the Theses for the Conference. We did not intend to give ready-made answers in all matters. We figured that new ideas and proposals would arise in the course of the discussion and that the Conference might take them into account. Its decisions then will really be a collective achievement of the whole Party and people.

It follows that the political objective of our Conference is to examine the period after the April 1985 Plenary Meeting of the Central Committee and the 27th Congress of the CPSU comprehensively and critically, to enrich the strategy and specify the tactics of our changes, and to define the ways, means and methods that would assure the steady advancement and irreversibility of our perestroika, and to do so in the spirit of Lenin's traditions and with reference to available experience.

27

Speech at the Closing of the 19th All-Union Conference of the CPSU

Moscow, July 1, 1988

Comrades, our Conference is ending. The documents we have just adopted on the outcome of the discussion, and the discussion of the documents themselves, relieve me of the necessity to deliver a long concluding statement. Still, the Conference is an event of such a scale that the work we have done in the past four days needs to be evaluated by the strictest of standards.

This is not in order to pay tribute to the once prevalent tradition of eulogizing every successive Party forum, but in order, in my opinion, to grasp the place of the 19th Conference in the life of the Party and of the entire country. A big event has occurred in the history of our Party.

First of all, as regards the atmosphere that reigned during the discussion. It was a true, open Party discussion about the things that matter the most, things that are troubling Communists and all Soviet people today. It was an attempt to find answers to questions which are bothering them. The Palace of Congresses has not witnessed such a discussion before, Comrades, and I don't think I'll be transgressing against the truth if I say that nothing like it has occurred in our country for nearly the last 60 years. We can, indeed, legitimately say that the Conference has been conducted in a Leninist spirit and that it was marked by a high sense of responsibility to the people and the revolution. That alone makes it especially significant.

I must mention the exceedingly high sense of involvement shown by the delegates. Indeed, the situation was anything but simple. There were nearly three hundred who wanted to speak. Unfortunately, not all of them could be given the floor. But the need to speak out was to some degree satisfied by the opportunity to speak in the drafting commissions. As I have already mentioned, nearly 150 people spoke at their sittings. This is something new for us. All in all, nearly once-tenth of the delegates took part in drafting the documents, so that many specific issues which arose during the discussion were examined and settled in a businesslike fashion.

The spirit that reigned at the Conference was very exacting. All issues were treated outspokenly, in a principled way, but, at the same time, the spirit was one of Party comradeship; I would even say of well-wishing towards each other. That, too, provides an example for the whole Party, the whole of our society, to follow. Indeed, that is as it should be among like-minded people who are tackling the great cause of perestroika and renewal, and who feel that hundreds, thousands and millions of their Party comrades, all Soviet people, are behind them and are following our work with enormous interest. In this sense, I dare say, the Conference reflected the political atmosphere taking shape in the country; it showed the degree of democratic development that the Party has attained, and not just the Party, but also all of Soviet society in the period since the April 1985 Plenary Meeting of the Central Committee.

Now about the content of our work. Its main outcome was that a programmatic political position has been worked out on all the fundamental issues discussed by the Party and the people on the basis of the Theses of the CPSU Central Committee, which thereafter became the topic of lively discussion in this hall. In so doing, the Conference did not simply endorse the proposals of the Central Committee, but enriched them in many ways through the experience of various Party organizations and work collectives. Let me say that all of us have, with tremendous interest and deep attention, followed whatever was said from this rostrum by workers, farmers, writers, actors, scientists and cultural workers, specialists in various economic fields, managers and Party functionaries.

In substance, the Conference covered the entire set of problems facing the Party and the country at the present stage. But I would single out the following as the most important topic of our discussion and the resulting resolutions. At the center of attention here was the role of the Party as the political vanguard. What could I say on this score if I were to sum up briefly the opinions of the delegates? We are all convinced that the Party has a clear-cut program of action—the one worked out at the 27th Congress and enriched by the already available experience of perestroika. It has the unconditional support of the people, who have accepted the policy of perestroika and will not allow it to be abandoned. As far as I can see, the Conference delegates have no doubt on this score.

The wish to see the Party still stronger has resounded here most passionately and resolutely. This can only be welcomed, and I think all of us are pleased. As put down in its resolution, the Conference demanded that our Party should in every respect be a Leninist party not only in content but also in its methods. In other words, it must renounce command-style method once and for all, and conduct its policy by means of organization, personnel and ideological work, in strict conformity with Soviet laws and the democratic principles of society.

There should be no duplication of the work of state bodies. There should be no dictating to trade unions, the YCL* and other public organizations, or to the unions of writers, artists, etc. Does this mean that the Party's leading role can weaken? Doubts of that kind have, indeed, been expressed. As I see it,

---

*Young Communist League. —Ed.

the Conference gave a sufficiently clear and convincing answer: No, the Party's leading role cannot weaken. As the ruling party, it has all the requisite levers to implement its leading role. And the most important lever of all are the 20 million Communists carrying out the Party's political line in all areas of life.

In the setting of democratization and glasnost, and with the functions of Party committees changing, the Party's authority, Comrades, will be put to a serious test. This test is already under way. Let's be frank: in the times of the command-style system, when the Party apparatus supervised absolutely everything, it was sometimes hard to discern where a Party committee and Party secretary had true leadership prestige, and where that prestige was at best the official authority obeyed merely out of necessity.

It is beyond doubt, Comrades, that perestroika and the reform of the political system are creating a fundamentally different situation. In the new conditions, the Party's leading role will depend entirely on its actual prestige, which at every point will have to be reaffirmed by concrete deeds. That is why it is absolutely essential for us to overcome even the slightest passivity shown by Party members. Every Communist must become a fighter for perestroika, for the revolutionary renewal of society. Let that be the chief mandate of our Conference.

On the whole, Comrades, the Conference is a major stage in the development of the Leninist course adopted by the April 1985 Plenary Meeting of the Central Committee and the 27th Congress of the Party, and in the deepening of the theory and practice of perestroika. This is what has determined its political scale and weight.

In this connection, I should like to express a fundamental thought. We have adopted a number of deeply considered and crucial decisions. But if we drag our feet in carrying them out —and that is one of the chronic maladies which we have not yet remedied (this also afflicted us in the first few years of perestroika)—much of what we have accomplished will fall by the wayside. This should be said loud and clear. Let's get rid of our old weaknesses and begin immediately to tackle the work ahead of us without waiting for additional decrees, injunctions, instructions and explanations.

The essential work of the CPSU Central Committee and the Presidium of the USSR Supreme Soviet should be properly organized. The coming elections in the Party should be based on the principles we have agreed upon here. Alterations in the structure of the Party apparatus should be introduced this autumn. And as concerns the reorganization of Soviets, the entire set of related issues should be examined during the autumn session of the USSR Supreme Soviet. Elections of USSR People's Deputies could be held in April 1989, and elections to the Supreme Soviets of Union and Autonomous Republics in the autumn of that year.

In view of the great significance of these issues, the Presidium of the Conference is submitting, for consideration by the delegates, a brief draft resolution on certain urgent steps to implement a reform of our country's political system.

That sums up the political results of the Conference. Upon returning home, each delegate will be able to tell his or her coworkers, Communists and non-Communists alike—all citizens—how we will work to implement its decisions.

To continue. The issue of democratizing society and radically reforming our political system was at the center of our attention throughout the deliberations of the Conference. I think that having defined its major aspects and parameters, we have answered the main question before us, the one about enhancing perestroika and guaranteeing its irreversibility. We have, therefore, every reason to say that the Conference has coped with its principal task.

Naturally, intensive organizational work to translate this reform into reality lies ahead. We will have to discuss everything thoroughly in our Party and in our society. But now we know how we should go about reforming the political system; we have arrived at a common viewpoint and articulated it in the form of policy guidelines.

Equally important is the resolve—which was forcefully expressed at the Conference—to continue and enhance our radical economic reform. Essential conditions for this were created by the decision of the June 1987 Plenary Meeting of the Central Committee and by the adoption of legislative acts, particularly the Laws on the State Enterprise (Association) and on Cooperatives. We focused our attention on the experience acquired by countless enterprises during the first months of operating according to the new principles and on the progress of the reform. And that is as it should be: everything occurring within the underlying infrastructure is of immense importance to society. We are dealing with the very foundations of perestroika.

As concerns the key landmarks of the discussion on these issues, the point is above all that after the Conference we must get down in earnest to the job of dismantling the mechanism which is holding us back. Representatives of virtually all delegations said that the bureaucracy was still showing its teeth, resisting and trying to sabotage things. As a result, the reform is hitting snags in many areas. That is perhaps one of the more important observations the delegates have made here, and it means that the phenomenon is widespread. Therefore, we in the Central Committee, in the Government and in central and local organizations must do everything we can to advance the radical economic reform more vigorously.

I think the delegates are unanimous in their support of those comrades who spoke about the present need to concentrate the bulk of our efforts on tackling the food problem, to make comprehensive assistance to our farmers and the revival of our agriculture a top priority. We should do everything we can during the current five-year period. We have already mastered a great deal and invested, via different channels, additional capital and resources into this sphere. It is important for all this investment to be used properly and effectively. Reviving our rural areas is, simply, our sacred duty. I think that after the Conference, we should become more demanding and keep a close watch over the entire effort to implement its guidelines about supporting the agrarian sector and its workers. Then we will succeed in solving the food problem without delay, too.

Another salient feature of the Conference, as I see it, is that it discussed the more urgent political and economic issues in close connection with the sphere of nonmaterial values, which gave it what I would call an ethical dimension. It is a sign of our profound awareness that at the current stage of social development, with the revolution in science and technology exerting an enormous influence on all social processes, no problem can be resolved without tapping the intellectual and moral potential of our people. Hence the elevated, I would even say super-elevated, tone of our discussion concerning science, education, culture, literature and art.

I cannot recall any other Party forum or even congress at which such a broad range of issues was discussed. Different views were expressed from this rostrum, reflecting the trends that run in concert but sometimes also clash in our public consciousness. That is natural. We are promoting a pluralism of views and reject having a monopoly on intellectual attitudes. But I think you will agree that there is a common basic idea in the diverse opinions that have been voiced at the Conference: we must be guided in everything by the interests of man, of the people, we must assert the humanitarian values of socialism. Then we will have a healthy moral climate in our society, a vigorous and creative intellectual quest and a truly flourishing culture.

What we need is not blind faith in a bright future but scientific projections based on a profound and precise knowledge of the inexhaustible potential inherent in a citizen of socialist society, in his work and his creative spirit. That is exactly why we refer to a new and humane imagine of socialism as the objective of perestroika.

Glasnost was one of the main subjects of the Conference— primarily because our debate was itself shaped by the climate of openness, frankness and sincerity that is spreading in our society. Another reason was that we were discussing how we should handle glasnost and whether it has reasonable limits. Although different views were expressed, I think that on this score, too, we eventually agreed that we must in every way support the mass media and their work to get rid of all kinds of negative phenomena we inherited from the past, and to encourage bold, original and interesting people, the true champions of perestroika.

On the other hand, there was an equally clear demand that journalists be more responsible for what they write, abandon parochial and departmental ambitions, likes and dislikes, and lay no claim to a monopoly on the truth. The people remember too well the times when the printed word became a docile tool of authoritarianism and arbitrary bureaucratic attitudes. Hence the great importance of learning, now that all spheres of life are becoming humanized, how to criticize and discuss things in a civilized, comradely manner. I think that on this score, too, the Conference did produce useful results. We all have gained a better understanding of the way a discussion in the Party should be conducted.

In connection with this discussion, I feel I must comment on the statement made by Boris Yeltsin. To begin with, I think we were right in giving him the floor. As I said, democracy calls for removing the veil of secrecy from such questions— although there is, in fact, no secrecy about this case.

In that part of his statement which was devoted to the specific issues discussed at the Conference, Comrade Yeltsin expressed views largely consonant with what was said both in the report and during the debate. In this sense, his proposals are part of the mainstream of our discussion. We should also note that, like other speakers, Comrade Yeltsin came out for continuing and promoting perestroika for the good of our society, our people.

What I cannot accept, however, is Boris Yeltsin's contention that we have launched perestroika without a sufficiently thorough analysis of the causes behind the phenomenon of stagnation or of the present state of our society, without an in-depth analysis of our history or of the Party's failings, that our perestroika is nothing but words.

During preparations for the Conference, during the discussion held in our Party and in our society, and at the Conference itself, we made a principled assessment of perestroika's accomplishments and problems and took stock of the work performed by Party and government bodies, by work collectives and by the country as a whole. Comrades, I hold that we were right to do that, because of the concern we all feel for perestroika. This concern has been felt here, too, and it has mobilized us and strengthened our commitment to act more resolutely in furthering the process of reform.

Nor do I regard as justified or acceptable Comrade Yeltsin's critical remarks about our failure to effect revolutionary transformations over the past three years. Of course, if one refers to the overall, long-term plan aimed at imparting, through perestroika, a new quality to our society, we cannot yet speak about revolutionary transformations. We have spent a great deal of time understanding the society we live in, the past in which many current phenomena are rooted, the world around us and our relationship to it. All this needed to be comprehended in order to prevent "revolutionary leaps forward," which are extremely dangerous, and to rule out improvisation in politics. We needed to involve society and its intellectual and scientific potential, in order to understand this, and, after serious and critical analysis, to work out the policy of perestroika and then to transform it into practical solutions in the main directions. That had to be done, and we needed to do it in a responsible way. So we proposed the policy of perestroika, to which there was no alternative. This in itself proved to be a great achievement to the Party during the past stage.

We share Comrade Yeltsin's concern for the accomplishment of the practical tasks which are uppermost in our people's minds, and I think the speeches we have heard here, particularly by representatives of the working class, have shown that the working people hope for a speedy solution of these matters.

I don't know why Comrade Yeltsin was critical of the Theses of the Central Committee as well, and questioned that they had been thoroughly and well thought out. This document has been regarded as a very serious one in the Party, in the country and in the world. Nor is his assertion that members of the Central Committee took no part in preparing the Theses understandable. I personally met with two-thirds of the Central Committee members, not to mention that they wrote and came forward with their suggestions. And finally, there was a plenary meeting which discussed the draft Theses. Comrade Yeltsin participated in its work, but said nothing and did not ask for the floor. The Central Committee members are present here, and they remember how it was.

I think, Comrades, our Conference, the way the discussion proceeded, and the documents we have adopted are the best proof that perestroika in our country is going on and is gathering strength.

While trying to look with good intentions into what is going on in the Central Committee and the Politburo—and this concerns the General Secretary in the first place—I cannot but go back to the history of the matter. When we recommended Comrade Yeltsin for the post of the First Secretary of the Moscow City Committee of the Party, we proceeded from the fact that it was necessary to improve the work of the Moscow Party organization, and that the general situation in Moscow called for improvement, too. An experienced and energetic person with a critical approach was needed for the job. We had seen that Comrade Yeltsin had these qualities, and so he was nominated for that post. Your humble servant had a hand in it, too. At first Comrade Yeltsin set about his work actively, did a great deal to invigorate it and launched a struggle against the negative phenomena that had accumulated in Moscow. We supported him in these efforts, realizing that the Moscow Party organization was facing no easy tasks, but at some point we felt that there was something wrong. That had begun when the time came for practical solutions to the problems of perestroika, for introducing it in every sphere of life when intensive and profound efforts were required to achieve radical change. There was too much work for the City Party Committee and its First Secretary to cope with. Comrade Yeltsin, instead of relying on the Party organization, on people and on collectives, adopted peremptory attitudes and command methods. That was followed by an endless shuffling of personnel.

At first we believed that this was, perhaps, justified, that the wrong personnel had been chosen, and the conference held in the city had failed to solve the personnel question correctly.

Most likely that was the case. Not everybody had proved capable of solving the new tasks or shouldering the leadership of the Party organization at that turning point in the development of the city and the country. But when he set to replacing personnel for the second and the third time, this began to worry us. I reproved Comrade Yeltsin at a Politburo meeting. I said then in a comradely manner that he should draw appropriate conclusions and take all that into consideration in his work. In other words, we offered assistance to him, nothing more than that.

What, in my opinion, is behind the drama of Comrade Yeltsin as a political worker? At the time, when it came to tackling practical matters, he did not have enough strength to do it, and so he fell back on high-flown talk and pronouncements and resorted to command methods. But even then—this should be made known to all and we should clear up this matter entirely—the Politburo did not consider Comrade Yeltsin a lost man and did not think that he could not go on working. So we continued to support him, which I said at the plenary meeting of the Moscow Party Committee, and big decisions concerning Moscow were adopted.

While on vacation in August 1987, I received a letter from Comrade Yeltsin, in which he asked to be relieved of his position as First Secretary of the City Committee of the Party. I decided that nothing should be done hastily, that things had to be sorted out carefully. The Politburo did not even know of the letter's existence. I decided to have a talk with Boris Yeltsin after my leave and suggested that he first see through the celebrations marking the 70th anniversary of the October Revolution, and after that we would meet and talk. He agreed to that. But contrary to that arrangement, he unexpectedly took the floor at the October Plenary Meeting of the Central Committee. I have already spoken about the import of his speech. And my speech at the plenary meeting of the Moscow City Committee was published—I didn't say anything more at that time. After the discussion, and when the comrades voiced their criticisms, Comrade Yeltsin admitted his errors.

Let me quote from the transcript of the plenary meeting and

an episode at the end of the meeting, after everyone had spoken.

"GORBACHEV: Tell us your view on the remarks made by the comrades in the Central Committee. They have said a lot and want to know what you think about it. They have to make a decision.

YELTSIN: With the exception of certain remarks, on the whole I agree that I let down the Central Committee and the Moscow City Organization by making a speech today—that was a mistake.

GORBACHEV: Have you got enough energy to remain in charge?

VOICES: He won't be able to carry on. He cannot be left in this post.

GORBACHEV: Wait a minute. I'm asking him. Let's be democratic about this. We all want to hear his answer before reaching a decision.

YELTSIN: I said that I let down the Central Committee of the Party, the Politburo, the Moscow Party Organization. I will repeat what I have said: 'I'm asking to be relieved of the post of Alternate Member of the Politburo and of the duties of head of the Moscow City Party Organization.' "

So these are the facts. After Yeltsin's speech was found to be politically incorrect—which he himself admitted—I still urged the Central Committee members: Let's not decide now whether or not to relieve him from the duties of Alternate Member of the Politburo, let's ask the Politburo to consider the question. But the situation had already evoked such a response that the matter could not be left unattended. We related all this at a plenary meeting of the Moscow City Committee, and the comrades there spoke far more critically of Comrade Yeltsin's work—you know about that.

On the whole, Comrades, I think that this is a lesson not only for Comrade Yeltsin, this is also a lesson for the Politburo, for the General Secretary of the Central Committee, for all of us. We must proceed firmly along the path of decisively reviving our Party on Leninist principles, on the basis of large-scale democratization, relying on the primary Party organization, the cadres and the elected activists. We cannot accomplish the great tasks of perestroika that we have set ourselves by employing the old methods which have been denounced not only by the Party, but by the whole of society, by time itself.

And there is another lesson. Comrades at the Conference have correctly remarked that people should have been informed and told everything, in which case the situation would not have developed as it did.

I will return to the question which is of the greatest concern to the delegates—I feel this as I hear the speeches and read the written notes. It is how to ensure the implementation of the decisions we have taken. Let us organize the entire activity of the Party in accordance with the Conference's resolutions and not wait for the next Congress to put all this in the Rules. There are the political guidelines of the Conference, and we shall follow them.

And another thing. Let us not put off the reform of the entire political system, as we need it to advance perestroika. It is coming up against the existing political system already now. We must not allow a repetition of what happened at the January Plenary Meeting of the Central Committee. That was an important meeting at which a profound analysis was made and the causes of what had happened in the country and in the Party were revealed. But we did not consider the ways of implementing the decisions of the Plenary Meeting. They "hovered in the air," and things did not proceed as we expected. The decisions of our Party Conference should under no circumstances be allowed to suffer the same fate.

Many of the questions that were raised here are not covered by the resolutions. I think all this should be summed up for discussion at a plenary meeting, and specific assignments be given and their fulfillment be verified. In many of their written notes the delegates suggested that a verbatim account should be published. We should do that by all means, in order to equip our Party and the whole of society with the ideas expressed during the Conference debate.

And one more issue, Comrades, raised shortly before and at the Conference—that of building a monument to victims of the repressions. You will probably recall that this was mentioned in the concluding remarks at the 22nd Congress of the Party and was received with approval. The question was also raised at the 27th Congress of the Party, but it was not given a practical solution. As noted in the Report, restoring justice with regard to the victims of lawlessness is our political and moral duty. Let us perform that duty and build a monument in Moscow. I am sure that this step will be supported by all Soviet people.

In conclusion, I want to go back once more to the question of how to deepen the revolutionary perestroika launched in the country on the initiative and under the leadership of the Party, and how to make it irreversible. All our work, all the proceedings, the final documents—all this has shown that a clear answer has been worked out by the Conference: democratization, economic reform and transformation of the political system will make perestroika irreversible. Through revolutionary perestroika our society will reach a qualitatively new state, and socialism will be given a new, humane and democratic image. We will go forward in a creative quest for ways and methods to attain this goal under the conditions of democracy and glasnost. We will work persistently to carry out our objectives.